The
Juárez
Myth in Mexico

The
Juárez
Myth in Mexico

CHARLES A. WEEKS

THE UNIVERSITY OF ALABAMA PRESS

Publication of this book was made possible, in part,
by financial assistance from the Andrew W. Mellon Foundation and the
American Council of Learned Societies

Library of Congress Cataloging-in-Publication Data

Weeks, Charles A., 1937–
The Juárez myth in Mexico

Bibliography: p.
Includes index.
1. Juárez, Benito, 1806–1872. 2. Mexico—History—
1821–1861—Historiography. 3. Mexico—History—European
intervention, 1861–1867—Historiography. 4. Mexico—
History—1867–1910—Historiography. 5. Mexico—
Presidents—Biography. I. Title.
F1233.J9W44   1987   972'.07'0924   85-16543
ISBN 0-8173-0285-9

Contents

Illustrations

Acknowledgments

Many people have contributed much to the preparation of this book. I want especially to thank Robert E. Quirk, David M. Pletcher, Robert H. Ferrell, and those anonymous persons who read earlier drafts and made many constructive suggestions regarding content, organization, and style. I am grateful to the late James R. Scobie for his insistence that I look deeper into the literature on myth and mythmaking; to Charles A. Hale of the University of Iowa for his encouragement when I was just beginning and for his continued interest in the project, especially as it touched on his important study of the development of nineteenth-century Mexican liberalism; to the late Stanley Ross of the University of Texas, whose knowledge of Mexico and Mexicans proved most helpful; and to Mexican historians who were helpful and cordial with regard to locating materials and people in Mexico: Luis González, Moisés González Navarro, Josefina Zoraida Vázquez of the Colegio de México, Edmundo O'Gorman, and the late Daniel Cosío Villegas. Carlos J. Sierra and the late Raúl Noriega were active in the organization of the 1972 Juárez centennial in Mexico, and I was most fortunate in having the opportunity to meet them in the context of that celebration. Laurens Perry of the Universidad Veracruzana sounded a note of caution about the undertaking, and Harold Parker, emeritus of Duke University, and Malcolm Partin of Davidson College provided helpful comments about national mythmaking in modern France and Germany. Librarians and their staffs on both sides of the border went far beyond the call of duty to help, and finally Malcolm M. MacDonald and his able staff of The University of Alabama Press provided expert guidance and care toward the end.

The
Juárez
Myth in Mexico

1

Mexicans and Their Juárez

Like many capitals the city of Mexico is a place of monuments—large monuments, small, ancient monuments, and new, representational monuments, and allegorical monuments—each bearing a message from the past. Among them is the Hemiciclo. It stands in a spacious, old, beautiful park, the Alameda Central, where the young and old of the city still promenade on Sundays and holidays as people do in the plazas throughout the country and, indeed, as people do in many parts of the world. Amid green trees and a great variety of flowers and shrubs and flanked by a semicircle of twelve doric columns of white Carrara marble stands the central pedestal of the Hemiciclo supporting the statues of three figures. One statue represents a former president of the republic, Benito Juárez, who appears solemn and grim as a Roman proconsul administering justice. Juárez the Lawgiver is seated, and surrounding him are two allegorical figures, also of marble, one representing Glory, who is placing a crown on Juárez's head, and the other, the Republic, who stands behind, resting her sword on the ground to signify the end of a gigantic struggle. Crowned by a doric frieze, the columns support a massive, ornate bronze urn at each end, and at the foot of the central pedestal, decorated in gold-plated figures and letters, below the national eagle, rest two marble lions. The letters of the pedestal read: "Al Benemérito Benito Juárez. La Patria."

Many years have passed since 1910, when the Mexican government built and dedicated the Hemiciclo after a design by the

The Juárez Hemiciclo, Mexico City. Courtesy of the Benson Latin American Collection, The University of Texas at Austin.

architect Guillermo Heredia. It was then the centennial year of the beginning of the independence movement, a year filled with many similar ceremonial functions for President Porfirio Díaz. Weighing seventy tons, and standing seven meters tall, the three sculpted figures required only seventy-five days to complete. The entire Hemiciclo used about fourteen hundred tons of marble, of about six hundred cubic meters. Like many other such monuments it is the embodiment of a myth.[1]

In life Juárez offered little to the mythologizers—he was never able to boast a military career, he often impressed people as reserved or even impassive, he stood a little over five feet; with small hands and feet and dark staring eyes, a coppery complexion that helped disguise a large scar across his face, of Zapotec Indian parentage, he was no striking figure. He did, however, lead Mexican liberals in the 1850s and 1860s in their titanic struggle against formidable opposition, both foreign and domestic, and in the years since his death his worshipers have gathered at the Hemiciclo, at his tomb, or in many other places in Mexico sacred

Benito Juárez, from a lithograph by Fernando Lara. Courtesy of the Benson Latin American Collection, The University of Texas at Austin.

to his memory, usually on anniversaries of his birth or death. For them Juárez is, in agreement with the golden inscription on the central pedestal of the Hemiciclo, "Benemérito de la Patria" or even "Benemérito de las Américas."[2]

A typical celebration was the ceremony at the Hemiciclo on July 18, 1947, when a great crowd gathered to honor the anniversary of his death. People carried banners advertising their school, labor union, Masonic lodge, or veterans' organization. Protestant and Catholic groups mingled. Banners and the ceaseless speeches, all suitably (perhaps unsuitably, some auditors would have said) amplified, referred not only to Juárez but to events a few weeks earlier in the city of Durango. There Catholic priests from all parts of the country had met for a Eucharistic Congress and, adorned in florid vestments, marched in violation of the Mexican constitution, which banned both the wearing of clerical garb in public and public religious processions. Their action alarmed speakers at the Hemiciclo, who, using the commemoration of Juárez's death as a forum, shouted that the "inheritance of Benemérito Juárez should not be stained." It was endangered, they said, by "hands outside the Constitution." According to one orator, "The people of Mexico, who fought for 137 years to construct a nation, would not allow a return to the time of tithes and taxes on first fruits, of ecclesiastical privileges and intolerance."[3]

The past was miraculously merged with the present as speakers recounted sacred episodes from Juárez's life and stressed their relation to the present. At one time, decades ago, according to the speakers, Mexico had experienced greatness of example, purity of motive, the possibility of leadership, all through the life of one of its most humble citizens. The speeches apotheosized the immortal Juárez almost as a Christ redivivus in nineteenth-century Mexico. The clerical defiance of the constitution prompted speakers to invoke earlier struggles that involved Juárez and his generation as people of that primitive day sought to establish the great principles of the supremacy of state over church and rule by law. General Rodolfo Sánchez Taboada, a veteran of Mexico's twentieth-century Revolution and president in 1947 of the nation's official party, extolled Juárez as a defender of the constitution and commented that fulfillment of the law "ought to be for us the product of our belief that the sacrifice of our ancestors was not in vain." Enrique Ramírez y Ramírez, described by the magazine *Tiempo* as a "youthful and militant intellectual of the labor movement," identified Juárez with nationalism and democracy and observed that enemies of these values desired only factional conflict and monarchy.[4]

On this occasion as on others Mexicans turned to the Juárez myth not just in a ritualistic, ceremonial gesture, but to argue, to protest, for they saw a link between events of the present and those that intimately involved Juárez. The past became present. They identified Juárez with their constitution and law; they believed Juárez had defended both and that the actions of the Eucharistic Congress and failure of the government to prevent such actions were challenges to these values. By describing him as a liberal they recalled his role as head of the Liberal party in the 1850s and 1860s, especially the party's effort to establish by law and practice the principles of separation of church and state and a republican form of government characterized by a strong legislature. Some praised him as the most important liberal of the nineteenth century. They characterized him as a nationalist and a patriot, unwavering in defense of Mexico and Mexican values that once again the Roman Catholic church seemed to be challenging by provocative words and actions. The liberal impulse, with its advocacy of a secular society, constitutionalism and rule by law, and nationalism requiring loyalty to Mexican law and government and stressing national tradition were some of the values associated with Juárez in 1947 on the anniversary of his death.

The speakers of 1947 were nothing if not imaginative. They interpreted key events in Juárez's life so as to make specific the abstract qualities of their beliefs and to meet the needs of the moment, which were to denounce the clerical behavior in Durango and admonish the government to do something. They pointed to Juárez's Indian parentage and his youth as an orphan in the mountains of Oaxaca to demonstrate that he was an authentic Mexican, whose blood was untainted by the blood of foreigners; they praised his decision to be a lawyer instead of a priest as evidence of an early commitment to liberalism. Citing his opposition to the government of that great nineteenth-century adventurer Antonio

López de Santa Anna, which took on the trappings of monarchy and dictatorship in the early 1850s, and his unfailing support for the Constitution of 1857 during the three-year civil war that followed its ratification, they showed a president unswerving in commitment to republicanism and constitutionalism. They recalled Juárez's reform decrees of 1859 and 1862 that forbade priests to wear vestments outside churches, turned birth and marriage into civil rather than religious functions, limited church processions and acts outside churches, banned monastic orders and nationalized their lands, secularized cemeteries, and generally separated church and state. They reviewed his leadership of the resistance to French intervention between 1862 and 1867, which they saw as the most important accomplishment in his life, establishing his credentials as Mexico's leading liberal.

Development of a Juárez myth has had all the classic characteristics of myths and mythmaking, especially the subjective view or image of a reality, whether it be of an historical figure, as in the case of Juárez, an event, an institution, or even a geographical region. Image or meaning ascribed to what is assumed to be a reality constitutes one of the main elements of myth and when manipulated to promote a cause assumes a reality of its own.[5] The apotheosis of Juárez projected a subjective view or image of the historical reality. In all myths, to be sure, the assumed reality is a feature useful to an individual or a group.

The subjectivity of myth derives from another element already alluded to, namely use. When Mexicans refer to Juárez as a champion of nationalism or democracy they treat the historical personality in such a way as to create a symbol, something that is itself and more. Mexicans have attributed meanings to Juárez that express what they want to believe about him and the time he lived. The result is a hero—or a villain—depending upon the particular set of values and beliefs of the speaker or writer. The myth creates an intelligible reality by breaking down distances between present and past and present and future so that in effect all is present; it thus satisfies a basic human need to make the present and the future more intelligible by references to the past.[6] Thus in a sense nations are the creatures of their mythmakers; it is their image of the past that produces an image of present and future.[7]

Mexicans use Juárez to understand the present or to promote a cause or to express views about an event or a condition, and this word "use" suggests yet another characteristic of the Juárez myth. Unlike a story or a tale about Juárez, which is merely told, the myth, which may consist of a narrative or several narratives, is used to satisfy the needs, psychological, social, and political, of the creators.[8] By seeming to justify the present, myth can satisfy a fundamental need for a sense of security or rightness. If historical precedent can be found for some action or idea, whether it be government policy or an act of rebellion or an ordinary and mundane event, it can be rationalized. The decision to do something may come first and then an attempt to support it by reference to a similar act in the past. Myth, in short, serves a psychic need for security, for integrating disparate moods and attitudes. It also fulfills a social function when it provides understanding and when it is seen as a language through which values, beliefs, aspirations and points of view are communicated.[9] Closely related to both psychological and social uses is a political purpose. Because myth simplifies, governments use myths to explain complex situations and communicate with citizens, and groups outside government employ mythmaking to praise or to criticize an incumbent regime.[10]

Because myth and mythmaking have taken important roles in human life they have been the object of much study, and one of the measurements of mythmaking is the fulfillment of a psychological purpose. Carl Jung has identified Jesus Christ as the most important myth in our culture because he represents the God image in man and has served for many centuries to objectify views of the human psyche.[11] In France the career of Napoleon Bonaparte has provided the raw material of a legend that has satisfied a need or desire for a sense of glory and greatness, often in time of national crisis. William Sater has applied some of the findings of social psychology to illuminate the way Chileans have used one of their heroes, Arturo Prat, a naval officer who died during the War of the Pacific, as a paternal figure and symbol of purity, especially in time of stress and conflict.[12] Inspired by publication in 1934 of Samuel Ramos's *Profile of Man and Culture in Mexico,* Mexicans in the 1940s and 1950s examined their myths and symbols to define a collective Mexican psychology or *mexicanidad*. Because some of them believed that their countrymen still lacked a sense of community, they added to these myths, as Jorge Carrión may have done in his discussion of the Virgin of Guadalupe as the little mother through whom Mexicans projected their religious and magical sentiments. Carrión saw the Virgin as a synthesis of the psychological characteristics of the Indians in contrast to those of the Spaniards. The Spaniards represented force, authority, order, law, and pain, and the Indians represented passivity, submission, and tenderness.[13] Man objectifies himself by myths and symbols, and the Juárez myth shows that what Mexicans say about Juárez represents what they want to believe about themselves, as individuals and as a nation.

If myth may project views of the self, another purpose of the process is social. Because people use myth to communicate values, beliefs, aspirations, and points of view, it is a form of language and can serve a community as a cohesive force. Communication in society is basically an attempt to create symbols whose use is believed to uphold social order, which has been described as a drama of social hierarchy in which people enact roles as superiors, inferiors, and equals.[14] Beginning with Emile Durkheim anthropologists and sociologists have recognized this quality of myth-making. Durkheim saw this characteristic as closely related to religion, which he defined as a system of myths, dogmas, rites, and ceremonies, and he argued that even the most barbarous and the most fantastic rites and the strangest myths translate some human need or aspect of life, individual or social. Because man shapes myths to satisfy needs, he argued, only through historical analysis can they be understood.[15]

Bronislaw Malinowski argued somewhat later for a social or cultural approach to myth, with a thesis that myth must be defined by social function. According to him, myth is a story told to establish a belief, to serve as a precedent in ceremony or ritual, or to rank as a pattern of moral or religious conduct. He rejected the idea of myth as "an imaginative and pseudo-scientific tale" and maintained that it must be studied in its "social, ritual, and ethical effects."[16]

Agreeing that myth forms a part of culture, E. R. Leach disagreed with the notion that a myth is static, and his study of the political culture of two highland Burma tribes concluded that societies are not in equilibrium and neither are their myths, which may consist of many and often conflicting versions suitable for groups with different positions and claims in society.[17]

Understandably, political scientists have been attracted to myth as a political phenomenon and have concluded that symbolic aspects of politics are important for political behavior and that myth defined as belief held in common by a large group of people, giving events and actions a particular meaning, has helped the emergence of political movements. They have concluded that because myth simplifies, governments form and reflect myths to explain complexity and communicate with citizens. A real source of myth is the incapacity of many people to hold abstract ideas and their consequent need to embody a myth in incident and in concrete shape.[18] Governments have found development and use of myth especially important in the promotion of nationalism; they have recognized that if a nation is to have what Sidney Verba and Gabriel Almond have described as a civic culture it needs symbols and myths.[19] Mexican governments have exploited the wealth of people and events their nation's history provides to try to secure a commitment to the nation and its governors, and if Verba and Almond's conclusions are correct they have succeeded. Especially in recent years Mexican presidents have sought to enhance their importance by frequent identification of their ideas, problems, and courses of action with those of Juárez.[20]

The approaches to myth are as diverse as its uses. Through a study of the Juárez myth, this essay will examine the question, What is the historical reality of myth? Although historians have studied the development and use of myths in history, often employing other terms such as "symbol" or "image," studies of myth have been more attractive to the anthropologist, sociologist, or political scientist, and although these social scientists have brought much insight and understanding to the use to which historical, geographical, or institutional reality has been put, they have not always seen, as Durkheim noted, that an important dimension of myth analysis is historical. That, of course, is a difficult if not impossible undertaking when one is studying a culture that has no history, for traditionally history has been the study of civilizations with written records. Many scholars such as Claude Lévi-Strauss have been interested therefore in the linguistic aspect of myth—the use of linguistic analysis for studying myths. One can be deluded, too, into thinking that myth is found only in primitive cultures and that modern man has passed beyond the mythic stage to think and act historically, that is, to separate past from present and see that each historical situation or period is unique and can be understood only in terms of itself and what went before.[21] A full study of myth in Mexico and elsewhere requires realization that myth develops through time and in response to changing social and political relations and needs, as Leach observed when studying a somewhat traditional society in Burma. The same stories may be retold with the same words, but if the telling is in a historical context, subtle and perhaps even major differences in meanings can be seen.[22]

The approach to Mexicans and their Juárez, therefore, has to be historical. It begins with the assumption that what can be called the Juárez myth in Mexico, the political and ideological uses of Juárez, has a clear history. It begins with the era when Juárez lived, for though it cannot prove in great detail who Juárez was or what he did, it must try to establish as fully and objectively as possible the historical reality with which the myth began.

The historical approach to the Juárez myth must be careful to show that at the outset Mexicans did not agree about what Juárez represented. The argumentative aspect of myth noted by Leach was much in evidence in the 1947 gathering at the Hemiciclo. Speakers condemned the clerical demonstration in Durango; they seemed almost more concerned with that event than with the ceremony honoring Juárez. Clerics and their sympathizers used Juárez in different ways, showing that what Mexicans say about him depends on their position in society and their ideology.[23] Drama caused by conflict and often characterized by polemic constitutes much of the style of the Juárez myth and supports a view of society that sees it as a drama of authority, a struggle by those in power to control symbols already powerful or to create new ones that will order relations that cannot be ordered through traditional symbols.[24]

Myth is a marvelous mirror of the social and political tensions in a society, and the study of its history reflects those tensions. Such study shows the inadequacy of the symbolism of the Hemiciclo. The monument is a man in the form of a marble statue, fixed, unwavering, unchanging. Although there is an enduring quality to Juárez, he continues to provoke debate and even polemic, for what he did raised up controversy and debate in a country with a short national history that continues to try to see itself in its past. In that sense he is alive, just as one can conclude that his myth is true in that it has survived and become larger and larger.

What Mexicans say about Juárez may not be true in a strict factual or historical sense, but we must pass over the factual content of what is said and concern ourselves with the interpretive and pragmatic. The particular mixture of time and circumstance have given to Juárez a special ability to provoke reaction from the present against the robust inventions of the mythologizers of the past.

Juárez looms large in Mexico. The year 1972 was known as the "Year of Juárez," and the great celebrations of that year made him truly Mexico's maximum official hero. "Juarismo" has become an integral component of Mexican nationalism, or at least that version of Mexican nationalism promoted by the government and inculcated in Mexican schoolchildren, for whom he stands out as the greatest of Mexico's great men and women.[25] He also serves as a means whereby Mexicans communicate and often disagree with one another. The development of the Juárez myth as a language of both argument and assent began when he lived in the midst of the tumultuous nineteenth century, from 1806 to 1872, and it will probably continue into the long future. To understand, therefore, what Juárez means to Mexicans, one must examine the man and his role in the events of his century and also what Mexicans have said and done in his name since 1872. These tasks are essential to a history of the Juárez myth.

2

 Triumph of the Republic

President Juárez stood on the central balcony of the National Palace overlooking Constitution Plaza, also known as the Zócalo, on July 15, 1867, to proclaim to the world the triumph of the liberal and republican cause. He and his government had returned to the capital after a long absence, having defended the rights and liberty of Mexicans and the sacred cause of independence from an iniquitous foreign invader, or so he announced. Querétaro, the last stronghold of the Emperor Maximilian, had fallen in May, and on June 19 the emperor died before a firing squad on the Cerro de las Campanas, together with two of his generals, Miguel Miramón and Tomás Mejía. The republic of Juárez emerged victorious.[1]

To what a scene the defeat of the foreign invader, the victory of Juárez, had led! There at the Cerro de las Campanas, which soon became a national shrine, the Emperor Maximilian and his generals stood before the firing squad, with soldiers backing up the sharpshooters, prepared for the coup de grace, and with perhaps four thousand troops gathered in ranks for the great ceremony of execution. After the emperor shook the hands of the men who were to kill him and gave each of them a coin, he took his place with the generals, not the place of honor, he insisted, but to one side, and the soldiers raised their rifles and fired. A photograph was made of the occasion for posterity, and it shows the ranks of soldiers and the crowd of onlookers, as the cause of Juárez triumphed over that of the effete Europeans. The faces in the photograph blur, and the trinity of victims stands out in pathetic resemblance of another trinity of long ago. But triumph it was, and a shudder ran through Europe when the news arrived that the New World had bested the Old.[2]

The liberal press of Mexico City thereupon joined the exuberant multitudes by heaping praise upon Juárez as the man who most deserved the gratitude of all those Mexicans who remained loyal to the republican and liberal cause. In *El Siglo Diez y Nueve*, the leading liberal newspaper of the capital, Pantaleón Tovar wrote that it was impossible to enumerate the toasts delivered to the president for his steadfastness and to his followers for their bravery and the results of their hardship. Adding to these sentiments in *El Monitor Republicano*, Gabino F. Bustamante described Juárez as the personification of the republic and announced in clarion tones that he was worthy of a thousand titles, of universal respect. Possessing enlightenment, patriotism, and experience, Juárez inspired unlimited confidence in the future of Mexico, a future secured by the death of the Conservative party and the victory of the nation over foreign domination. These and other encomiums put Juárez at the pinnacle of his political career, for the opposition, foreign and domestic, had been silenced and a chorus of harmony sang praise. As a Mexican historian wrote many years later, he seemed the only national figure to emerge from the wars of the 1850s and 1860s.[3]

Running through the rhetoric of praise and thanksgiving was an immense sense of relief and of hope—relief that the great trial was over, hope for years of peace and unity and economic progress. For more than twenty years of struggle associated with one event, the Reform, liberals had attempted a new course for Mexican history, after three decades of what they saw as drift. Beginning with the overthrow of the Santa Anna regime in the revolution of Ayutla (1854–55), the Reform produced the Juárez and Lerdo laws in 1855 and 1856 to abolish ecclesiastical and military privilege and end corporate landholdings by the church and Indian villages. These two laws aroused the wrath of the church and stirred peasants to rebellion in some parts of Mexico when their land was seized by large hacendados. A new constitution appeared in 1856–57. After a violent three-year civil war, from 1858 to

1861, Mexican conservatives turned to the government of Napoleon III in France and attempted to thwart all further reform efforts by establishing an empire in Mexico. This effort promised success in 1864 and 1865, but it could not survive Napoleon's decision in 1866 to withdraw his troops from Mexico. Forced to rely on a conscripted and disloyal army, the regime soon collapsed, and Maximilian was executed in 1867.[4]

Today, more than a century later, for Mexicans who still feel allegiance to one or the other of the two major groups involved in the struggles of those years, the conservatives and the liberals, their legacy means a great deal. For partisans of the liberal cause, past and present, the Reform represents a victory for the ideals of a strong, secular state and a modern economy: government by law and not by men, separation of church and state, freedom of press and speech, national sovereignty, the free circulation of property. For conservatives the Reform undermined institutions and values that defined Mexico: the church and its religion, the communal life of Indians, freedom from a materialism and greed often associated with the United States. For both groups Juárez is a figure to be reckoned with in the shaping of the Reform.[5]

Who, then, was Juárez, and what was his relationship to the Reform, that event that now ranks with the Independence of the early nineteenth century and the Revolution of the twentieth century as a seminal event in the emergence of a mythology of Mexican nationalism? Like another nation's hero, Abraham Lincoln, who was his contemporary, Juárez enjoyed humble origins, as mythmakers of both countries often stressed.[6] The Mexican president was born in the village of San Pablo Guelatao in Oaxaca on March 21, 1806, just three years before Lincoln's birth in a frontier cabin in Kentucky. Juárez's parents were Zapotec Indians. By the age of four he had been orphaned; relatives cared for him until he was twelve, but he could neither read nor write then and was ignorant of the Spanish language. Then he went to the state's capital, the city of Oaxaca, walking the almost forty miles, to live with a sister, and began his education under the guidance of a Spanish priest. He entered a seminary in Oaxaca, but withdrew to further his studies in the Institute of Sciences and Arts, which had been founded in 1827 and whose professors imbued a generation of young men with liberal and secular values and ideas. Eventually he took a law degree.

His political career began with election to the municipal council of Oaxaca in 1831, and he served in the state legislature for a short time beginning in 1832 and then in the national congress during the liberal regime of Valentín Gómez Farías. He was named secretary general to the governor of the state of Oaxaca in 1844 and again served in the national congress in 1846. As a member of congress he supported the government's initial efforts to raise funds by taxing ecclesiastical property to help finance the war against the United States. From 1848 to 1853 he was governor of Oaxaca. In 1853 the adventurer Santa Anna, back for the last of his many residences in the National Palace, removed Juárez from the governorship and forced him to leave the country, and Juárez spent most of the next two years with other Mexican exiles in New Orleans.

The liberal revolution of Ayutla that broke out in 1854 led to a rise to the top, the presidency of Mexico. Santa Anna resigned in 1855 and went into exile, and the leader of the revolution, Juan Alvarez, briefly assumed the presidency. Calling Juárez back from exile and appointing him to the post of minister of justice and ecclesiastical affairs in the national cabinet, he enabled Juárez to issue the famous law that did away with special privileges for soldiers and clerics. That law was complemented in the following year by a decree from Miguel Lerdo de Tejada, the treasury minister, ordering the sale of all corporate property except that used directly by the corporation. This Lerdo law destroyed the economic basis of church power and caused many Indian communities to lose land. While the constituent congress of 1856–57 ratified these two laws and worked out a new constitution, Juárez returned to Oaxaca to resume his governorship. Then opposition to the work of the congress quickly developed and plunged Mexico into a civil war, and the task of defending the new constitution and other liberal measures fell to him. Ignacio Comonfort, elected president under the constitution, was ousted by a conservative coup after vacillating between support for the document and opposition, and Juárez as president of the supreme court and ex officio vice-president under the constitution succeeded to the presidency of the republic.

Juárez became president in January 1858 and held office until his death in 1872, and his tenure was anything but tranquil, for barring Santa Anna and a few Mexican presidents thereafter he was probably the most mobile of Mexican chief executives, though not by preference. The conservative revolt that ousted his predecessor forced him to flee Mexico City; and after stops in such inland cities as Guanajuato and Guadalajara he and his government took ship for Veracruz, which became the liberal capital until Juárez was able to return to Mexico City in 1861. During the French intervention Juárez and his government ranged over much of northern Mexico—San Luis Potosí, Saltillo, Chihuahua, and Paso del Norte (now Ciudad Juárez). Finally, in July 1867, he returned to Mexico City to stay until his death five years later.[7]

Juárez's interest in reform may well have come out of his wanderings, when in yearning for the National Palace the itinerant president may have come to believe that if he promised reform— and the promises necessarily had to be just that, with no immediate possibility of fulfillment—he might end his travels. Certainly it was during the presidential years of turbulence that the Juárez government announced reform. It brought reform to its most radical extreme by issuing in Veracruz in 1859 the first of the so-called Laws of the Reform. By carrying further the reforms of the Constitution of 1857 and the earlier Juárez and Lerdo laws, the president stirred up wrath from those who saw their privileges slipping away. The reform decrees confiscated all wealth administered by the regular and secular clergy, abolished all brotherhoods and regular orders, and prohibited new monasteries. Laws followed in 1859 and 1860 to secularize cemeteries and make marriage a civil contract. As head of the liberal government during these hectic years, Juárez laid the basis for his later exaltation as head of the Reform, the Moses of modern Mexico.[8]

The president emerged as the victor from his trials and tribulations, much as if he were a modern-day Saint Sebastian, who removed the slings and arrows that afflicted him and entered again into the daily life of this world, but he jeopardized his achievement by two controversial decisions. At the moment of his triumph Juárez was able to contemplate problems that would threaten his position as chief executive of Mexico. Never could he be sure of success. One problem that led to trouble involved money. To help the Mexican treasury and eventually to secure investment capital, technology, and protection, Juárez had supported in 1859 the negotiation of the McLane-Ocampo treaties with the United States that pledged Mexico to cede transit rights across the isthmus of Tehuantepec and from the Rio Grande to the Gulf of California. Although most liberals saw these agreements as a triumph for the Juárez government, conservatives were quick to label him a traitor, a charge that reappeared long after his death.[9] His willingness to cede transit rights and the right to use military force to the United States provided the basis for this charge, even though the liberal government argued that it desperately needed the several million dollars that the United States agreed to pay for the cession and that close and friendly relations with the United States were essential for future Mexican development. Although the United States Senate rejected the treaties, many Mexicans continued to regard them as stains on Juárez's reputation.[10]

The other problem raised the specter of dictatorship, symbolized by Santa Anna. Juárez may have not possessed the malevolence and self-centeredness of Santa Anna; yet during his presidency the dictatorial Santa Anna was not yet a memory, and people everywhere were inclined to weigh the possibility that Juárez might become another Santa Anna. In the context of civil war and foreign intervention Juárez concluded that both the interests of the liberal cause and the security of Mexico as an independent and sovereign state required his continuation as president. But that decision was reminiscent of Santa Anna, for Juárez's long presidency conflicted with the ambitions of others and also seemed to threaten the liberal goal, expressed in the Constitution of 1857, to put an end to strong-man governments by concentrating power in the legislative rather than the executive branch. His tenure as president began in January 1858, when he succeeded Comonfort, and he served the remainder of Comonfort's term that, according to the constitution, expired in 1861. Juárez stood for election, opposed by Miguel Lerdo de Tejada and Jesús González Ortega, and during the campaign he faced threats of a coup d'état, a problem he met by governing with a grant of extraordinary power from congress until May 1861. Surrender of power and skillful handling of cabinet problems won support and facilitated his election.[11]

The presidential succession again became an issue in 1864–65 in the midst of the French intervention, and at this dire time González Ortega challenged Juárez. As president of the supreme court and de facto vice-president, the same office Juárez held in 1858 when Comonfort resigned, Ortega claimed the right of succession. Juárez took steps to prevent him from realizing his claim. Based on the extraordinary powers once again granted by congress, he extended his term until such time that elections could be held. He also laid the basis for judicial proceedings against Ortega, who had voluntarily abandoned his post as president of the supreme court and, because he was a general, had deserted his men to flee to the United States in 1865.[12] Many liberals supported Ortega's candidacy in 1865, for they thought that only removal of Juárez from the presidency would help oust the French, preserve the constitution, and bring peace. Juárez retained enough support to extend his presidency and imprisoned Ortega when the latter returned to Mexico in 1867.[13]

Rival images, then, emerged from this period of the Reform. The first projected a good Juárez, the man who through courage and tenacity defended Mexico and its republican constitution. Liberal Mexicans used this image on July 15, 1867, to express their exuberance over the triumph of the republic. The other image, which returned as soon as Juárez began to deal with the mundane tasks of government, depicted a bad Juárez, who used political and legal maneuvers to perpetuate his presidency, who almost compromised the national sovereignty in exchange for Yankee dollars, and who helped undermine such important Mexican institutions and values as the church and communal landholdings as well as the new constitution.

Earlier controversies were forgotten for a moment and unity prevailed in July 1867, and Juárez the leader benefited. Opposition to the cause had been roundly defeated, the Conservative party discredited, and foreign intervention defeated.

Within a short time disunity returned when controversial measures by Juárez after the return to Mexico City in July 1867 and his persistent refusal to vacate the National Palace produced opposition among liberals, who remained skeptical of executive power and wanted no concessions to or accommodation with the church. They thought the liberal attempt at parliamentary democracy was failing, to be replaced by another solution to the problem of law and order—the "constitutional dictatorship."[14] In August 1867 the Juárez government issued a proclamation setting a date for national elections for president, members of the supreme court, and deputies. It asked electors to approve important amendments to the constitution in a way not authorized by the constitution. Because the amendments proposed to strengthen the executive branch of the government they reminded Mexicans of earlier attempts by Juárez to extend his control of the presidency. They provided for a senate, a veto power by the president, written executive reports to congress instead of the verbal interpolation of ministers, limits on the right of congress to call special sessions, and determination of the presidential succession beyond the president of the supreme court. Juárez argued that events of the Reform and French intervention demonstrated a need for a much stronger executive branch. Many liberals opposed the amendments because they feared return to dictatorial or caudillo rule.[15]

Not only did Mexicans object to the amendments, but they criticized the proposed manner of ratification and who should vote. Article 127 of the constitution specified that amendments should pass by a two-thirds vote of congress and required ratification by a majority of state legislatures. Juárez's proclamation stipulated that the people either accept or reject the amendments as general propositions when they voted for candidates. In addition to a controversial mode of ratification, Juárez's proclamation granted the clergy the right to vote, allowed them and federal employees to be deputies in congress, and eliminated the residency requirements for deputies.

With many Mexicans describing Juárez's proclamation as a coup d'état, a phenomenon well known in Mexican history, there came a terrible tempest of protests. *El Siglo Diez y Nueve* condemned one article of the proclamation as "a strong attack on the sovereignty of the states that cannot be tolerated" and warned that the government would lose "the glory and laurels it enjoyed only a month earlier if it failed to listen to the criticism of the press and abandon the scholastic subtleties it uses in the most solemn of proceedings." The proclamation of February 1857 provided the model instead of this new and revolutionary one, *El Siglo* said in defense of the constitution. One of the antagonists of Juárez and his government, Manuel María de Zamacona, used the terms "dictator" and "dictatorship" to characterize the government.[16] Juárez, defender and personification of the constitution on July 15, now seemed the enemy.

Despite the controversy over the August proclamation, Juárez remained the leader and principal symbol of the liberal cause. Because Sebastián Lerdo de Tejada as minister of foreign relations and government drafted and promulgated the document, Juárez avoided some of these attacks, and occasionally liberals forgot the animosities this controversy provoked when they recalled their unity when opposing the conservatives and the French. Clearly referring to Lerdo, who invited caricature as a Jesuit because of his intelligence and appearance, *El Siglo Diez y Nueve* published an article titled "List of Objects, Things, and Persons That Could Be Suppressed with Convenience in Our Society"; included were "the Jesuits who may be in the ministry." Alfredo Chavero in *El Siglo Diez y Nueve* described a "moving incident" at a party late in October 1867 in the National Palace when Ignacio Altamirano, often a critic of Juárez, made a toast to the president and said that before foreign nations the Liberal party did not have divisions. Juárez in response praised the "frank and loyal" opposition.[17]

Although many liberals opposed the reelection of Juárez in 1867, he won an absolute majority in the December election and again served as a symbol of unity. Francisco Zarco often criticized Juárez but rallied liberals to support a Juárez whom Mexicans approved by the election—a "personification of nationality and the resistance of the republic." Zarco attributed other qualities to Juárez, including support for abolition of ecclesiastical privileges to achieve equality of citizens before the law and determination to restore republican institutions of government. "The reelection of Juárez has in our view great political significance, both with respect to foreign and domestic concerns," he continued. "Juárez will again

"Luck should decide, but without tricks," cartoon from *El Padre Cobos,* June 1871. The three contenders for the presidency, Juárez, Díaz, and Lerdo, watch a roulette wheel spin the presidential chair that each hopes to win. Courtesy of the Benson Latin American Collection, The University of Texas at Austin.

be the representative of legality and constitutional order. . . . The majority reelected Juárez because they have confidence in his antecedents and his patriotism. The dictator of yesterday is now a magistrate of limited functions to execute the laws."[18]

Such manifestations of liberal unity disappeared after 1867, when Juárez's decision to run again for president brought him into conflict with two other ambitious men, both of whom had fought alongside him during the Reform. Sebastián Lerdo de Tejada became a key member of Juárez's cabinet during the 1860s but resigned in 1872, retaining the presidency of the supreme court.

"Reelection," cartoon in the pro-Díaz *El Padre Cobos*, June 1871. Juárez is strangling the people with the garrote of another reelection.

By 1871 he had held almost every important office available to an ambitious and talented politician and felt he deserved to succeed Juárez. Similarly, Porfirio Díaz had served in almost all important positions—local deputy, federal deputy, governor of Oaxaca, cabinet minister, military hero in his capacity as a general during the Reform and Intervention (on April 2, 1867, he led victorious Mexican troops into the city of Puebla).[19]

The political history of the 1867–72 period centered largely around the conflict among these three men. As one writer puts the situation in a biography of Lerdo, in regard to Mexico's destiny in general and the presidential chair in particular, Juárez believed he was indispensable, Lerdo regarded himself as infallible, and Díaz saw himself as inevitable.[20] Juárez's reputation as the tenacious defender of the constitution and selfless patriot who led Mexico to victory over foreign and domestic enemies again diminished in the context of this struggle, and no euphoria of triumph, no underlying feeling of unity helped him as he again attempted to win reelection in 1871. His term had been tumultuous, with frequent revolts and requests by the president for grants of power. The Liberal party divided, as did the liberal press. *El Siglo Diez y Nueve* supported Lerdo, and porfiristas founded *El Mensajero* to support Díaz. The juarista press *(Diario Oficial, La Paz, El Federalista,* and *Correo del Comerio)* backed the administration.[21] Critics complained that Juárez subverted the constitution by ruling with grants of power and building a machine to ensure his perpetual reelection, and they used such epithets as "dictator" and "ambitious power-seeker."[22] *El Siglo Diez y Nueve* often ran articles portraying Juárez as a dictator and a tyrant; and another critic, Ignacio Ramírez, urged no reelection—government, he said, had degenerated into favor-giving. Military men, said Ramírez, received medals for servility rather than deeds of valor. Merchants had to solicit patents of contraband from the National Palace so as to avoid ruin. "We must never forget," he warned, that "the tyrant knew how to colonize cemeteries; for the sake of the living and the dead there should be no reelection."[23]

Juárez failed to win a majority of votes, the choice passed to congress, where he did have a majority, and he secured victory but at the cost of estranging Lerdo and provoking Díaz to launch a revolution. The Juárez government suppressed the revolution, only to be confronted by others. Juárez asked for an extension of the powers voted him by congress in December 1871.[24]

He seemed unable to govern with the constitution, and his enemies attacked him as a subverter of the law—democracy, they said, was dead so long as Juárez remained. A liberal journalist, Julio Zárate, concluded that "the majority of the representatives of the people have just legalized the titles of the stupid, immoral, and oppressive six-month-old dictatorship," a harsh judgment after the election in response to congress's approval of Juárez's request for an additional extension of powers in May 1872. Arbitrary government supplanted constitutional government, Zárate charged; never before had democratic institutions been so endangered by those who instead of governing the nation oppressed and impoverished it. The "indefinite and irresponsible dictatorship of Sr. Juárez" led to "disappearance one after another of the patriotic aspirations that were born in the souls of all during the victorious and radiant triumph of the republic in 1867."[25]

Death now interceded on Juárez's behalf. Early in the morning of July 19, 1872, the inhabitants of Mexico City awoke to the roar of artillery followed by cannon shots every quarter hour to signal the death of the head of government.

Once again unity characterized public discourse, for the grand state funeral erased the animosities of the past years. Orations delivered at the cemetery of San Fernando near the Alameda revived Juárez's identification with the liberal triumph; speakers lauded him as "Messiah" and "Redeemer" and as defender of the constitution and hero of American democracy and leader of the Reform and savior of independence; even the journal of the Catholic Society, normally hostile to Juárez and other liberals, praised him as the savior of the republic, "the celebrated head of a party," the "memorable author of the Reform."[26] Juárez alive provoked controversy; dead he was victorious; the hero image prevailed. As part of the political legacy of the Reform—the Constitution of 1857, the development of a constitutional dictatorship, the subordination of powerful corporations to the will of the state, and the final defeat of conservative ideology—Juárez and many of his liberal colleagues became synonymous with Mexican nationalism.

Mexicans built monuments, erected statues, named plazas and libraries, and held two national celebrations to commemorate the centennials of his birth and death.[27] They often invoked his name. Sometimes the image of a bad Juárez appeared, but far more often his name represented to Mexicans what ought to be, for their country and, indeed, for the world.

3

 Juárez and the Politics of the Porfiriato

A deafening discharge of artillery awakened the residents of Mexico City early on the morning of July 19, 1872, to announce the death of Juárez the night before. The president was dead; long live the republic! In this manner a chapter ended and all subsequent chapters began. Fifteen years later, on July 18, 1887, the noise of cannon again stirred the city, this time heralding the first major commemoration of the president's death, and throughout the day the batteries sounded every quarter hour. Parades, speeches, and newspaper commentaries revived memory and dramatized the relation of Juárez to Porfirian Mexico, raising the myth to a new level of importance.

El Siglo Diez y Nueve contrasted the events of 1887 with earlier anniversaries and suggested a need to see Juárez as a standard. After his death, *El Siglo* commented, Mexicans tended to forget his work. Only members of his family, his close friends, and "reformers of the old guard" had gone to lay flowers at his tomb. After revolutions discredited the administration that had succeeded Juárez, a new regime at last had assumed power, bringing an era of peace and material progress. The major questions that divided the people disappeared, and a sense of unity and purpose took hold. The Republican party, *El Siglo* continued, believed that it had triumphed, but the defeated conservatives of course revived and were threatening the work of the Reform. Juárez now intervened, in death as in life. He was a "lighthouse built upon a granite rock capable of withstanding the waves of tempest." He could guide the government of Porfirio Díaz on the right course. Commemoration would rekindle the light and ensure the constitution and the principles of the Reform.[1]

Other papers made similar assessments, observing that conditions required a new look at Juárez, and among the celebrators both the government and its critics figured prominently. Beginning in 1887, official manipulation of a Juárez myth by means of celebrations, eulogistic studies, and textbooks sought to link government policies with those of Juárez, for, although there had been no major commemoration of him until 1887, the former president stood as a major Mexican hero, and the regime of young Díaz, committed to office, was eager to stress the connection between itself and Juárez, even though the two leaders had been enemies. In 1887 the regime's opponents saw an equal need to revive Juárez as an anticlerical symbol and thereby broadened their campaign against Díaz.

Although newspapers sometimes failed to remind Mexicans of anniversaries of Juárez's death, *El Siglo Diez y Nueve* exaggerated the supposed lack of interest during the first years after his death, years that were vital for setting forth ideas that were important in 1887 and in the years that followed. In April 1873, the Mexican congress decreed that Juárez should be "well-deserving of the fatherland"; that his name should be inscribed in gold letters upon the session chamber of the congress; that the national flag should be displayed on public buildings on March 21 and July 18, the momentous anniversaries of his birth and death; that the president should spend ten thousand pesos for a burial monument for Juárez and his wife and fifty thousand pesos for a national monument that should bear his statue and be finished by May 5, 1874; that pensions be arranged for members of his family; and that the president should appoint a commission to award a prize of two thousand pesos for the best biography.[2] Although construction of the national monument had to await the 1910 centennial celebration of Mexican independence, President Díaz was able to help dedicate the burial monument in the San Fernando cemetery in 1880; and by 1887 a portion of the route Juárez and his followers took on their triumphal entry into the Mexican capital in 1867 had been named the Avenida Juárez.[3]

In 1874 a liberal member of congress and dramatist, Gustavo Baz, published a biography linking Juárez with liberalism and describing his life as the vindication of a social class. Baz said that Juárez owed his fame to his unwavering support for the Reform and Mexico's sovereignty, causes intrinsically noble and just. Comparing him to Washington, Hidalgo, Garibaldi, Kosciusko, and Toussaint, Baz pointed to Juárez as an American and revolutionary as opposed to a European and traditionalist. Juárez indeed personified the difference between the political histories of Europe and America in that he defended the principles of government by law as opposed to government by a monarch. Baz acknowledged that Juárez had been controversial while alive (he and his government erred in the proclamation of August 1867) but insisted that the Juárez regime always respected the rights and interests of the opposition. Above all, Juárez served as a lesson to those who in the future must take up the cause of justice and progress. He proved, Baz said, an eternal example to imitate in the noise of combat over social transformations and in defense of national integrity. History treated the past, Baz wrote, but it served as a guide to action in the present and future.[4]

Others supported these projects and sentiments. In a pamphlet written in 1873 but not published until 1887, Marcial Aznar depicted Juárez as the symbol of a race and the nation, claiming that he had saved democracy in moments of supreme crisis, given force to a system of popular representation, saved independence, put Mexico on an equal footing with European nations, and issued the Laws of the Reform to combat ecclesiastical errors. Juárez vindicated the "indigenous race," Aznar wrote; before him Mexico had been the "plaything of European powers."[5] Similarly, *El Monitor Republicano* devoted a long editorial in 1874 to praising Juárez for his role as "the spirit of national defense" during the Reform and the Intervention; and in the late 1870s and early 1880s his name assumed importance in the pages of *La Libertad* and other newspapers as they debated the nature and future of liberalism as both an ideology and a program in Mexico.[6]

By the late 1870s political and ideological forces in Mexico created a climate for the use of the myth in debate rather than merely as support for a hero symbol. Sebastián Lerdo de Tejada succeeded Juárez in 1872, and although he briefly enjoyed support, his popularity declined because he was unable to subordinate the factions and individuals in local areas to the national government—and also because of Díaz's lust for power. In January 1876, Díaz proclaimed the Plan of Tuxtepec, which asserted the principle of no reelection and called for the expulsion of Lerdo and other officials chosen in the election of July 1873. Presidential elections took place during the summer of 1876, but the president of the supreme court, José María Iglesias, declared them invalid and proclaimed himself president. The Díaz revolt continued and succeeded; by the end of the year both Lerdo and Iglesias had fled the country, and the Díaz forces occupied Mexico City.[7]

The indomitable Díaz—he was to become an idol in Mexican politics, although not of the mold of Juárez—now began thirty-five years of domination of the country's political and economic destiny. Adhering only once to the principle of no reelection, he allowed a loyal friend of almost twenty years to succeed him in 1880; but then resolution if not revolution triumphed, and with the help of constitutional amendments and an effective political machine Díaz served continuously as the president of Mexico from 1884 to 1911.[8] He adopted a policy of conciliation toward the church by tolerating violations of the Laws of the Reform, which had been incorporated into the Mexican constitution in 1873. Soon, and to the dismay of many liberals with vivid memory of the anticlerical struggle of the 1850s, the black cassocks of the clergy became a familiar sight in the streets, along with such public religious acts as the coronation of the Virgin of Guadalupe and pilgrimages to the grandiose shrine near Mexico City.[9] Díaz sought to develop a friendly press through coercion, subsidy, and establishment of semiofficial newspapers—*El Partido Liberal* (1885–96) and *El Imparcial* (1896–1911).[10]

Under Díaz, peace, order, material progress, and executive centralism became the objectives of government, a commitment Juárez himself had undertaken when he returned to Mexico City in 1867. The emphasis seemed to require rejection or modification of important elements of liberalism, a change many Mexicans did not want. Although Díaz carefully identified himself with the liberal tradition in Mexico, his approach to government, like that of Juárez before him, was pragmatic, for he understood the contradictions between many older liberal values and Mexican tradition. Nevertheless, he and his followers could exploit and change Mexican liberalism to support the lifelong presidency to which he committed himself in 1887 and provide an ideology for the regime. Both before and during his first administration (1876–80) and that of his successor, Manuel González (1880–84), Mexican liberalism was shaped so as to provide the ideological foundation of a Díaz dictatorship.

How then could Díaz's opposition use the Juárez myth against the wily dictator? For both the old liberals and the new pragmatic or scientific liberals, Juárez became a symbol to manipulate. Díaz and the new liberals continued to celebrate the leadership of Juárez during the Reform and the Intervention; they also realistically viewed him as the man who laid the basis for the presidential government that was carried to the ultimate extreme by the dictatorship of Díaz. Recognizing the dimensions of Juárez as a national idol and praising him as a man of great courage and accomplishment, they cautiously described similarities between Juárez and Díaz by playing down the young Díaz's early opposition to Juárez and drawing the general as carrying on the task begun by his great predecessor.[11] But other liberals regarded Juárez as quite different from Díaz. They preferred to overlook the Juárez of the restored republic, who after the experience of the Reform and the Intervention saw a need for a strengthened executive, and to emphasize his earlier, more radical and patriotic role as defender of the constitution of 1857 and sponsor of the Laws of the Reform and as champion of republicanism and Mexican independence during the Intervention.

Although the ideal of a secular national state built upon anticorporatism and utilitarianism formed the heart of the ideology of all liberals, some of them were especially attracted to positivism and conservative Spanish republicanism. These new ideas and models helped change their views of Juárez and Mexican history. While Juárez was alive, and on the anniversary of the beginning of the Mexican independence movement in 1867, Gabino Barreda, a student of the French positivist Auguste Comte, delivered a speech in Guanajuato in which he applied the notions of his mentor to advance a new interpretation of Mexican history. Characterizing history as a science subject to laws that made possible both an explanation of the past and an anticipation of the future, he described Mexican history before 1867 as emancipation from the colonial order, when liberals freed Mexico from religion. The next stage, he said, was beginning and would produce a social order guided by liberty and progress.[12] Inspired by these ideas, Juárez appointed Barreda as director of the new National Preparatory School, a positivist model for similar schools throughout Mexico.[13] Other liberals began to argue that the older, more reform-oriented liberalism needed to be modified to fit a new reality. They viewed the restoration of the republic as the opening of a new national era in which emphasis should be on a strong president, a centralized state, and economic growth rather than individual liberties.[14]

For Barreda and many others 1867 seemed a crucial year for Mexican liberal ideology and institutions; and the following generation saw the defeat of both Lerdo and Iglesias in the 1870s as further evidence of the disappearance of an old age. Such men as Justo Sierra and his brother Santiago, Telesforo García, and Francisco Cosmes viewed their defeat as the end of an older, jacobin, theoretical, dogmatic liberalism that served Mexico well during the Reform but now seemed inappropriate. In 1878 these men founded the newspaper *La Libertad* and used it to argue for a scientific, pragmatic approach to politics and to work out a new liberal program for Mexico.[15] They provided Díaz with the theory and program of a centralized, capitalistic, and authoritarian state, but in the process they alienated many who objected to changes in the sacred text of Mexican liberalism, the Constitution of 1857. *La Libertad* sought liberal unity; instead it contributed to division.[16]

Writers for *La Libertad* found the Juárez of the August 1867 proclamation particularly important, even though they conceded that he and his advisers might have erred in the means they proposed for carrying it out. They characterized the proclamation as a profound observation about the needs of the country and used it to call for an extension of the presidential term to six or seven years, establishment of a suspensive veto, and temporary legislative powers for the president. Excessive individualism and faith in democracy led to anarchy, they thought. As Justo Sierra explained, individual rights were not absolute or separate from the needs of society; the individual and society are two great organic realities, he intoned, inseparable.[17] Reforms in the Constitution of 1857, a document these men characterized as an "ideal law made for abstract man" and the product of a "literary liberalism," would make it "a Mexican law adequate for our present condition."[18] Such reforms, they maintained, would strengthen the central government and within it the president, and only in that way could Mexico achieve the liberty, order, and progress that Barreda called for in his civic oration of September 1867. Mexican aptitude for democracy, they concluded, was, in a rather unattractive metaphor, merely a germ surrounded by elements of death.[19]

La Libertad saw the Juárez of the 1867 proclamation as a model but criticized him for personalism—a bane of Mexican politics generally and the Liberal party in particular, a blight it hoped to overcome by a program that would make the party something more than an instrument for personal ambition. Liberals, lamented a writer in one of the first issues of the paper, were *juaristas* or *lerdistas* or *iglesistas* or *porfiristas* first and liberals second. Juárez's reelection in 1867 was justified, for "the entire country was eager to glorify their own country in the person of the benemérito Juárez"; but the great man erred in seeking reelection in 1871, for it could be accomplished only through pressure and "shameful parliamentary coalitions."[20]

La Libertad's liberal critics could agree with this evaluation of the 1871 reelection, but they found distressing characterizations of the Constitution of 1857 as "celestial music" or "literary liberalism" and the changes proposed by *La Libertad.* Expressing themselves in such newspapers as *La República* and *El Monitor Republicano,* these liberals found the Juárez who defended the Constitution of 1857 and who led liberals to their triumph in 1867 to be an increasingly important symbol in the polemics of 1878–84 with *La Libertad* and in the years that followed. The old liberals attacked the new by describing the latter men as embracing a system that denied absolute truths and the proposition that the "rights of men are found in principles of liberty and equality before the law."[21]

As Mexican intellectuals used Juárez to debate the nature of liberalism, other Mexicans began using him as a way to claim status or to disagree with government policies. Workers' organizations adopted Juárez as one of their heroes, and *El Monitor Republicano* praised a commemoration in 1875 in Mexico City on the anniversary of his death. In 1876 the Gran Círculo de Obreros de México conducted a similar event. Founded in the early 1870s, this organization attracted members from all parts of Mexico and by 1874 had acquired several thousand. Because many people accused it and other labor organizations of communist inclinations, they took every opportunity to identify themselves with Mexican heroes. The 1876 event consisted of a demonstration in the morning at the tomb of Juárez and a literary party in the evening. A baker and a tailor gave speeches praising Juárez for the Constitution of 1857, the basic law that guaranteed freedom of association, and for his advocacy of the Laws of the Reform and unswerving defense of the rights of Mexico before the threat of the foreigner.[22] This ceremony began a long tradition of worker participation in the Juárez myth, an involvement that included active promotion of the erection of monuments to both Miguel Hidalgo y Costilla and Juárez in the Paseo de la Reforma during the commemoration year of 1887.[23]

Critics of the government found it useful to invoke Juárez for protesting the opening of the country to foreign investment and laxity in enforcement of anticlerical laws. In 1884 a newspaper called *La Voz de Juárez* attacked the government's policy of promoting economic development by granting concessions to foreign companies, citing Juárez for resisting offers of arms and money for railroad concessions.[24] In 1875 *El Monitor Republicano* protested a religious procession in Toluca that was held without permission of the governor and the governor's acquiescence to popular demand that the priest and other religious-minded paraders be released from jail. "We desire that the law be fulfilled by everyone," the paper editorialized on the anniversary of Juárez's death, "above all so that the government shall be respected by all those who inhabit Mexican territory."[25] Ten years later the Benito Juárez Society of Toluca admonished the government to adhere to a liberal and reformist creed, an effort that *El Monitor Republicano* described resignedly as vain.[26]

Two prominent liberals who opposed *La Libertad* and its program in the 1880s published important but different evaluations of Juárez and his role in Mexican history. The leader of Mexico's literary renaissance after 1867 and a veteran of the battles of the Reform and the Intervention, Ignacio M. Altamirano, saw Juárez as an important political leader who had left a legacy of accomplishment and failure. He described Juárez as courageous and brave but lacking initiative and judgment, possessing only modest talent and "scarce and imperfect learning." Juárez, he said, hesitated to accept the advice of his ministers, who possessed far more talent, and he introduced such undemocratic practices as coalitions with governors of states for imposition of official candidates and refused to dismiss ministers even when their measures suffered defeat in the legislature. Little economic progress occurred during his presidency. Altamirano praised Juárez for respecting the press and noted the widespread sympathy and shock of Mexicans when they learned of his death. Seldom did the death of a man so rapidly silence the criticism raised against him, Altamirano concluded.[27]

The image of Juárez the hero interested and attracted an old liberal, José María Vigil, who sustained a long polemic with Justo Sierra and other editors of *La Libertad* between 1878 and 1882. Vigil provided a tribute to Juárez in the final volume of the monumental *México a través de los siglos,* published between 1886 and 1889. Edited by Vicente Riva Palacio and incorporating some of the ideas of the new liberalism, this work was the first liberal survey of Mexican history. The last volume recounted events of the Reform and concluded with generous praise: "Depository of the law and the most sacred rights of the nation, he revealed nothing in his conduct that would suggest vacillation or distrust." Enemies of that worthy man, Vigil continued, looked in vain with a "malevolently critical microscope" for something to insult. Juárez, however, was one of those colossal figures that grows and shines more and more as time passes because the disappearance of the hatreds of faction makes his services to the fatherland and humanity more obvious. Juárez was a worthy successor to such liberals as Gómez Farías, José María Morelos, and Hidalgo and the man most responsible for leading liberals to their triumph in 1867.[28]

All liberals supported the 1887 commemoration, organized by friends and associates of President Díaz. After Díaz's decision to stay in office for at least another term and the successful amending of the constitution in early 1887 to make that possible, the government was particularly eager to identify its fortunes with the man who now seemed to be a major national hero. Such association would be awkward, for Díaz had been Juárez's principal adversary after 1867. As Joaquín Casasús pointed out during debate on the amendment permitting reelection, if death had not removed Juárez in 1872, the Díaz revolution of La Noria, which Casasús called the "daughter of the popular will," might have toppled him.[29] Díaz's reelection in 1888 and in following years made him an heir. Of course he wanted to be viewed as the legitimate leader, the man most qualified to guide the goals of Juárez toward fulfillment.

To help achieve this grandiloquent object, two Díaz constituencies, the press and the Oaxacan colony in Mexico City, cooperated to organize a commemoration on July 18, 1887. Responding to a suggestion by Gustavo Baz, José Vicente Villada, the editor of the semiofficial *El Partido Liberal,* in early July published an invitation to Mexico City's liberal press to take part in a manifestation. Its purpose, Villada said, was "to tighten the bonds of union among liberals by reaffirming before Juárez's tomb the eternal oath of never to compromise with the enemies of liberty and the Reform, those remnants of a party that wander amid the shadows like lepers of the Middle Ages who found themselves exiled from all cities." Citing the Juárez decree of amnesty of 1867 that permitted the return to Mexico City of Archbishop Pelagio Antonio de Labastida y Dávalos, the cleric who led the revolt against the new constitution in 1857, *El Partido Liberal* sought to allay liberal discontent with Díaz's conciliation toward the church by pointing to similarity between conciliation and the moderate policy after 1867. At the same time Oaxacans, led by Felix Romero, who served as a member and president of the Mexican supreme court during much of the Porfiriato, announced a meeting to plan the commemoration of 1887. In the context of the recent debate over reelection and the substantial opposition to accommodation with the church, Villada and Romero saw Juárez as a symbol to unify the liberals and perhaps even all Mexicans.[30]

Members of the liberal press agreed to participate, but many of them saw an opportunity to revive anticlericalism and remind the government of the law. "Only the name of Benito Juárez can unite the various elements of the Liberal party," commented *El Monitor Republicano*. "The manifestation will be national in scope with impact not only in the capital but in the states." *El Siglo Diez y Nueve* stressed an anticlerical theme, lauding public power as a guarantee that functionaries would defend the constitution and principles of the Reform. *El Diario del Hogar*, edited by Filomeno Mata, a harsh critic of the Díaz regime, evaluated the event as an act of a nation to deify one of its heroes: "The religion of cultured people ought to be the deification of their great men." In its view Mexico had arrived at a time when Juárez deserved deification as the author of the second independence and the Reform and placement in the pantheon of Mexican national heroes.[31]

The conservative Catholic press reacted differently, interpreting the affair as hostile to Catholics—the great majority of the nation—and instead celebrating Agustín Iturbide, who died on July 19, 1824. *El Nacional* announced that although it acknowledged Juárez as a major figure in the history of the Mexican people, it could not take part because of the anti-Catholic nature of the proceedings, and *La Voz de México*, the Catholic daily of the capital, said Mexicans ought to honor Iturbide, who sustained the Christian constitution of society that Mexico enjoyed under viceregal government. According to *La Voz de México* and other Catholic journals and organizations, Iturbide had formulated the Plan of Iguala ending the independence struggle in 1821 by guaranteeing independence, equality for those born in America and Europe, and respect for the Catholic church, and he thereby signified Mexican acceptance of a Catholic and Hispanic tradition. Thus rivalry between the anniversaries of these two men became an important aspect of the myth.[32]

The great manifestation of 1887 began as a liberal undertaking to promote both liberal and national unity, but the result was discord. Pro-Díaz liberals saw the event as a way to muster support for the government in the context of increasing discontent over policies, notably the decision to amend the constitution to permit one reelection of the president and to allow conciliation toward the church, but other liberals saw it as a means to remind the government to adhere to the Reform laws and both the letter and spirit of the constitution. Conservatives felt left out. All participants used this and subsequent commemorations to promote their interest or view.

The sound of artillery and the raising of the national flag to half mast on all buildings early in the morning of July 18, 1887, began a day filled with oratory, parades, meetings, and banquets. The city took on a grave and serene aspect. The School of Mines, where the parade to the tomb of Juárez began, displayed three large white and black wreaths, and streamers of black cloth hung from the national palace. A veritable forest of streamers, flags, and hangings festooned the Calle de los Plateros (today the Avenida Madero), which joined Constitution Plaza and the Alameda and merged with the recently named Avenida Juárez. Balconies displayed portraits. The east side of the San Fernando cemetery contained a double row of three-colored masts crowned with streamers. Floral offerings abounded, on and around the tomb of Juárez.

Departing from the School of Mines and representing many groups, the procession moved slowly through the streets. A band was in the vanguard, survivors of the Congress of 1856–57, *inmaculados* (those who accompanied Juárez to Paso del Norte and never were in territory subject to imperial rule), veterans of the War of the Reform, representatives of liberal newspapers and of the Oaxacan colony in Mexico City (a group of Oaxacans invited Díaz and cabinet members), the Benito Juárez Society of Toluca, representatives of schools, Masonic lodges, labor, and a delegation from the Gran Congreso Obreros de la República. Paraders moved to the corner of Calle de Moneda, where Juárez had his apartments in the National Palace and where he had died, and in the presence of President Díaz officials unveiled a plaque. Then the group moved around Constitution Plaza and down the Calle de los Plateros to the Avenida Juárez and the San Fernando cemetery where members of the Juárez family waited.[33] Shortly after ten in the morning the president and his retinue arrived and the ceremony began.

A Oaxacan, godfather of one of Juárez's daughters and in 1887 minister of foreign relations, Ignacio Mariscal, together with Guillermo Prieto, a staunch Reform liberal and intimate of Juárez, who had served in cabinets with and under Juárez, gave the principal speeches. Mariscal stressed the need for unity in liberal ranks. Extolling Juárez as a defender of the constitution and author of the Reform, he said Juárez would be remembered for leaving a free and independent Mexico, autonomous government, and republican institutions. Republic and independence were the values most closely associated with Juárez: Juárez was the symbol and central value of Mexican life. Prieto displayed more belligerence by setting out the anticlerical theme, expressing the views of many liberals not associated with the government: "The Mexican people answer in mass the calumny and the diatribes of hate, sacrilege, and profanation against this tomb and these ashes." He saw a "priesthood" threatening all ideals of liberty, equality, talent, justice, independence, and fatherland, all symbolized by Juárez. He seemed to express best the sentiments of the old or jacobin liberals. Francisco González echoed these views in reference to the "great event of July 18" to condemn as hypocrisy the decision of the town council of Mexico City to allow enemies of the Reform to have a demonstration on the day of the coronation of the Virgin of Guadalupe.[34]

Caricatures published for the July 18 event made very graphic the verbal comments. One entitled "Los mochos en la tumba de Juárez" showed rats representing the "clerical reaction" climbing over Juárez's sepulcher; in the next frame, "July 18," the people arrived, carrying banners reading "Long live Juárez!" and the *mochos* scurried into the "tombs of the reaction." Another caricature entitled "Painting Lesson" showed Díaz, with help from his teacher "Public Opinion," trying to make a copy of a picture of the bust of Juárez. Such words as discretion, constitutionalism, and patriotism surrounded Juárez. Another caricature showed the state governors at work at their easels in the studio of Public Opinion, who stood behind them with a lash, forcing them to produce exact copies of the model of a good liberal, Juárez.[35]

As a regional group, Oaxacans found value in promoting the memory of their native son, and even before the 1887 commemoration they often went to the tomb to leave flowers and pay homage. Because of Díaz's Oaxacan associations they operated as

"Rats at the Tomb of Juárez," from *El Hijo del Ahuizote*, July 24, 1887. Courtesy of the Benson Latin American Collection, The University of Texas at Austin.

"A Painting Lesson," from *El Hijo del Ahuizote*, July 24, 1887. Courtesy of the Benson Latin American Collection, The University of Texas at Austin.

"A Portrait Lesson," from *El Hijo del Ahuizote,* July 31, 1887. Courtesy of the Benson Latin American Collection, The University of Texas at Austin.

a powerful group in Mexico City during the Díaz era and helped give the Juárez myth a regional cast.[36]

Future commemorations of both Juárez's birth and death attracted participation of all these groups, and often their involvement enhanced the polemical aspect of celebrations. With Díaz and his ministers appearing regularly and José Vicente Villada continuing his role as one of the principal organizers, official participation dominated after 1887. *El Universal* joined *El Partido Liberal* in 1888 to reflect official views by celebrating Juárez as a hero, describing him as responsible for national independence and lauding Díaz for establishing peace, well-being, and progress, arguing that the two men attained greatness not as revolutionaries but as leaders of government.[37]

Liberal opponents found the annual commemorations useful to criticize the government and try to separate the two men. *El Monitor Republicano* and *El Diario del Hogar* described Juárez as a reformer and revolutionary, a pure liberal who championed separation of church and state and the cause of secular democracy.

Despite harassment by the government, *El Diario del Hogar* was unrelenting in these themes: Juárez's authorship of the Laws of the Reform contrasted with Díaz's failure to enforce them; Juárez's defense of the constitution versus Díaz's profanation by failure to enforce its anticlerical provisions, his addiction to reelection, and his disrespect for the press.[38]

The 1887 commemoration began as a demonstration of liberal and national unity, and such celebrations became forums of argument. Conservatives saw the affairs as hostile and either ignored them or honored men they considered more authentic heroes such as Iturbide. Groups close to the government tried to use the commemorations for their own purposes. Liberals not associated with the government saw the anniversaries as useful opportunities. Juárez thus was far more valuable to all Mexicans dead than alive.

4

The Centennial—1906

The extraordinary recognition of Juárez as a hero that began in 1887 culminated in 1906 with a national celebration of the centennial of his birth. This exalted affair, and four years later the centennial of the beginning of Mexican independence, elevated the memory of Juárez to the level of a cult. It enhanced Díaz's prestige by linking him with his illustrious predecessor. Ironically, as this and the two subsequent chapters will show, it also encouraged his opposition.

Many countries besides Mexico have attached social and political meaning to commemorations and public festivals, which leaders use to enlist support for national causes. Such events that manipulate past heroes and events to encourage sentiments of patriotism, loyalty, national identity, and belief in the virtue and inspiration of the contemporary civil order have come to define what many observers have called civic religion.[1] Before the French Revolution Jean Jacques Rousseau recognized the usefulness of myths, rituals, and festivals to explain and dramatize the origins, principles, rules, and destiny of a free people, and he recommended that rulers pattern festivals after those of republican Rome. Public festivals, he thought, could make people love their country and the government charged with preserving public peace. Festivals could be used in much the same way as the liturgy, for the modern state required pageants to define the abstract ideologies of republicanism and nationalism. During the French Revolution the Jacobins put his theories into practice by raising the

43

tree of liberty, enthroning the goddess of reason, and pointing to the rays of the sun as symbols of republican virtue. They enlisted painters, musicians, and writers to glorify the new order. Subsequent regimes built triumphal arches and monuments in Paris to commemorate anniversaries in the Revolution. In 1880, not too long before the Juárez centennial, the French began to celebrate July 14, the greatest national festival of all.[2]

Germans and Americans meanwhile were creating their own traditions. An early advocate of the public festival in Germany was Friedrich Ludwig Jahn, a high school teacher in Berlin, who worked to free Germany from Napoleonic rule and who organized the Turnverein, a gymnastic association to build strength and fellowship among young people of all classes and to promote German nationalism. He advocated festivals that, like the carnivals of Rome, would enable people to give of themselves without direction from above. In 1810 Jahn saw such festivals as an expression of the new nationalism he was promoting; he believed they also gave concrete form to the people as a primeval force without any representative intermediaries to help accomplish their purpose. After German political unity was achieved in 1871, the nobles and businessmen started a national festival society to overcome social differences and draw people into political life. They attempted to surmount public indifference to remembrance of Sedan, the site of a victory over the French during the war of 1870–71. This form of celebration came to a climax years later during the Nazi era when Germany's rulers sought to direct what earlier had been described as spontaneous events: on the Nazi party's Day of Martyrs every man in Germany became a living symbol of the community.[3]

Americans developed a set of symbols and holidays, as well as monuments to heroes and glorious accomplishments. Like the early German endeavors, much of the effort was spontaneous and popular, although the government recognized the importance of heroes and holidays. George Washington, the first citizen of eighteenth-century Virginia, became a national hero-symbol, and the Fourth of July was celebrated as the nation's greatest holiday. Early in the nineteenth century the historian George Bancroft began his survey of American history to lend historical support to the exaltation of Washington and others of the Founding Fathers. Americans, he argued, were God's chosen people, and they had a duty to further the cause of liberty, democracy, and Christianity. As the village of Washington became a full-fledged city, monuments and public buildings imitating the styles of Greece and Rome were built as if to proclaim that America embodied the principles of the Roman republic or Greek democracy.[4]

In Mexico the Díaz government, seeking to enthrone itself, memorialized what it regarded as important people and important days in Mexican history. It began to subsidize the writing of history. Suitable schoolbooks, of course, assisted the few who learned to read. But annual commemorations of such timeless events as the death of Juárez, the victory over the French at Puebla on May 5, 1862, and Hidalgo's 1810 proclamation that began the independence movement appealed to a public that loved spectacle. The government built the monuments and put up the statues as permanent memorials. In the early 1880s it constructed statues of leaders along the Paseo de la Reforma in Mexico City and in 1891 dedicated a statue in the National Palace to the hero of the Reform, Benito Juárez. Fashioned with bronze taken from cannons used by conservatives during the War of the Reform and with metal from a piece of artillery employed by the French during the Intervention, this statue enabled the Mexican government to provide yet one more reminder to Mexicans of those events and Juárez's huge role in them. At the dedication, duly attended by Díaz, a member of the cabinet, Manuel Dublán, spoke of the transcendental meaning of Juárez in the life of Mexico.[5]

Mexican intellectuals joined the government in promoting the hero symbols and use of festivals to give unity and loyalty to the regime. The leading intellectual of the Porfiriato and secretary of education and fine arts in the Díaz cabinet for several years, Justo Sierra, urged the adoption of days of the year as holidays. He thought November 2 should be set aside to recall the heroes of independent Mexico, including Hidalgo and Juárez. That day, he argued, would remind Mexicans of such aspects of their history as the devotion of both men. In a speech before the chamber of deputies in 1880 he pointed out that Mexico's enjoyment of an era of work and peace after the tumultuous battles of earlier years required the nation to honor those men who had helped the country attain its felicitous present state. The editor of *El Partido Liberal* and principal organizer of the 1887 Juárez commemoration, José Vicente Villada, urged the government to continue to exploit the symbolic value of Juárez; and responding to an attack on Juárez, the positivist historian Francisco Cosmes argued that countries with large illiterate populations need hero worship to secure the allegiance of the masses.[6]

Building on an already well-developed tradition of festivals, Mexicans began to plan and organize a centennial in 1903. Individuals and organizations took part in the planning, but by 1906 the government had assumed responsibility for the celebration. On March 21, 1903, a provisional commission that included such veterans of the congress that drafted the Constitution of 1857 as Felix Romero, Justino Fernández, and Benito Gómez Farías met to form plans for a centennial. This group called for an assembly to choose a national commission consisting of one representative from each state and territory to prepare the program. Instead, the government named the National Commission for the Juárez Centennial, headed by Romero, and it in turn named delegates and subdelegates in the states.[7] Objecting to this government involvement, *El Diario del Hogar* asserted that the government feared an honest election (the sixth reelection of Díaz loomed in 1904) and decided that the Interior Ministry rather than a national assembly should determine the composition of the national commission.[8]

Without achieving the spontaneity and unanimous approval that some desired, the commission began in the summer of 1903 to make the celebration appear as popular as it could by requiring participation from all levels of government and encouraging activities that would involve large numbers of people. The Mexican congress cooperated by suspending import taxes on statues and busts of Juárez that state and municipal governments purchased abroad for public buildings and plazas. The commission sponsored a literary competition for books on Juárez and his era, and the secretary of public instruction announced a competition for a hymn to Juárez and a biography suitable for reading in public schools on the day of the centennial. The commission attempted to carry out the 1873 authorization for a national monument in

Mexico City, but construction had to await the 1910 independence celebration. Meanwhile, it recommended that locomotives display large banners with pictures of Juárez on the day of the celebration and that free tickets be issued to individuals traveling to commemorations.[9]

With more than two years devoted to preparation for the centennial, few could escape awareness of Benito Juárez in Mexican history. Juárez came to life in the oratory, parades, pantomimes, and other spectacles of the celebration. Plazas, streets, and public buildings and institutions assumed the name "Juárez," and practically every town and city added at least one statue or monument.

Three days of events in the capital of the northeastern state of Tamaulipas, Ciudad Victoria, typified the activity throughout Mexico. An atmosphere of carnival dominated the city. Adorned and brilliantly illuminated throughout the three-day festival, the Plaza Libertad became Plaza Juárez, and owners and tenants of buildings facing Juárez, Hidalgo, and Morelos streets decorated their properties and illuminated them at night. Young and old, high officials and lowly artisans and vagabonds—all celebrated the fiesta of the hero. A scholastic festival, which involved boys and girls from public and private schools, and a fireworks display had prepared townspeople for the full schedule of events on March 21. At dawn of the twenty-first, salvos from artillery, pealing bells in church towers, locomotive and factory whistles, and music from three bands accompanied the raising of the national flag on all public buildings. At eight o'clock teachers and students met to unveil portraits of Juárez and plaques commemorating the grand day; these ceremonies were led by the governor of the state, the director of public instruction, and the municipal president. At nine in the morning the governor dedicated the Plaza Juárez that contained a column and bust, as well as public works. From nine to ten a student group marched, and at noon there was a repetition of the dawn ceremonies. With the governor presiding, another ceremony, highlighted by speeches and playing of the national anthem, took place at four in the afternoon. Participants marched down Hidalgo Street to the Plaza Hidalgo for homage to Miguel Hidalgo y Costilla, hero of Mexican independence. At six a ceremony accompanied the lowering of the national flag. Evening events consisted of a grand serenade from eight to eleven in the plazas Hidalgo and Juárez. Bands of the state and the institute played, and fireworks added sparkle throughout.

The festivities at Ciudad Victoria continued the next day, March 22. From nine to eleven in the morning the city enjoyed a musical matinee in Hidalgo and Juárez plazas and beginning at four a cavalcade of wagons and carriages decorated to be allegorical moved from the Juárez Plaza to the Alameda, where an orator gave the discourse. Then a great civic march moved down Hidalgo Street to the Plaza Hidalgo, followed by a parade in front of the state government building. Serenades filled the evening hours in Hidalgo and Juárez plazas. Three times during the three-day celebration officials raised gas-filled balloons carrying honorific inscriptions from the period of the Reform.[10]

Similar activities went on throughout Mexico, and in many cities and towns officials used the occasion to dedicate public works. In Ciudad Juárez the government initiated a potable water system, a new school, a public garden, a wider street, and a school of agriculture valued altogether at more than a million and a half pesos. Streets, buildings, and institutions assumed the glorious name Juárez, as did a barber shop and a restaurant.[11] Evidence perhaps that the policy of conciliation with the church enjoyed some success, the Caballeros de Colón joined masonic lodges, government employees, members of scientific organizations, and many others in a parade, serenades, and fireworks displays in Mexico City.[12] A public dinner attracted ten thousand of the capital's poor to the Porfirio Díaz park so that they could feel some material involvement in the great event. Assuming a "profoundly altruistic" and a "highly democratic character," according to *El Mundo Ilustrado,* city officials thereupon offered a meal requiring eleven thousand loaves of bread, eighty thousand tortillas, sixteen cattle, seven hundred kilograms of rice, a thousand liters of beans, three thousand pounds of fish, twenty sheep, and five thousand pastries—all donated by stores—as well as ten thousand bottles of beer thoughtfully donated by the Cervecería de Toluca. Felix Díaz together with the son of Juárez, then a member of congress from the state of Oaxaca, and other dignitaries shared the repast, although they dined in a special area.[13]

The drama of these events appealed to large numbers of people, from schoolchildren and poor and illiterate to government elites. Publications endeavored to provide a more permanent homage and contributed to the continuity of the myth that many liberals were developing in their books and in pages of such papers as *La Libertad, El Partido Liberal, El Universal,* and *El Imparcial* beginning in the late 1870s. They all characterized the Juárez era as one of transition, which broke the power of the church, defended the independence of Mexico, and began a pragmatic reassessment of the Constitution of 1857. Many observers linked Juárez and Díaz by showing Juárez as a precursor. Prizes were awarded in the competition sponsored by such organizations as the National Commission for the Juárez Centennial and government ministries. Other Mexicans not so friendly to Díaz found the official manipulation distasteful and stressed the discontinuities between Juárez and Díaz, especially with regard to the Constitution of 1857. They identified Juárez as representative of the older, purer liberal who led the attack on the church and other privileged orders and defended the independence of Mexico and the constitution as drafted in 1857.

A primary school teacher in the state of Guerrero, Francisco Figueroa, submitted a eulogistic biography of Juárez to the secretary of public instruction, who selected it as winner of the competition for a biography suitable for reading in state primary schools on the day of the centennial. Stressing themes already associated with Juárez, projecting him as a model Mexican, and exhorting Mexican schoolchildren to emulate him, Figueroa emphasized Juárez's rise from humble origin to a position of respect and achievement not only in Mexico but in the world. He pointed out that Juárez had sided with the good men of Mexican history, the liberals, and was unswerving in his dedication to the cause. Figueroa related present and past by noting that Juárez prepared the way for the present time of peace, overthrowing the regime of privileged military and clerical classes and overcoming the backwardness that impeded liberty of conscience, work, education, and belief. Figueroa noted Victor Hugo's praise of Juárez as the savior of Mexico to show that the hero had won for Mexico international fame and respect.[14]

In the competition sponsored by the commission, Ricardo García Granados's *La Constitución y las Leyes de la Reforma en México* won first prize. Like the Figueroa biography it described the age as a transition during which the liberals broke the power of the church and established the separation of church and state as a prelude to the Díaz era of peace and stability. García Granados focused attention on the Mexican constitution and stressed its idealistic and theoretical character under both Juárez and Lerdo. Defining a constitution as a pact among the powers that constitute the government of the nation, he found the Constitution of 1857 a system of political philosophy with limited applicability, a statement of aspirations rather than a real constitution.

A real constitution, he argued, reflected the habits and customs of the people, and in Mexico that meant central government rather than democracy, which could operate only with equal and universal suffrage. Only Switzerland had attained that happy condition. The administrations of Juárez and Lerdo witnessed the substitution of neofeudalism for centralism and militarism. Díaz destroyed the system of *cacicazgos* or political feudalism, however, and assured peace and national unity. Under Díaz an idealistic written constitution gave way to a more realistic government by power. On balance, the Laws of the Reform provided the more important legacy of the Juárez era, not only because they helped separate church and state but because they provided an example of strong executive government.[15]

Andrés Molina Enríquez's *Juárez y la Reforma,* which looked to the social instead of the political aspects of Mexico during the Juárez age, won a prize. Molina accented the role of racial elites during two key periods. Creoles, he said, dominated during the disintegration that followed independence, whereas the more progressive Indian and mestizo elements wielded power during the present period of integration. He characterized the Reform as a transition during which the Constitution of 1857 defined Mexican nationalism and finally triumphed after the victory of Capulalpán. Molina considered Juárez the hero of the Reform, for as a member of a racially progressive elite he became the true founder of Mexican nationalism, the personification of the civil hero.[16]

A literary explosion marked the Juárez centennial, and the Díaz regime took care that the celebration of history included suitable apostrophes to the present. Writers analyzed Juárez not merely as the personification of an era but as the forerunner of the present, the foundation to Díaz's claim to be the legitimate heir to the revolution of the mid-nineteenth century. Rafael de Zayas Enríquez in *Benito Juárez: Su vida—su obra* concluded that Juárez achieved a lifelong goal to end the "repugnant theological-military regime that had weighed upon Mexico since colonial times." Leonardo S. Viramontes described Juárez as a reformer but emphasized the last phase, from 1867 to 1872, for facilitating the rise of a new social class that supported Díaz. Viramontes described the Juárez age as a step in the social evolution of Mexico, a period that moved toward the present era of peace and prosperity. Another prize winner in the literary competition, Porfirio Parra's *Estudio histórico-sociológico sobre la reforma en México,* praised the Reform and its herculean leader for making possible a time of "integral peace and tranquility," external credit, secure highways, quick communication, and a stable budget.[17]

To celebrate the centennial (as well as to refute an attack on the cult of Juárez by Francisco Bulnes), Justo Sierra in 1906 published a large biography in collaboration with Carlos Pereyra, complementing Sierra's famous *La evolución política del pueblo mexicano* in that both books enabled him to apply positivist notions of historical evolution to Mexican history as well as draw attention from Mexico's past to people and events he earlier had urged be remembered. Like other books published during the centennial, the biography carefully described Mexican history divided by stages and emphasized similarities and differences between Juárez and Díaz. It interpreted the age of Juárez as one of liberty and social emancipation, that of Díaz as orderly and progressive. Describing both men as progressive forces in Mexican history, thus meriting celebration in the "rites of our civic religion," the biography presented Mexicans with a lesson in civic patriotism.[18]

For Mexicans of strongly Roman Catholic persuasion, the centennial was no occasion for joy. To them Juárez was unacceptable as a hero, and they preferred either to ignore him or to use the centennial as they had employed earlier commemorations, as an opportunity to bring to the attention of their fellow citizens those aspects of Juárez's career that remained controversial. The Catholic press in Mexico City deplored the proceedings of the year 1906— for them the new statues were insult, the books almost beneath contempt, the fiestas and parades juvenile. If liberal and progovernment newspapers filled their pages with eulogistic articles and poetry, *El País* on the anniversary of Juárez's death published on its first page the text of the hated 1859 treaty with the United States and described it awkwardly as "one of the more glorious episodes from the life of don Benito Juárez."[19]

Unwilling to let well enough alone, *La Voz de México* ran an article in March 1906 analyzing the treaty, noting its threat to Mexican nationality, and concluding that the centennial distorted history. The truth was not so friendly to Juárez, it argued. Like a music teacher, history ought to lead us to harmony, but if "we listen to the liberals extol Juárez, we get dissonance, for their purpose is to reopen the wounds of the past." The centennial constituted only another of many public acts that refight the battles of the past, concluded *La Voz*.[20]

To Mexicans who considered themselves defenders of an older and purer liberalism, Juárez also stood for a cause betrayed. Aroused by the official manipulation of Juárez during the centennial, they made the myth a language of argument rather than harmony. José María Iglesias's son Fernando stressed differences between the past and the present by describing Juárez as an adherent of the written law and Díaz as one who looked upon the law as merely his will. Juárez defended the national integrity; in contrast, at the time Fernando Iglesias Calderón was writing, the invasion of North American capital endangered the fatherland.[21] Newspapers of the independent liberal press used the centennial to protest government participation and attack the regime. *El Dictamen* of Veracruz commented that in that city the people honored, exalted, and celebrated Juárez without coercion of official pressure, and *El Diario del Hogar* continued its criticism by protesting the tendency to make the centennial official by claiming that the work of Benito Juárez was in eclipse; official participation was hypocrisy, for Juárez had preserved national honor without stain and proclaimed separation of the spiritual and temporal powers. *El Paladín* complained that government sponsorship made the centennial a joke, although it cautiously praised the commemoration as a "solemn protest of a people who knows how to love its heroes and benefactors."[22]

Non-Mexicans found the exploitation of the Juárez myth by the aging dictator far easier to comment on than did Mexicans, and hence it is interesting to read the forthright judgments of John Kenneth Turner, an American writer who was well acquainted with Mexican politics. After visiting Mexico in 1908, he produced *Barbarous Mexico,* a scathing indictment of the Díaz regime. Sympathizing with Mexican exile groups in the United States, Turner had sought to learn the truth about the Díaz dictatorship, and upon returning he published the series of articles in the *American Magazine* that became his book. The articles caused an uproar among Díaz's supporters in Mexico and throughout the world, for Turner openly described the "overwhelmingly popular idolatry of the patriot Juárez." Díaz, he wrote, while professing to respect the institutions that Juárez and Lerdo had established, had "built up a system in which he personally was the central and all-controlling figure, in which his individual caprice was the constitution and the law, in which all circumstances and all men, big and little, were bent or broken by his will."[23]

Increasing numbers of Mexicans shared this view, and their dissent found expression in the centennial—which, like the 1887 commemoration, exacerbated the nation's social, economic, and political discontent by its attempt to use Juárez as a symbol of union. In the Mexico of Porfirio Díaz, the Juárez myth so carefully championed by the sycophantic administration of Díaz, so schemingly twisted to the service of the Porfirian status quo, became a rhetoric of dissent and dispute.

5

The Bulnes Polemic

The commemoration of 1887 and the 1906 centennial, taken together, dramatized the Juárez myth in Porfirian Mexico, for the Díaz government exploited it to the utmost to attract support, and Díaz's enemies attacked the aging dictator's effort to project himself as Juárez's worthy successor. During preparation for the centennial, a leading supporter of the dictatorship, Francisco Bulnes, published a pamphlet and two books that raised discussions of Juárez to the level of major polemic. Ironically, this publication succeeded in accomplishing what the centennial failed to do, for it unified the liberals as the factions rose to defend Juárez from Bulnes's attack.

Bulnes sought to use analyses of Juárez to indict individual liberals whom he regarded as dangerous to the Díaz regime and to Mexico. He believed the myth had been fabricated by liberals whom he described as jacobins, men who sought to protect and defend an older, purer, reform-oriented liberalism from the inroads of scientism. As earlier chapters have shown, changes in Mexican liberalism had begun even while Juárez lived and had received his endorsement as he turned from leading and defending a revolution to the more difficult task of governing after the enemy had been defeated. More changes had occurred in the late 1870s, when Justo Sierra and other liberals, including Bulnes, collaborated in the pages of *La Libertad* to define the fundamental tenets and program of a liberalism and a scientific politics that would support order, stability, peace, and economic growth that were

54

desperately needed after the reform and revolution led by Juárez in the 1850s and 1860s. To the extent that they discussed Juárez they lauded him as the leader of the Reform and the defender of Mexico against the French and characterized him as laying the groundwork in the years that followed 1867 for the Díaz dictatorship, a government that subordinated political debate and conflict to effective administration.

As these liberals, the advocates of scientific politics, developed their ideas and as the Díaz dictatorship consolidated itself, dissenters appeared, who turned to Juárez as a representative of values they thought were being betrayed. The Juárez of the Reform and the Intervention was their hero; they rarely talked of Juárez as president after 1867. Two arguments thus defined the liberal myth of Juárez by 1903: that employed by the scientific liberals, most of whom were pro-Díaz, emphasized continuity between the Juárez of the Reform, the Intervention, and the restored republic, and Díaz; that used by Díaz's liberal critics, who were sometimes called jacobins, stressed continuity between anticlericalism, a strong legislature, the individualistic liberalism championed by Juárez during the Reform and the Intervention, and their indictment of the dictatorship. The conflict in the Juárez myth came to a climax during the period between publication in 1903 of Bulnes's pamphlet, which argued that Díaz should be seen as the man who successfully completed the work that Juárez began after 1867, and his subsequent two books in 1904 and 1905 that sought to destroy the jacobin liberal myth that celebrated Juárez as the personification of the earlier Reform and Intervention.[1]

Bulnes's scathing attack on what he regarded as the jacobin distortion of Mexico's history and Juárez's role must of course be seen not only in the context of the continuing political and ideological controversies of Porfirian Mexico but as the characteristic outburst of a highly individualistic and controversial polemicist writing in a country that seemed to delight in polemic. Born in Mexico City in 1847 and educated as an engineer, Bulnes had a political career that spanned more than thirty years, from the administration of Sebastián Lerdo de Tejada to that of Francisco Madero. Serving as either a deputy or a senator in the Mexican congress, collaborating with such newspapers as *La Libertad, El*

Siglo XX, México Financiero, and *La Prensa,* he achieved both fame and notoriety as a journalist-politician. By 1904 he had established a reputation as a formidable lecturer, whose every speech was, in the words of one observer, an oratorical triumph. Although a *científico,* he attacked this group as well as his fellow Mexicans who adhered to traditional liberalism and conservatism. Nonconforming, skeptical, paradoxical, often just irascible, perhaps "one of the most evasive, designing, and deceitful writers that Mexico has produced," but one who surely understood the political life of his country as did few others, Bulnes acted as a gadfly in Porfirian Mexico by attacking any orthodoxy, regardless of its ideological content.[2] The Juárez tempest may have been to him only a high point in a life of storm and turbulence.

During the 1890s and the first decade of the present century, Bulnes was regarded as a *científico,* often used as a term of opprobrium to describe intellectuals, politicians, and businessmen who both criticized and collaborated with Díaz. The *científicos* emerged as a political faction in 1892, when they formed the Liberal Union to support Díaz's reelection and to set forth a program of reform to strengthen his accomplishments. Drawing upon the ideas and program outlined in the pages of *La Libertad,* they urged reorganization of the administration, a better tax system, suppression of internal tariffs, and policies to promote the economy. Above all, they advocated an independent judiciary and reform in the presidential succession to make government less personal and unstable.[3] They presented most of these proposals to the Mexican congress, but the Díaz administration opposed them.

Because Díaz recognized the talent and importance of these men, he shrewdly used them by appointing them to important offices and manipulating them, as he did other factions, thus fostering division among his opponents and enhancing his power, so that they indeed came to be regarded as the principal defenders of the regime. As one newspaper observed, "General Díaz knows very well these *científicos* and knows to what extent he can trust them." It then pointed out that most of them were taking not only the major political positions but those of the great commercial establishments.[4] Many *científicos* supported the ambitions of

Díaz's minister of hacienda after 1893, José Yves Limantour, and opposed those of Bernardo Reyes and Teodoro Dehesa. All of these officials entertained notions of succeeding Díaz.[5] Because of their elitism and especially because of their willingness to profit personally from the miseries of Porfirian Mexico, they seemed by 1910 to epitomize the oligarchic nature of the regime and its betrayal of the liberalism of the Reform and the Intervention.[6]

Bulnes's judgments about Mexico, its society, its political system, and its heroes, contributed to the unpopularity of the *científicos*. Agreeing with such men as Ricardo García Granados, Justo Sierra, and Emilio Rabasa, he believed the democratic provisions of the Constitution of 1857 had to be modified for Mexico to maintain order and prosperity. His criticism of democracy did not preclude support for government by law or institutions rather than men; it meant that he and others believed that democracy, which he equated with an omnipotent legislature, could not work in a society of illiterate Indians and mestizos. Only an enlightened or liberal dictatorship could provide Mexico with a government that above all stressed effective administration over politics.[7]

These views angered those liberals who included the editor of *El Diario del Hogar*, Filomeno Mata; the editor of *El Hijo del Ahuizote*, Daniel Cabrera; Juan Sarabía; Camilo Arriaga; and many others whom Bulnes derisively called jacobins. Echoing the views of other *científicos*, Bulnes characterized their liberalism as metaphysical or theocratic and attacked them for refusing to understand or accept the insights of the new liberals into the reality of the country and for continuing to insist that Mexico adhere to the Constitution of 1857 as formulated in that bygone year.[8] Throughout the 1890s the jacobin liberals opposed the reelection of Díaz and his manipulation of the constitution. They grieved over the subservience of congress, which institution they described as a barracks of invalids or a depository of officials, a kind of natural history museum in which one could find an example of every extinct species, including state governments and the press. They protested the lax official attitude toward the church, its violation of anticlerical laws, and the suggestion that Mexico should accept the contributions of the Spanish and admit to the country's pan-

theon such men as Iturbide and even Hernán Cortés.[9] After 1900
they began to win the support of regional governors and to organize liberal clubs.

In his two books on Juárez and in almost all his other works and
speeches, Bulnes attacked many of these views of Mexico and the
regime, and because of the belligerence of the onslaught he irri-
tated just about everyone—fellow *científicos,* traditional conservatives, jacobins, and patriotic Mexicans. His assessment of the
capacity of Mexicans and other Latin Americans to make achieve-
ments in government seemed negative; his distinctly racist pro-
clivities made it impossible for him to accept Juárez as a hero. In
his two books published in the late 1890s, he attributed Latin
America's political and social deficiencies to Spanish and Indian
elements in the population. Because of reliance on a diet of corn,
he said, the Indians were inferior and could achieve nothing.[10] He
found the Spaniards vain and fanatical, characteristics deriving
from Catholicism; the Spanish conquest contributed nothing positive to the region, and indeed it introduced anarchy, clericalism,
antisemitism, jacobinism, and militarism, all banes of Latin American society. The mixture of Spaniards and Indians spelled disaster;
jacobin democracy could not take root in such miserable soil.[11]

If the Indians whom Bulnes maligned were silent about his
commentaries and probably did not even know of them, conservatives objected to his unpleasant evaluation of Spaniards and
Catholicism, and *científicos* often found his views and belligerent
language impossible. One of the latter, Francisco Cosmes, could
agree with the evaluation of the Indians but disagreed with the
view of the Spaniards, whom he regarded as agents of civilization
in Mexico, responsible for enabling Mexico to join the free nations
of the world. Both Cosmes and Bulnes thought the Indians inept,
as Cosmes described them in a significant pro-Spanish tract published in 1896. Cosmes went on to urge that Mexicans see Cortés
as the true father of the country (a controversial recommendation
but one that typified attempts by Mexican intellectuals of the time
to reconcile liberalism and conservatism) and venerate him along
with Iturbide, Hidalgo, and Juárez, whom Cosmes described as an
exceptional and enlightened Indian.[12]

Impervious to criticism, Bulnes continued to make his provocative points. An example is his speech of 1903 before the National Liberal Convention, described as a notable oratorical piece and one that produced an immense sensation.[13] The group had met to endorse the candidacy of Díaz in the election of 1904 and to advocate the new office of vice-president and an extension of the presidential term to six years. Recognizing Bulnes's exceptional oratorical skill, delegates from several states chose him to endorse Díaz's candidacy. But he did much more, as was his wont; he managed to provoke reaction from almost every political group in Mexico. Employing the new liberal interpretation of Mexican history of the nineteenth century, Bulnes said that Mexico had enjoyed two political developments: the work of demolition, which lasted seventy years, and the work of reconstruction, lasting twenty-four. He credited the jacobins, especially the great ones of 1856–67, with glorious demolition of the old regime inherited from Spain and perpetuated by conservatives in the three decades after independence. Their immortal work consisted of the Laws of the Reform and defense of the country during the French invasion. All errors of this group, he continued, appeared in the vain and pompous words of history as imperceptible insects in an immense field of grain. Yet if the jacobins were strong and effective as revolutionaries, they were weak and ineffective as men of government, for they erred in believing that government could guarantee individual rights, which all liberals agreed was its function, by means of the popular assembly.[14]

Warming to his subject, Bulnes began to make his points with some fervor, and the most provocative portion of the speech came toward the end, when, after praising Díaz for leading the work of reconstruction and giving Mexico glory, peace, and wealth, he called for a conservative party that would challenge liberals and enable them to be strong, robust, and healthy. Such a party would be one of many institutions that would help Mexico overcome the chief weakness of the Díaz regime and its predecessors: excessive personalism and militarism, the rule of caudillos and caciques.[15]

Those Bulnes and others had dubbed jacobins now rose in wrath. Filomeno Mata's *Diario del Hogar* described Bulnes's suggestion of a new conservative party as a true political crime, and, as the annual commemoration of Juárez's death approached, he urged true liberals to gather around the sepulcher to help erase the scandals provoked by this impudent and shameless talker.[16] A liberal who considered himself neither a *científico* nor a jacobin attacked Bulnes's suggestion that *científicos* were descendants of jacobins and doing what the jacobins could not and noted that Bulnes's diatribe against rule by caudillos and caciques was impaired by excessive fear that Bernardo Reyes, a general and the governor of Nuevo León, would be a candidate for vice-president.[17] The Catholic *El País* characterized the speech as a recantation by a liberal in the presence of victorious conservative criteria.[18]

To meet such criticism as that expressed particularly by *El Diario del Hogar*, Bulnes calmly prepared a defense and amplification of his speech in which he reiterated his endorsement of another term for Díaz and went on to attack the jacobin use of Juárez. Defining jacobins as all foolish Mexicans who were enslaved to the principle of an omnipotent legislature and who hated executive power, he said they distorted history by associating democratic government with Juárez, for in the time of Juárez, he maintained, there was neither democracy nor personal government but legal anarchy. Although he praised Juárez for authoring the Laws of the Reform and defending Mexico in the 1860s, he concluded that the governmental work of Juárez was a failure, not because of personal shortcomings but because of jacobinism.

Not yet ready to attack Juárez directly—the year was 1903 and centennial preparations were just beginning—Bulnes linked Juárez and Díaz. Between the two he beheld a logical succession, not opposition, as the jacobins argued. The two presidents carried out distinctive tasks, admirably correlated; the work of Díaz fulfilled that begun by Juárez. Jacobins distorted history by trying to separate the men and their accomplishments. Both presidents saw a need for central government with a strong executive, and both could act despotically. Bulnes described as despotic the work of the Reform, including the Laws of the Reform and the Constitution of 1857; because the majority of Mexicans in 1856 desired religion and not liberty, the Liberal party was able to impose those measures only by taking advantage of the inertia of the Indians to convert them into unconscious military masses fighting on behalf of the liberal cause. The Liberal party saved the country "through one great despotic act."[19]

Bulnes continued his assault on the jacobins in *Las grandes mentiras de nuestra historia,* published in 1904, and laid the groundwork for the open attack on Juárez as a jacobin hero that he began that very year. In these books he confronted what he considered jacobin distortions of Mexican history. Mexican children often learned fables, legends, and apologies for a sect, rather than true history. National vanity had made Mexican history a den of bravado and lies. This conceit made even Santa Anna a hero. *Las grandes mentiras de nuestra historia* examined the role of Santa Anna and the Mexican army in three wars (the Spanish invasion of Mexico in 1829, the war over Texas in the 1830s, and the so-called Pastry War with France in 1838) and concluded that the Mexican army showed only incompetence and that Santa Anna, who led the army, displayed a nice combination of cowardice, cruelty, and selfishness. Such historians as Lucas Alamán, Guillermo Prieto, and Luis Pérez Verdía overlooked the problems of Mexico (praetorianism, social megalomania, excessive national pride, provincialism, absence of institutions of government) in an effort to make the country look as good as possible.[20] In this book as well as in the speech before the National Liberal Convention, Bulnes argued that personalism went too far when it converted men into divinities; Mexico's approach to history and politics in an era of science must be empirical and objective.

In 1904, then, Bulnes had established a reputation as an individualist. With other so-called *científicos,* he shared a belief that Mexico required a central government with a strong executive. He shared their skepticism about the capacity of Mexicans and other Latin Americans to develop self-government and displayed little tolerance of Catholics and liberals who had not accepted a scientific liberalism and politics. Orthodoxy and rigidity bothered him, and he stood poised, rhetorical armor buckled on, verbal broadsword in hand, to enter the lists on the side of the unpopular, unorthodox, and novel.

Hence the appearance of *El verdadero Juárez y la verdad sobre la Intervención y el Imperio* and its sequel, *Juárez y las Revoluciones de Ayutla y la Reforma.* By 1904 the figure of Juárez had assumed almost godlike dimensions for many Mexicans (they were fond of speaking about the apotheosis of Juárez), and they had begun preparations for the centennial. Two national congresses on the teaching of history had concluded that children should be introduced to history by the study of the lives of great men, and in the 1890s Mexican law recognized the importance of the hero and endorsed such august figures as Cuauhtémoc, Hidalgo, Morelos, and Juárez as divinities in Mexico's civic religion.[21] Juárez personified an immensely important period in Mexican history, and in the context of yet another reelection and the pro forma extension of the presidential term to six years, he represented the model of a good liberal or, perhaps, the most colossal of the jacobins.

El verdadero Juárez attempted to establish the truth about Juárez during the French intervention and the empire of Maximilian. Unlike the *Defensa y amplificación,* which focused on Juárez after 1867, this book conceded little. Bulnes concluded that as a leader Juárez possessed neither intellect nor skill; he did not qualify as the personification of the Reform. His resistance was merely decorative. The principal liberal general during this era, Santos Degollado, had a more legitimate claim, and Bulnes described Juárez as a bad organizer who could have avoided the French intervention by paying Mexico's debts. He called him an inert president and charged that he had considered exchanging Mexican territory for help from the United States. Juárez committed two cardinal errors: he believed that Maximilian could establish an empire in Mexico and that Mexicans could defeat the French.

Bulnes doughtily continued his criticism to show that Mexicans could not defeat the French without help. He drew on earlier assessments sometimes only to contradict himself. Despite his argument in the *Defensa y amplificación* that liberals depended on an Indian army to carry out the Reform, he now described the Mexican army as ineffective during the Intervention and attributed its weakness to its Indian composition. As for the middle and upper classes, he said they possessed bureaucratic hunger, a craving for government jobs, a predilection for praetorianism, and, of course, vanity. These characteristics prolonged the empire.

Burdened with such liabilities, Mexicans had to rely on external factors, forces apart from the Juárez government and the leaders and soldiers of the republican army, to assure the success of the republic. Pressure by the United States on the French, the corruption of interventionist forces, scorn of the French for the Mexican soldier, national resentment of French militarism and tyranny, and above all, the weak and indecisive character of Maximilian were the factors that assisted Juárez, according to Bulnes.

Bulnes arrived at what he considered a more accurate assessment of Juárez's role in the events of 1861–67, concluding that Juárez should be seen as a "subjective idol of liberal veneration, formed piece by piece with political subterfuge and legendary material extracted from the volcanoes of our illusions, always on fire but never to illuminate us, only to calcine our spirits." Mexicans should not call Juárez a democrat (he would not have run for reelection in 1867); neither should they see him as a dictator, for he had the temperament of an Indian and the calm of an obelisk. Thanks to jacobinism, he had been transformed into a Zapotec and lay Buddha.[22]

Bulnes's attack on the sacred Juárez brought an enraged storm in the press, most of it highly adverse. After publication of *El verdadero Juárez* in August 1904, the semiofficial *El Imparcial* pledged "to refute all the charges levied against the *Patricio*," and the journalistic voice of anti-Díaz liberals, *El Diario del Hogar*, described Bulnes's characterization of Juárez as blasphemy and asked whether the author should be a member of congress because of his attacks on that symbol of union, Benito Juárez.[23] The two major Catholic dailies in Mexico City, *El País* and *La Voz de México*, reacted differently, praising the book for "reducing to its true proportions the gigantic figure of Don Benito Juárez."[24]

Meetings and demonstrations protested the treatment of Juárez. Students of the National Law School held a meeting in his honor. The son of the former president, Benito Juárez Maza, sought to determine whether he had been personally attacked and what steps he should take. Headed by a nephew of Díaz, Felix Díaz, the Patriotic Liberal Committee met to decide on a response. The Circo Orrín was the scene of a tumultuous meeting, and later in the same day groups at the San Fernando cemetery heard speeches at the tomb of Juárez. Oaxacans rallied, as did so-called patriotic women, concluding that a "solemn moment had arrived when we should demonstrate that sentiments of gratitude move not only the hearts of the masculine sex but also the feminine." They invited

Unos miopes estudiantes
Por temor á un acto libre,
Bajaron de sus pescantes
A tipos de este calibre.

El Colmillo Público, which means "the public outrage," September 25, 1904, describes student reaction to *El verdadero Juárez.*

women of the Mexican capital to sign a register in the office of the Juárez Mining Company.[25]

Groups loyal to Juárez met in other cities and towns of Mexico, and an animated discussion ensued in the Mexican congress. Juaristas in Cholula gathered to call Bulnes a megalomaniac, traitor to the fatherland, plaza orator, sacristy rat, chameleon, recalcitrant conservative, and lunatic. In Pachuca, Hidalgo, Antonio Ramírez, owner of a bookstore, complained of harassment by liberals and expulsion from the association of booksellers for advertising Bulnes's book.[26] A member of the Chamber of Deputies, Juan Dublán, called for censure of "this perpetrator of libel," while others demanded his expulsion. Bulnes eluded the attacks by going to the United States.[27]

In quest for historical truth, Bulnes may have desired impartiality, but the substance and the tone of his book belied this motive. Catholics liked what he wrote in *El verdadero Juárez.* For a long time they had been saying that Juárez was only a liberal, not a Mexican hero. "We have been filled with admiration," *El País* commented, "because the liberal party had removed the personality of Juárez from all critical examination" by saying that such treatment would be injurious to the nation. *El País* found the book as "exotic as a banana plant weighted down with clusters of fruit on the summit of Popocatepetl."[28] Liberals defended Juárez and pledged to publish supportive books and pamphlets, several of which had appeared by the end of the year. Both *El Imparcial* and the *científico* writer Genaro García challenged Bulnes's credentials as a historian. Beginning in August *El Imparcial,* as promised, published articles dealing with the charges; according to them, Bulnes had accused Juárez of possessing a weak character, of being a poor organizer, of prolonging the Intervention by resistance, of encouraging treason; Mexicans should view Bulnes not as a historian but as a passionate and combative man who ignored all that took place before 1861—all the difficulties Juárez faced. Genaro García charged that Bulnes had little historical talent and wielded a passionate pen. He analyzed Bulnes's points and concluded that each rested on either misuse of evidence or bad logic. He attempted to show Juárez's "immaculate probity."[29]

On and on went the battle. Such liberals as Hilarión Frías y Soto, Justo Sierra, and Carlos Pereyra published evaluations, albeit emphasizing the danger to national unity by attacks on heroes. Dedicating his book to Díaz, Hilarión Frías y Soto placed Bulnes among the conservative enemies of Mexico and said that Bulnes's book ought to carry the name of the prominent conservative historian and politician of the Santa Anna era, Lucas Alamán. Frías y Soto asserted that Juárez had prepared Mexico for the present era, for had Juárez not decreed the Laws of the Reform and stood behind the execution sentence of Maximilian, "the Republic would not be what it is in 1904." In his biography of Juárez, published to refute Bulnes and to honor Juárez in the context of the centennial, Justo Sierra again emphasized the need in every country for a civic religion to make great men into divinities. The duty of a people is to worship, not criticize, he wrote. Carlos Pereyra, who collaborated in the writing of Sierra's biography and who had agreed with Bulnes's argument that Juárez's greatness derived from anticipation of the Díaz "civil dictatorship," lamented that Juárez belonged to the passion of contemporaries and urged that Juárez have neither detractors nor panegyrists, as when he lived.[30]

Díaz's foreign minister, Ignacio Mariscal, and the historian Fran-

"Thus history is written, when it is written by Bulnes," commented *El Colmillo Público* on September 18, 1904; the result is libel against Juárez paid for by the church.

cisco Cosmes stressed the importance of heroes, and, although they could agree with many of Bulnes's ideas regarding Mexico and its society and government, they found his direct attack on Juárez unacceptable. Mariscal argued that Juárez, serene, dispassionate, and judicious, deserved imitation and that he personified two episodes in the history of Mexico, the Reform and the Intervention, which he described as Mexico's second independence. Mariscal concluded that "sad is the task of the ugly pedant who endeavors to diminish the character of a hero in order to usurp the right to abhor him." Cosmes thought a country such as Mexico needed legends and heroes to encourage national unity. A legend, even false or absurd, ought to be respected when it contributed to "fortification in the spirit of the masses the sentiment of love of country." Legend fulfilled the same needs as religion; it constituted human religion.[31]

Juan Pedro Didapp presented a different view. In 1903 and 1904 he served as an apologist for Bernardo Reyes, whom cientíﬁcos regarded as an ominous figure and as a critic of the cientíﬁcos, and he considered Bulnes's attack an attempt by the cientíﬁcos to eliminate a figure who embarrassed them: "To accept Juárez as the greatest man in Latin America would be to condemn usurious ambitions and those who do not respect any human law." The cientíﬁco party, which included Bulnes, had demonstrated cowardice, ineptitude, and incapacity to fulfill the law. Juárez represented the law that transcended the purest glorification of the republic. The Zapotec Indian attained immortality by sustaining the Constitution of 1857, a dead letter under Díaz, and by defeating clerical power.[32]

Bulnes once again attempted to meet criticism, in letters to Victoriano Agüéros, the editor of El Tiempo. After objecting to the description of him as unpatriotic or as a traitor, he complained of the religious fanaticism that colored interpretation of Juárez. Juarism, he said, had been transformed into buddhism. The jacobins insisted that he be regarded as the Buddha of Mexico and refused to tolerate anyone who dissented. Claiming to be a liberal of the school of Ramírez, Altamirano, Melchor Ocampo, even Juárez, he said he refused to be a slave or an idiot before any religion with cults, rituals, or idols. One must approach liberalism as one would mathematics. Mexican law proclaimed freedom of religion. Mexicans could choose to follow or to reject the beliefs of any sect. Why substitute slavery to one cult for slavery to another? One should not be accused of being a bad Mexican or a traitor for trying to exercise judgment: "The cult of the Fatherland is not dogmatic and is not opposed to truth."[33]

Bulnes repeated these views in *Juárez y las Revoluciones de Ayutla y la Reforma,* published in 1905, which examined the life of Juárez up to the revolt that overthrew Santa Anna in 1855 and, more substantially, Juárez's career from defeat of Santa Anna to the Intervention. As in *El verdadero Juárez,* Bulnes criticized the jacobin worship of Juárez; addicted to personalism and the religion of the state, with its saints, liturgy, altars, and hierarchy, jacobinism encouraged the writing of "literary caramels," he said, biographies of Juárez by Gustavo Baz, Francisco Sosa, and Anastasio Zerecero that were "stimulants of hilarity for persons of sane critical judgment." The faults, weaknesses, and errors of Juárez had been suppressed, and history had been distorted, he said.

To show that Juárez could err, and that his role in the Reform had been minor, Bulnes defined the Reform as passage from the old regime to the modern, expressed by destruction of privileges recognized by law and custom. In Mexico the process had begun in colonial times and continued after independence. It did not involve Juárez, who at that time was a cleric rather than a rebel against the church: "Born an Indian, educated by a priest, instructed in a pontifical seminary, reconfirmed as a fanatic by an Institute with the science of the Spanish universities of Oviedo and Salamanca, Juárez could not be a progressive or a reformer of pure blood."[34] Before 1852 the Reform in Mexico had two leaders, Morelos and Gómez Farías.

Bulnes the historian was nothing if not specific. After 1852, Juárez did little to distinguish himself as either a reformer or a patriot. He lived as an exile in New Orleans while Alvarez and Comonfort led the Revolution of Ayutla. The Juárez law, promulgated while Juárez served as Alvarez's minister of justice, did not abolish ecclesiastical and military privileges. That was accomplished by a *pronunciamiento* issued in Zitácuaro in December 1852. Bulnes described Juárez as a satellite in the cabinet of

Alvarez. He did not attend the congress that framed the Constitution of 1857, a work that failed. Moderates carried out the reforms of 1857; by allying himself with the radicals, Juárez became a counterreformer. Bulnes described Juárez as insignificant during the Reform and argued that Santos Degollado did more. Two events during this period made Juárez's behavior shameful: negotiation in 1859 of the McLane-Ocampo treaties with the United States and the Anton Lizardo affair of 1861 during which Juárez granted permission to Americans to apprehend vessels bearing the Mexican flag in Mexican waters. Juárez thus condoned foreign intervention in Mexican territory.

As for jacobin criticism, Bulnes repeated his views of Mexican social reality and the potential for democracy. Juárez could not be called a democrat because his Indian, Spanish, and Catholic background made it impossible to be one. Democracy could never thrive in the Mexico of Juárez's day. Democracy, Bulnes argued, required a society of classes. Passivity characterized the popular class in Mexico and in all Latin America, supporting tyranny or liberal dictatorship. Bulnes rejected the words "democratic" or "jacobin" to describe the authentic Reform, preferring "colonial" and "national"; the Reform, he said, owed its progress to generations of educated men and to social classes open to progress, and three men had led this movement: José María Morelos, Valentín Gómez Farías, and Santos Degollado. Juarism sought to divest these illustrious Mexicans of their merits in order to create a Juárez of jacobin mythology.[35]

Perhaps because of exhaustion from their assault on *El verdadero Juárez* or perhaps because they thought the centennial would provide the opportunity for a more appropriate response, few liberals prepared reactions to this book, although *El País* published articles that criticized Bulnes for his statements about the church and Catholicism. It praised him for his characterization of Juárez, but it said that he began with wrong premises by rejecting theology as incapable of sustaining liberty or criticism and failed to see that civilized nations derived from Christianity. Liberalism regardless of variety (jacobin, radical, Masonic, positivist) was a lie.[36]

If Mexicans of all persuasions reacted to Bulnes's statements about Juárez between 1903 and 1906 as they had to his earlier writings and speeches, Bulnes may only have enhanced the standing of Juárez among liberal Mexicans, especially those who were increasing their criticism of Díaz. Controversial statements about Juárez and Mexico invited reaction, and arguments revealed discontent with Mexico at the height of the Porfiriato. The polemic, one must conclude, sharpened disagreement over what Mexican liberalism meant during the first decade of the twentieth century and encouraged more elaboration of Juárez as a symbol of conflicting values and interests.

6

 Juárez, Symbol in
a Revolution

In September 1910, Porfirio Díaz presided over the dedication of the Hemiciclo, Mexico's national monument to Benito Juárez. Although the Mexican congress had authorized its construction in 1873, complications over design, location—many thought it should be placed in one of the glorietas of the Paseo de la Reforma—and purpose delayed completion until 1910, the year of the centennial of the beginning of the Mexican independence movement. For Díaz the month had been filled with dedications and formal appearances; it seemed to be a year of fulfillment for both him and Mexico. Certainly that was the principal motive for sponsoring this centennial and the one to Juárez four years before and for spending millions of pesos on monuments, ceremonies, and a host of invited dignitaries.

The appearance was deceptive. The regime desired its guests to receive the impression of a prosperous Mexico, and so the beggars were pushed off the streets; and while champagne flowed for the few, Mexicans by the tens of thousands suffered from malnutrition. By 1910 the contrasts and tensions could no longer be contained, not even by a national fiesta, and Díaz was in trouble. Some months later he resigned and set sail from Veracruz, to spend the last years of his life in Paris as an exile, a victim of the revolution he so often had proclaimed.[1]

Díaz's opponents rejoiced, and the old guard liberals among them used the next annual Juárez commemoration to express their pleasure over the events that had led to his overthrow. *El Diario*

71

President Díaz inaugurates the national monument to Juárez, the Hemiciclo, September 18, 1910. Courtesy of the Benson Latin American Collection, The University of Texas at Austin.

del Hogar, which had survived years of harassment by the dictator's censors and whose editor, Filomeno Mata, had been arrested many times for his doughty criticism of the regime, rejoiced that the good name of Juárez had been vindicated. No longer would liberties be trampled, no longer would he suffer from that "monster of wickedness and hypocrisy" who had persisted in coming up before the hero's tomb annually and solicitously depositing flowers and presiding over the acts of glorification.[2]

And so it came to pass that even though the Díaz regime had shaped popular thinking so that Mexicans would see continuity between Díaz and Juárez, beholding an orderly, prosperous, just Mexico, its version of the Juárez myth failed. Its sponsorship of commemorations and prizes for meritorious books had served only to arouse the political opposition, which had developed its own continuity argument stressing similarities between itself and

Juárez. Order, prosperity, and justice had eluded Díaz, as they had Juárez; as official manipulation of the myth increased, so had opposition to the regime.

During the decade from 1900 to 1910 that preceded Díaz's overthrow and the chaotic and bloody one, from 1910 to 1920, that followed, numerous factions attempted to use Juárez as a means to attract support to their causes and to denounce enemies as traitors. Juárez's myth thus became all things to all people.

Catholic conservatives, always outside the range of Díaz's manipulation of the myth, had been doubtful about the dictator's policy of conciliation. Although they never attacked him directly, they remained uneasy about the status of the church in a Mexico and a world that seemed increasingly liberal and secular, and they had expressed this discontent by attacks on Juárez as a national symbol. The detested Laws of the Reform continued as part of the constitution and were an ever-present threat to whatever power the church possessed after the conservative defeat in 1867. Through extensive discussions of the McLane-Ocampo treaties of 1859 and relaxed dealings with the United States, pro-Catholic newspapers endeavored to show that liberals and the government had distorted history by describing Juárez as a patriot. They maintained that because of his support for policies hostile to the religion of a majority of Mexicans, Juárez could not be viewed as a nationalist. Although the Díaz government moderated liberal anticlericalism, its support for the Juárez cult belied a commitment to Catholicism. Wide acceptance of a scientific liberalism, which furthered liberalism's secular tendencies, together with Bulnes's diatribes against Catholicism made peace between church and state extremely difficult. In the first decade of the twentieth century, groups within the church increasingly sympathized with the plight of the lower classes in Mexico and supported a program of social action that shared many of the same goals of Díaz's critics among liberals.[3]

But the principal opposition to Díaz had come from the many groups of liberals who opposed his reelection, his willingness to tolerate infractions of the anticlerical laws, the opening of the country to foreign investment and domination of the economy, the censure of newspaper opposition, and his identification with the *científicos*, who seemed to monopolize the direction of economic policy. After the publication of a speech by the Catholic bishop Ignacio Montes de Oca y Obregón in the Catholic newspaper of San Luis Potosí, Camilo Arriaga and other Potosí liberals called upon liberals throughout Mexico to organize liberal clubs to combat the resurgent clericalism and recommended that these clubs send representatives to a national congress, which would assemble in February 1901 on the anniversary of the promulgation of the Constitution of 1857.[4]

Liberal opposition to Díaz thus changed from words to organization, but it continued to refer to Juárez and other liberals of that era to sanction its cause. As preparation for the congress drew to a close, *El Hijo del Ahuizote* published a cartoon that showed the liberal congress of San Luis Potosí personified as Jesus Christ driving from the temple of the constitution the two despised cler-

"Preparations for the Liberal Congress of San Luis Potosí," from *El Hijo del Ahuizote,* February 10, 1901.

ics, Montes de Oca and Regis Planchet. The shadowy figures of Santos Degollado, Sebastián Lerdo de Tejada, Melchor Ocampo, and Benito Juárez look down with satisfaction.[5]

Radical liberals in Mexico City, Diodoro Batalla, Jesús and Ricardo Flores Magón, and others, meanwhile established the Liberal Reform Association and the newspaper *Regeneración*, which became an important organ of radical opposition to Díaz. In February 1903, Enrique Flores Magón and Alfonso Cravioto issued a manifesto calling for social reform, so as to attract support of more than just jacobin liberals. Government concern with the increasingly radical views of this group and its newspaper forced an exodus to the United States in 1903, and for several years *Regeneración* was published north of the Rio Grande.[6]

To revive the work of Benito Juárez and Sebastián Lerdo de Tejada and to devise new programs, these expatriates formed the Mexican Liberal party, and in St. Louis in 1906 they published a manifesto proclaiming "Reform, Liberty, and Justice." Invoking Juárez and describing the Reform as a cause betrayed, the manifesto urged a democratic regime based on the institutions of the Reform and its illustrious hero, Juárez. It went further than advocating a political program and included economic and social change. In addition to restrictions on the power of the executive, abolition of the senate and reelection, and suppression of the political power of the boss system—all changes of a political nature needed to end the dictatorship—the manifesto called for a labor law, an eight-hour day for workers in industry, regulation of employment of children and women, a minimum wage, and workmen's compensation. For agricultural workers, few of whom owned the land they worked, it asked for agrarian reform that would nationalize land not cultivated by landowners and turn it over either as private parcels or in the form of collective *ejidos* to those who did not own land.[7]

The manifesto's words fell on a multitude of sympathetic ears, for conditions in Mexico cried out for such a program. During the Juárez centennial year of 1906 disgruntled workers expressed their grievances and thereby shattered the industrial peace of the country by means of several major strikes. Confrontations in the cotton textile mills of Orizaba, Puebla, and Tlaxcala climaxed with the infamous Rio Blanco strike in Veracruz and a major strike in the Cananea mine in Sonora. The government ruthlessly suppressed both the Rio Blanco and Cananea strikes.[8]

Shortly afterward, in 1908, Díaz added immeasurably to the unrest and sense of change by foolishly telling the American journalist James Creelman that he might not run again in 1910. Liberal organizing increased as Mexicans took this speculation as a green light to proceed with political activity for selecting a president other than Díaz in 1910. Because Díaz's advisers warned of anarchy if he did not run, he ineptly decided to run, but his decision came too late to check the increased political activity. Mexicans thereupon formed antireelectionist clubs, many of which were named after Juárez. Supporters of Bernardo Reyes, the political chief of the northern Mexican state of Nuevo León, much feared and disliked by those close to Díaz, produced the Democratic party dedicated to promotion of his vice-presidential candidacy. Díaz's minister of hacienda and major businessmen and industrialists favored the reelection of Ramón Corral as vice-president, and they established a Reelectionist party and the newspaper *El Debate*. In November 1909 Díaz pressured Reyes to resign as governor of Nuevo León and accept a military assignment to Europe, so as to guarantee Corral the vice-presidential nomination and continued control of the government by Díaz's cronies. That action turned out to be another miscalculation.[9]

Although opposition groups were many and drew support from all parts of Mexico, Francisco I. Madero of the northern state of Coahuila soon emerged as the principal anti-Díaz leader, and as is well known, managed to oust Díaz in 1911. A member of a prominent and wealthy landholding family, Madero briefly had supported the Mexican Liberal party, but by 1908 he had developed his own political platform, which had supported antireelectionist clubs. He assumed leadership of the Anti-Reelectionist Center in Mexico City in 1910 and ran for president. To further his cause, Madero employed Juárez as a symbol of the values important to his movement, and for a time the Madero political organization, which came into being shortly after publication of Creelman's article, took the name of Benito Juárez Democratic Club. Madero alluded to Juárez in his political tract, *La sucesión presidencial en*

1910, by dedicating it to the heroes of Mexico, independent journalists, indeed all good Mexicans. Although he described Juárez as an example of a leader who could err if given too much power (Juárez had compromised Mexican interests in the McLane-Ocampo treaties), he saw him as the representative of worthwhile values.

Madero admired Juárez especially as the incarnation of law and the representative of legality. Juárez, Madero wrote, had succeeded as a civil president, for with his patriotism he "seduced the haughty military men who served him, and with his unquenchable energy he dominated those headed by General Díaz who rose against him." Madero saw Mexico's problems as political, and consequently reform for him meant a return to the principles of the Reform, including those of the Constitution of 1857.[10]

The polemical literature in support of Madero often described him as a modern Juárez, and one pamphlet went so far as to describe Madero as a businessman and an intellectual who had come forth from the masses as had Juárez. Another portrayed Madero as a true heir of Juárez, in contrast to the radical Ricardo Flores Magón.[11] A ballad of the time echoed these sentiments by stressing the dedication of Juárez and Madero to the principle of government by law and the special role of Madero in fulfilling the laws that Juárez guarded lovingly from his tomb:

> Benito Juárez desde su tumba umbría
> guarda sus leyes en su pecho amoroso
> y en Francisco Madero se confió
> que las cumpliera, ¡haciéndose glorioso![12]

> (Benito Juárez from his shadowy tomb
> guards his laws in his loving breast
> and he trusted that Francisco Madero
> would fulfill them, making him glorious!)

Two antireelectionist newspapers that supported Madero linked their cause with that of Juárez. *El Anti-reeleccionista* referred to the execution of Maximilian as the last act in the bloody drama that saw the conquest of enemies of the constitution and said this event assumed great symbolic significance for those Mexicans who since then had stood for liberty of suffrage, faithful observance of the constitution, and no reelection. *El Constitucional* liked to invoke Juárez as a symbol of integrity and of faith in justice, democratic liberty, abnegation and vigorous patriotism, democracy, and republicanism. It sponsored demonstrations in honor of Juárez and celebrated his simple possessions then on display in the national museum of history (a black coat, a silk hat, a red chair, and a small tricolor sash) in contrast to the elaborate trappings of the aristocracy, such as the enormous banquet table of Maximilian. Juárez was a man of the people, said *El Constitucional;* despite his rise to the post of first magistrate, he never forgot his humble background or relinquished his simple way of life.[13]

Madero and his supporters promised moderate reform in Mexico and toleration for dissent, both regarded as a legacy of Juárez but still denounced by radical anticlerics. During the election campaign of 1911 that followed Díaz's overthrow by a few months, Madero used the anniversary of Juárez's death to proclaim himself a liberal in the sense understood by Juárez. Speaking to an audience gathered before the Juárez monument in Puebla, he pledged support for liberalism, especially respect for the beliefs of others, including all political and religious convictions. That comment aroused Madero's opponents, who also claimed to represent that Juárez legacy. Reacting to this speech, Jesús Ceballos Dosamantes called Madero's emphasis on toleration an effort to mutilate the Laws of the Reform. Juárez, Ceballos wrote, fought the clerics and left the rich inheritance of the Laws of the Reform, whereas Madero only mystified the nation by claiming allegiance to this tradition.[14] But the Madero interpretation countered these arguments by heatedly repeating its own.

Madero was elected in October 1911 in one of the most honest, clean, and enthusiastic elections in Mexican history. Yet he entered office with diminished prestige. He had postponed assuming office as a victorious revolutionary. The interim period allowed opponents and even partisans to develop ambitions of their own, and after taking office he lost support by attempting to limit the revolution to political objectives. During the short time he occupied the presidency, Madero made little use of the Juárez symbol.[15]

As a result, therefore, of Madero's failure to make a dramatic

"Over the Constitution, no one," says Juárez in the context of ten tragic days that saw the fall of Madero and the advent of Huerta. *El Ahuizote,* February 1, 1913.

impact, especially in the countryside, and the growing ambitions of regional leaders, the revolution against Díaz turned into a civil war, during which Mexico experienced violence and chaos unprecedented in its turbulent history. Factions and ambitious individuals, some representing ideologies and programs, others merely opportunistic, competed for control of the capital and its government. The followers of Emiliano Zapata pushed for continuation of the revolution as a social and economic movement, insisting on a return to villagers of land that had been alienated under Díaz and his predecessors. Felix Díaz and Bernardo Reyes, former allies of Díaz, opposed Madero. Finally, in February 1913, one of Madero's generals, Victoriano Huerta, joined them to oust Madero, who was then killed. By means of the Pact of the Ciudadela, Huerta succeeded Madero in the presidential chair. A broad coalition to oppose Huerta quickly formed under the leadership of Venustiano Carranza, a former governor of Coahuila. Calling themselves constitutionalists, they pledged by means of the Plan of Guadalupe to restore constitutional government according to Madero's Plan of San Luis Potosí. Because of pressure by the constitutionalists, other groups, and the government of the United States, Huerta resigned in July 1914 and followed Díaz into exile. After the drafting of a new constitution in 1917, a document that included many of the demands of Zapata and the Flores Magón brothers, Carranza became president, only to be cut down by an assassin's bullet in

1920. Peace returned with the advent of Alvaro Obregón to the presidency in 1920.[16]

Throughout this confused era references to Juárez served as a means whereby various factions expressed their goals and appealed for support. As each revolutionary group tried to claim it was carrying on the revolutionary cause of Juárez and that opponents were jeopardizing it, Juárez became ever more important. Revolutionaries, even the most radical, always wanted to establish continuity between their cause and the Reform.

Juárez dead was worth more than Juárez alive. The Vázquez Gómez brothers, Emilio and Francisco, supported Madero for a time, but then broke with him and tried to develop a power base of their own, and to advance their cause Leonardo Ballesteros in 1911 published short laudatory biographies of both Benito Juárez and the Vázquez Gómez brothers that attempted to show a similarity between them and Juárez. He argued that all three were self-made men who had overcome primitive and humble antecedents and advanced through diligence and stoicism.[17]

Another northern revolutionary, Pascual Orozco, tried to strike out on his own, and he too invoked Juárez. Orozco had been one of the initiators of the revolution against Díaz in the state of Chihuahua, and for a time he had supported Madero. In 1912 he turned against the federal government and appealed both to Juárez and to Cuauhtémoc, the last Aztec emperor, who died resisting the Spanish. in his plan of March 1913, he used the Mexican past by appealing to the virile and rejected sons of Morelos and Juárez.[18]

In the state of Morelos, Emiliano Zapata headed one of the most important movements opposing Madero. *La Voz de Juárez,* edited by Paulino Martínez, served as its journalistic voice in the Mexican capital. *La Voz* had been founded in San Antonio, Texas, in 1892, where it functioned as a critic of the Díaz government. It continued this role in Mexico City after 1910, supporting Madero at first but insisting that agrarian reform must be an object of his revolution. The origin and object of the revolution of Ayutla in 1854 had been agrarian, it asserted in August 1911, and so must be the present revolution. *La Voz* criticized both Madero and the Carranza movements when they failed to emphasize this aspect of the revolution. In 1914 it referred to supporters of Carranza as nothing more than offshoots of the *científicos*, who had been sheltered under the wings of Madero and Huerta. The plight of the Indian provided a related cause for *La Voz*, and in this regard it could better connect with Juárez whose European-based liberalism had supported those policies that laid the basis for the present need for agrarian reform. For *La Voz* the Indian in Mexico was a perennial object of bourgeois and military exploitation and the "eternal martyr of the fierce cacique."[19]

Rejecting the moderate liberalism of Madero but continuing to claim allegiance to Juárez and the realization of his ideals, the Flores Magón brothers headed the revolutionary faction associated with *Regeneración* and the Mexican Liberal party, and they tried to distinguish their brand of liberalism from Juárez's by pointing out that it suited contemporary needs better than did the ideas of Juárez or Madero. Contemporary liberals required action rather than law to achieve economic emancipation of the worker, Ricardo Flores Magón wrote. Radical liberals shared Juárez's goals; they differed only in regard to means. Juárez believed that by law (Article 4 of the 1857 constitution) the worker could achieve economic emancipation, but for a half century the worker had continued a slave. For the worker to benefit from his work, he must seize the land and the tools of production. Only in this way could he realize the just distribution of wealth authorized by the constitution. If Juárez were alive today, he would be on the side of the disinherited and would apply force of arms to achieve expropriation. The Juárez myth thereby acquired elements of anarchism, syndicalism, and revolutionary socialism.[20]

The Mexican Revolution eventually incorporated the goals of both Zapata and the Flores Magón brothers but under the nominal leadership of one who claimed to be a more traditional and moderate liberal. Venustiano Carranza became the first president under the Constitution of 1917, a document that included clauses affecting landownership and the rights of labor. Carranza stressed the moderate emphasis of his liberalism in his speech opening the convention that drafted the new constitution in Querétaro in late 1916 and early 1917. Here he pointed to Juárez as one who had seen the importance of law as the balance between dictatorship and anarchy, a theme that he often heard struck during the commemorative exercises that he regularly attended at the Hemiciclo.[21]

The Querétaro convention created opportunities for further elaboration of the Juárez myth within an emerging myth of the Revolution. The draft constitution that Carranza submitted did not contain provisions for radical reform desired by many, both within the convention and outside; hence the principal debates focused on proposals to lend constitutional sanction to a land reform that would restore village lands alienated from peasants under the Lerdo and other land laws, implement an advanced labor code, and separate church and state more effectively, particularly in education. Within the context of debates on these and other proposals, the Juárez legacy was viewed as a mixture of bad and good.[22]

From the standpoint of Alfonso Cravioto, a moderate who above all supported freedom of instruction and opinion, Juárez too often stood for rabid anticlericalism. Cravioto opposed including in the new constitution an article that would completely exclude the church and religion from schools, for, as he put it, such exclusion not only would violate those freedoms, it would also divide the nation further into juaristas and antijuaristas, into jacobins and clericals, juaristas and iturbistas.[23] Clearly for him the memory of Juárez as a strong advocate of separation of church and state was one to be suppressed as Mexicans worked to put their nation back together on a firmer foundation.

A more positive view of Juárez and what he stood for emerged during consideration of the powers of the executive. Once again Juárez became a symbol for those supporting a strong president. Apparently taking their cue from Carranza, who in justifying his call for a new constitution had suggested that the old one had made possible executive abuse of power leading to tyranny, some delegates questioned the provisions in the proposed new constitution that would allow the executive to exercise extraordinary powers in time of emergency. Other delegates welcomed the prospect of a strong president and sought to allay the fears of tyranny by stressing the qualities of both Juárez and Carranza. Rafael Martínez de Escobar was confident that Carranza, "a Juárez," would be the next president and like Juárez before him would give Mexico a necessary and beneficial "democratic" dictatorship.[24] Zeferino Fajardo invoked Juárez as "the best president of the Republic" to argue that provisions for the granting of extraordinary powers were necessary to confront emergencies. Between 1860 and 1867 Juárez could not have governed without such powers, he said.[25]

Because Carranza seemed firmly in control in 1916 and destined to become president under the new constitution, speakers before the convention tended to emphasize his heroic qualities and to reinforce them by allusions to what they saw as similar traits in both Juárez and Madero. A representative of the Liberal party of Querétaro, for example, in a speech welcoming the preliminary sessions in November 1916, depicted Carranza as the man chosen by destiny to carry on the great work of Juárez, who, although he was a "man of iron," could not suppress entirely the "hydra" of the priest, the latifundista, the cacique, and the military who rose again to threaten the political and civil rights of Mexicans. That task fell to the "great apostle" Francisco I. Madero and now to Venustiano Carranza. Madero had been characterized as a modern Juárez, and now Carranza was assuming that role.[26]

The process of linking Juárez and Carranza had begun long before the Querétaro convention. While Huerta occupied the presidency in 1913, Isidro Fabela referred to Carranza as the new Juárez of Mexican history, who would also save the country from tyranny. During a speech on the anniversary of Juárez's birth in 1916, Manuel Garrido grandiloquently described Carranza as a man who embraced the cause of Benito Juárez, and in that same year the painter Gerardo Murillo, better known by the pseudonym of Dr. Atl, lent support to Carranza's cause through his newspaper, *Acción Mundial*, by arguing that the work of Carranza and the constitutionalists fulfilled the revolution begun in 1810 and continued during the Reform led by Juárez.[27]

Other newspapers promoted Carranza by comparing him to Juárez. *El Pueblo* distinguished two types of revolutions and hence two kinds of revolutionaries: the "project, the conspiracy, the intrigue" as one type, headed by "usurpers" or "conspirators" such as Díaz or Huerta; and the "great movements" or "profound undertakings" that "glowed in the efflorescence of such great men as Hidalgo, Juárez, and Carranza, who were naught but creations of the latent and profound desires of the Mexican masses," as the other. These three men, said *El Pueblo*, lived with a soul formed from the sentiment, idea, and persevering will of the generations that gave them life—identification with the spirit and will of the Mexican people made them true revolutionaries. *El Pueblo* interpreted the July 1918 commemoration of Juárez's death as homage to both Juárez and Carranza.[28] A new *El Universal*, which began publishing in 1917 and became one of the three principal daily newspapers of Mexico City, emphasized the civil aspect of the current revolution and drew parallels between it and the movement headed by Juárez. Referring to a Hemiciclo ceremony of July 1918 presided over by Carranza, it editorialized that Mexico was coming out of the most formidable crisis in its life as a nation, the greatest of civilian revolutions headed by a personality developed independently of the military barracks.[29]

Antonio Rivera de la Torre published a book in 1918 to show similarities between Juárez and Carranza by describing parallel problems and their solutions. Both men had to combat foreign intervention (Juárez the French, Carranza the American in 1914 and 1916). Both men distinguished themselves by courageous and patriotic defense of national interests. They shared problems of archaic prejudices, the gold of political bosses and entrepreneurs, debts, tyrannies, conservative reactions, bad economic conditions, and the challenges of social revolution. Both responded in ways characteristic of the civil temperaments of liberal caudillos, in accord with three great liberal plans of Mexican history: Iguala, Ayutla, and Guadalupe. Above all, concluded the flowery Rivera de la Torre, the two men were constitutionalists in that they believed in government sanctioned by written constitutions. Juárez defended the document of 1857 from foreign and domestic enemies; Carranza performed the same role for the document of 1917. The liberal and conscientious people who helped Juárez were now supporting Carranza, and they would continue to support him, Rivera de la Torre concluded, "for they see him as the defender of their rights, and the powerful enemy of the reaction who will unite the Mexican family that so strongly yearns for peace and rational progress."[30]

Supporters of Ignacio Bonillas in 1920 stressed the civil aspect of Juárez's government, as had Carranza's followers, and tried to identify their candidate with it. A popular general during the civil war that followed Madero's overthrow, Alvaro Obregón opposed Bonillas. Although Obregón had at one time supported Carranza, many Mexicans resented his candidacy in 1920 because they believed the Revolution had attempted to purge Mexico of military involvement in politics and the election of a general would be a step backward.[31] Obregón defeated Bonillas and began a phase of Mexican history in which some of the radical provisions of the new constitution were carried out but official interest in Juárez declined, not to revive in an important way until the 1950s.

During the first two turbulent decades of the twentieth century, from about 1900 until 1920, when Mexicans fought and debated over who should rule and what ideology and program should guide, Juárez was the symbol for those who wanted legitimacy by claiming continuity with the past. Radical groups ascribed new meanings (he championed land reform, or he would sanction direct action to obtain justice for the propertyless workers of Mexico), but more moderate elements in the Revolution associated with Madero and Carranza seemed to find closer identity of cause and interest. In a time of confusion and proposals for radical change, Juárez thus became important as a way for Mexicans to see a continuity in their history. Juárez became, strangely, a force for order as well as, simultaneously, for revolution.

7

 Mexican Painters
and Juárez

Before 1920 Mexican politicians, writers, and caricaturists promoted a myth around Juárez, whom they saw as a useful symbol of the conflicting goals, values, and discontents of Mexicans during the period of the restored republic, the Porfiriato, and the Revolution. After 1920 the brushes and pigments of painters joined the pens and inks of writers and caricaturists to continue the mythologizing in an effort to incorporate Juárez along with other Mexican historical figures into an interpretation of the Revolution, which had just concluded its violent and destructive phase and for which its heirs needed a myth to lend support to their often controversial programs and policies.

Painters as well as sculptors and architects had not ignored Juárez before 1920, for with support from the government they had attempted to provide Mexicans with suitable memorials of Juárez as a national hero rather than as a symbol of division and change. Miguel Noreña in 1891 had produced the statue for the National Palace, and Guillermo Heredia in 1910 submitted his design for the Hemiciclo in time for its completion during the centennial celebration of the independence movement. José Escudero y Espronceda, Federico Rodríguez, Pelegrín Clavé, and Santiago Rebull painted portraits of Juárez that modified his dark, copper color and Indian features in favor of a white, European aspect.[1] Imitating patterns employed in Europe and the United States to memorialize men and events, all these interpretations reflected official preference toward style and content. Artistically

Portrait of Juárez by José Escudero y Espronceda, painted in March 1872. National Palace, Mexico City.

as well as economically, Porfirian Mexico looked abroad for stimulation and inspiration, and as a result treatments of Juárez differed little from those of other prominent figures.

Toward the end of the Porfiriato, Mexican artists became disenchanted with the artificiality and imitativeness of officially sanctioned art styles and subjects, and many rebelled against or simply ignored the style of art taught at the National Academy of Fine Arts. During the 1910 centennial several of them sponsored a counter-art show highlighting native accomplishments to offset the government-sponsored exhibition, which featured the work of a Spanish artist, and in 1911 students of the national art school began a strike that lasted for two years. To dramatize rejection of the official philosophy, one of these dissidents, Gerardo Murillo, changed his name to Dr. Atl (after the Aztec word for water) and in 1911 began planning a large mural for the Anfiteatro Bolívar, a project that he and others hoped would revive the Indian and colonial tradition of large-scale wall paintings. In 1916 Carranza, who was determined to enlist the talents of artists in defining and evangelizing the values of the Revolution, appointed him director of a reformed national art school.[2]

After the turbulent years of 1910–20, Mexican painters turned enthusiastically to mural painting as the principal means to express their emancipation from foreign art styles and project an ideology for a revolution they had supported. Building on Carranza's initiatives, Mexico's new president, Alvaro Obregón, and his minister of education, José Vasconcelos, backed them enthusiastically. Vasconcelos, sometimes called the *deus ex machina* of Mexican art, believed that culture should integrate, order, and harmonize knowledge and that the proposed murals should be civic altars before which the people would go to reaffirm their faith in the new order. He saw mural art as a significant force in a country wracked by civil war, whose population was plagued by inequality and illiteracy.[3]

Agreeing with Vasconcelos, Mexican painters in 1922 formed a syndicate under the leadership of David Alfaro Siqueiros and dedicated themselves to a philosophy of art that called for abandonment of easel painting in favor of the mural, stressed content as much as style, and would be accessible for all to see and experience.[4] Another important participant in this mural renaissance, José Clemente Orozco, later observed that the mural painters were fully aware of the historical moment in which they worked and the relation of their art to the world and the society around them.[5] Diego Rivera agreed by condemning pure art and advocating revolutionary art imbued with political content. Pure art, he thought, meant class art, whereas mural art belongs to everyone.[6] Above all, the muralists proclaimed themselves members of a new, revolutionary Mexican society that required interpretation and direction. In the early 1920s that meant painting the Revolution so as to relate it to the past and define it as a guide to the future.

Seeing Juárez as the leader of the Reform of the nineteenth century and a precursor of the twentieth-century Revolution, muralists used him extensively in their interpretations of Mexico's past in painting. For them he stood out as a leader in the national-liberal tradition, which, according to the muralists, began with Cuauhtémoc's defiance of the Spaniards and continued with Hidalgo, Morelos, and Guerrero of the period of independence, with Gómez Farías in the 1830s, and then with Juárez, Ramírez, Altamirano, Ocampo, and Manuel Doblado in the 1850s. It culminated with the Revolution of 1910 and its leaders: Madero, Carranza, Zapata, and the others. Opposing them as the villains of Mexico's past were such figures as Cortés, Santa Anna, Miramón, Mejía, and, of course, Díaz, followed by the usurper who overthrew Madero, Huerta.

Beginning with a mural commission from the American ambassador to Mexico during the Calles years, Dwight W. Morrow, Diego Rivera painted three murals depicting Mexican history. He displayed few doubts about right or wrong in Mexico's past. As one critic pointed out, Rivera painted his revolutionary desires almost empty of reality.[7] His strongly ideological murals enlisted the aid of the Mexican past to dramatize their message and to transform Mexico's history into one of the great myths of the twentieth century. In this endeavor he accepted uncritically a belief in a dialectical history, characterized by class conflict deriving from unequal distribution of wealth.[8]

Between 1929 and 1935, Rivera continued this project with a mural in the National Palace that synthesized the history of Mexico from the ideological perspective of class struggle and historical materialism. He divided Mexican history into three general periods: a remote past, an immediate past, and a prophecy of the future. More specifically, he treated Mexico before the Spanish, the colonial period, independence, and the Revolution, which merged with the present and anticipated the future. Rivera used the mural as a vehicle to teach by means of pictorial narrative the struggle between progressive and reactionary forces, between oppressors and oppressed.

The panel depicting the Juárez era sustained this message in a

Santa Anna, the Clerical Dictatorship, and the Reform of 1857, by Diego Rivera. National Palace, Mexico City. Courtesy of the Benson Latin American Collection, The University of Texas at Austin.

very obvious way by making Juárez the dominant figure of a group that included Ignacio Altamirano, Ignacio Ramírez, Melchor Ocampo, Santos Degollado, Ignacio Comonfort, and others, all of whom represented the progressive forces of Mexico in the middle of the last century. They defended the Constitution of 1857, which embodied the principles of liberalism, challenged by Santa Anna and others who represented the clerical dictatorship. Rivera caricatured those of the clerical and military dictatorship; he painted Santa Anna as a general to represent the military and close to him a fat and ugly monk and a smiling bishop to stand for the clergy and the church. His arrangement of figures and symbols heightened the contrast. He pointed one of Juárez's hands toward the bishop's miter, which contained a brightly painted cross. In Juárez's other hand and over the bishop, Rivera placed a scroll labeled "Constitution of 1857 and Laws of the Reform."

For Rivera, Santa Anna and the clergy represented the forces of reaction, a coalition of military men and priests who monopolized the wealth of Mexico to the detriment of the country. Rivera believed that Juárez and his allies had conquered them, but in other sections of the mural he depicted the emergence of other forces of evil and reaction to threaten the legacy. Mexicans reacted to these by means of the Revolution of 1910, portrayed in the center archway of the main staircase of the National Palace. Rivera put the leaders of Mexico's independence movement, Hidalgo, Morelos, Allende, and others of the liberal pantheon, behind such leaders of the Revolution as Emiliano Zapata, Felipe Carrillo Puerto (a radical governor of the Yucatán in the 1920s), and others.[9]

Departing somewhat from his earlier narrative and didactic style to provide an impressionistic view of Mexico's past, Rivera included a study of Juárez in the mural he did in the lobby of the Hotel del Prado in Mexico City. Called *Sunday Dreams in the Alameda*, the mural focused on the Alameda, the park in front of the hotel where the Hemiciclo to Juárez is located, and the four centuries of history associated with it. The section featuring Juárez shows him in the center with Altamirano on his right and Ramírez on his left. Juárez carries a document, the Constitution of 1857. Like so many of Rivera's murals this one caused a stir when Rivera placed in Ramírez's hands a scroll with the words "Dios no existe" (God does

Sunday Dreams in the Alameda, by Diego Rivera. Hotel del Prado, Mexico City. Courtesy of the Benson Latin American Collection, The University of Texas at Austin.

not exist). He later removed them, protesting that people did not understand the meaning Ramírez intended by the statement.[10]

José Clemente Orozco's 1948 mural for the Sala de la Reforma of the Museum of History celebrated Juárez as the hero of the Reform and the Intervention. Stylistically different from Rivera's murals, its theme harmonized with both artists' interpretations of the Mexican past. Orozco painted Juárez as a symbol rather than as a subject of a narrative. Juárez's head dominates the mural and the room. On one side a soldier stands, with the symbolic "57" on

Juárez and the Fall of the Empire, by José Clemente Orozco. Museum of History, Mexico City. Courtesy of the Benson Latin American Collection, The University of Texas at Austin.

his helmet; on the opposite side soldiers carry the national flag. Figures below represent the debris of empire. The grotesque cadaver of Maximilian stretches horizontally the length of the painting. A crown has fallen from his head. The principal enemies of Juárez (the politically minded clergy, conservative imperialists, and even Napoleon III) support the corpse.[11]

Called *Juárez and the Fall of the Empire,* the painting represents what Orozco believed to be the meaning of Juárez and his era. Unlike the Rivera paintings about Mexican history, these included little narrative. As a Mexican critic wrote later, when Orozco turned his eyes to the pages of history (Juárez, for example), he chose not to narrate anything but rather to analyze the greatness of the man and the peculiar circumstances that surrounded him. Juárez and his two companions in the mural represented the forces that killed the empire, symbolized by the dead Maximilian. The power of the Juárez idea (government by law defended by Mexican soldiers) proved too strong. Orozco accented the dialectic of the Mexican past, an important feature in all the murals. He painted Juárez in bright colors and his enemies with dark hues. He depicted a serene and self-confident Juárez, whereas he made Juárez's enemies, the conservatives and the imperialists, grotesque. Orozco seemed to want the painting to function as a clear call to Mexicans to remain ever vigilant in the face of old enemies. Maximilian might be dead, but his supporters still live, he intimated.[12]

Orozco's murals in Guadalajara introduced a sense of skepticism about the genuineness of revolutionary leaders and their claims and in so doing enhanced the stature of both Juárez and the hero of the 1810 independence movement, Hidalgo. In the mural celebrating Hidalgo in the legislative chamber of the government palace, Orozco linked the two men by painting Hidalgo as the author of "Liberty" and Juárez of "Reform." The carnival of ideologies of the Guadalajara mural describing the contemporary social struggle suggested that men and their ideologies can be false and deceptive. Here Orozco showed both Hidalgo and Juárez as prophetic figures who stood for good principles but who did not share fully in the Revolution.[13] Orozco had witnessed much ugliness in the Revolution, and like many other Mexican artists and writers he maintained a critical detachment and skepticism toward those who claimed to be revolutionaries or heirs of the Revolution.

Like both Rivera and Orozco, David Alfaro Siqueiros treated the history of Mexico by means of mural painting but in his own unique style. According to one critic, Siqueiros took a highly individualistic approach to all problems, political or otherwise.[14] More perhaps than either Rivera or Orozco he lived the drama of the Mexican Revolution, and he continued to live it even to the extent of conflicting with Mexican political authorities.[15] He took a more subtle approach than did Rivera and assumed a more positive view of the Revolution than did Orozco.

Siqueiros's 1941 study of Juárez reveals the subtlety that he could employ without detracting from a didactic intent. More than any other treatment of Juárez by the leaders of the muralist movement, it integrates Juárez into the Revolution. In 1941 Siqueiros went to Chile, where, under the auspices of the Mexican ambassador, he painted a large mural with an anti-imperialist theme. Entitled *Death to the Invader*, the mural reflected Mexico's recent experience with foreign powers over the petroleum expropriation,

Death to the Invader (detail), by David Alfaro Siqueiros. Santiago, Chile.

as well as concern with the expansion of Germany, Italy, and Japan. Siqueiros portrayed Juárez as a predecessor of Lázaro Cárdenas, the Mexican president who authorized expropriation of foreign oil properties in Mexico. He did this by superimposing the head of Juárez on the figure of Cárdenas, for he saw a parallel between Juárez and Cárdenas as reformers and defenders of Mexico against foreign encroachment. Cárdenas had championed Mexico's interests in a confrontation with the United States over expropriation of petroleum wells and refineries; Juárez had defended Mexican sovereignty in face of a French invasion. For Siqueiros both Juárez and Cárdenas represented a struggle for liberty epitomized in the central figure of the mural, Cuauhtémoc.[16]

Other muralists followed the examples of Orozco, Siqueiros, and Rivera, among them Jorge González Camarena, who did a mural in 1957 for the chamber of the Mexican senate. González Camarena expressed the mural's theme of national consolidation through law by means of architectural scaffolding. To depict the history of Mexican society, González Camarena devised a system of cells suggestive of architectural styles prevailing in Mexico at various times in the past. He associated with each style and period a law or set of laws that affected the major social transformations in Mexico's history. He portrayed Juárez, along with Morelos, Gómez Farías, and Carranza, as a great lawgiver, the man responsible for the Laws of the Reform.[17]

Those closely associated with the muralist movement used Juárez as the subject for oil paintings, as did others. Inspired by Orozco's Museum of History mural with its emphasis on the features of Juárez's head, Siqueiros completed a study of Juárez in 1956 that focused on certain physical features of his head and avoided any political or ideological comment. But Rivera attempted by means of an oil painting to make a further statement about Juárez's role in Mexican history. Painted in 1948, the work depicted Juárez as an architect and a builder. Rivera showed Juárez wearing the presidential sash with two large hands resting on sheets of paper on top of a table. (In reality, Juárez's hands and feet were small.) In one hand Juárez holds a pen and in the other two drawing instruments. Over his right shoulder and in the background, Maximilian and his two Mexican generals face a firing squad. Over his left shoulder two men wield pickaxes as a farmer cultivates a field behind them. For Rivera, Juárez's decision to execute Maximilian symbolized the destruction of the old order and made possible a new. Rivera depicted Juárez as the architect of this change.[18]

Younger Mexican painters have dealt with Juárez and emphasized his role as president and association with the Laws of the

Reform, the Constitution of 1857, and the triumph of the republic in 1867. In addition to his senate chamber mural, Jorge González Camarena painted Juárez and the 1857 constitution in a portrait that now hangs in the Museum of History in Chapultepec castle. Antonio González Orozco reminded Mexicans of Juárez's involvement in the triumph of the republic in a painting that provided the cover for the Mexican government's pamphlet recounting the events of the centennial celebration of the triumph of the republic in 1967. He showed a victorious Juárez, accompanied by José María Iglesias and Sebastián Lerdo de Tejada, entering the Mexican capital on July 15, 1867. A jubilant crowd throws flowers before them. Leopoldo Méndez, a printmaker, deeply indebted, as others, to the genius of José Guadalupe Posada, has found Juárez a favorite subject, and in 1971 a painter whose specialty is Indian subjects, Jorge Leguizamo, produced his *Juárez an Indian*.[19]

One Mexican painter dissented from the almost fanatical use of

July 15, 1867 in Mexico City, by Antonio González Orozco, showing the triumphal return of Juárez, along with Sebastián Lerdo de Tejada and José María Iglesias, to Mexico City. National Museum of History, Mexico City.

Homage to Juárez, by Rufino Tamayo. Museum of Modern Art, Mexico City. Courtesy of the Benson Latin American Collection, The University of Texas at Austin.

art to mythologize the past. Although he did not remain apart from the muralist movement, Rufino Tamayo did oppose the view that art must be political or nationalistic. Readily acknowledging the Mexican qualities of his paintings, Tamayo always preferred to think of himself as a cosmopolitan painter with Mexican roots. His *Homage to Juárez*, painted in 1932 on a commission from the government, showed very clearly this rejection of political art. Although Tamayo did the painting for the government, it defies analysis according to any ideology or interpretation of the Mexican past. Clearly, Tamayo admired Juárez (both were Oaxacans); yet Juárez's role in specific events receives no emphasis—he is projected as a monument blending with the gray neoclassical buildings of a provincial square. A native girl in a white dress watches a paper balloon rising—symbol of hope and homage to Juárez.[20]

After 1920, then, Mexican painters made a large contribution to the development of a Juárez myth in Mexico. Like writers, government officials, and caricaturists, they found Juárez a useful way to express views of Mexico's past, present, and future. Above all, they reinforced the view of Juárez as a force in Mexican history, a symbol worthy of adulation.

The result—although perhaps any theme would have brought an equal result, considering the talent of these painters—was some of the most gorgeous artistic creations of the twentieth century, a testimony of the coming of age of art in Mexico. No longer did Mexico and Mexicans need to feel as if their culture was inferior to those elsewhere. They stood out in their own right. And surely part of the reason for their prestige was the decision to use local myths and local arguments in place of importations of foreign examples. In this sense the myth of Juárez served the country well.

8

 Mexican Governments and Juárez after 1920

In March 1953 Mexico City witnessed yet another demonstration on behalf of Juárez, but this one dwarfed all the others as an estimated two hundred thousand people gathered in front of the monument to the Revolution—a structure that had been intended by the Díaz regime to be the dome of a new building for the Mexican congress but became instead a monument to the revolution that overthrew him—to pay tribute not only to Benito Juárez but to two other Mexican presidents, Adolfo Ruíz Cortines and Lázaro Cárdenas. This triple homage honored the memory of Juárez on the anniversary of his birth, exalted Cárdenas as the man who had secured Mexico's economic independence by expropriating the petroleum industry on March 18, 1938, and acknowledged by means of a rally of the masses (mainly members of various labor organizations affiliated with the government) attempts by the new administration to check a rampant inflation. Ruíz Cortines had just been inaugurated, and Cárdenas had served from 1934 to 1940.[1] Sponsors and participants invoked memories of past leaders and their accomplishments to lend support to a contemporary leader and his program.

Prompted by dissatisfaction with the previous administration of Miguel Alemán, the labor organizations that sponsored the rally called upon Mexicans to "affirm their loyalty to and solidarity with the new government of Don Adolfo Ruíz Cortines."[2] Loyalty and solidarity were the watchwords of the commemoration. *El Universal* commented that the presence of Ruíz Cortines and his cabinet proved his intention to link the government "with the revolutionary postulates of all periods of our history, enhancing thereby the value of the nationalization of petroleum as the principal factor of economic independence and therefore the political independence of Mexico."[3] The most conservative of the big three daily newspapers of Mexico City, but like the others a supporter of all revolutionary governments, *Novedades*, affirmed that the occasion rendered homage to a president "who in the few months of his government has distinguished himself by determination to heed public clamor favoring a reduction in the cost of living."[4]

Such triple celebrations, as *Novedades* described this one, continued throughout the Ruíz Cortines administration and those of Adolfo López Mateos, Gustavo Díaz Ordaz, Luis Echeverría Alvarez, José López Portillo, and Miguel Hurtado de la Madrid that followed. Participation by these presidents signified restoration of government involvement in the Juárez myth to the level it had attained during the time of Porfirio Díaz. As the government and groups identified closely with it continued to organize demonstrations such as this one, Juárez once again became a symbol of identification: governments used him to assert support for the interests of the people, and individuals and groups used him as a means to express claims on the government. He emerged once again as an official symbol of continuity with the past at a time when stability, consolidation, and economic growth rather than reform became the chief concerns of public policy.[5]

Although in the 1920s and 1930s Mexican governments had sponsored some of the mural paintings that exalted Juárez and other Mexican heroes, presidents and cabinet members rarely participated in annual observances of Juárez's birth and death; only low-ranking officials took part. Newspapers in the capital found little to write about. Journalists—especially provincial ones—from time to time lamented the absence of fervor in the Juárez cult, both in the capital and in other parts of Mexico. *El Heraldo de México,* a Mexico City newspaper, described as monotonous the March 21, 1921, event; *El Porvenir* of Monterrey reported that the July 18, 1927, anniversary passed almost unnoticed in Mexico City; *El Siglo de Torreón* noted in 1927 a decline in Mexico City of the cult of heroes, a sentiment echoed with alarm by *El Dictamen* of Veracruz in 1934; and *La Raza* of Mexico City chided the government for cynicism in its failure to sponsor a commemoration in July 1922.[6] The nadir of governmental participation in these acts of homage came during the administration of Lázaro Cárdenas.

There may be several reasons for this official neglect of Juárez. One may be that the regional bias of Mexican governments had shifted away from Oaxaca. Writing for the anti-Revolution and antigovernment newspaper *Omega*, Nemesio García Naranjo suggested that the beneficent oaxacanism of Díaz and Juárez had been replaced by the tyrannical sonorism of Adolfo de la Huerta and Alvaro Obregón.[7] Plutarco Elías Calles, Obregón's successor in 1924, also came from the North, and together the three constituted what Mexicans called the Sonoran dynasty. The assassination of Obregón shortly after his second election to the presidency in 1928 encouraged a movement to project him as a hero at the expense of Juárez. Because the anniversary of Obregón's death fell on July 17, manifestations in his honor throughout the late 1920s and 1930s always overshadowed those for Juárez.[8] The Revolution produced a regional shift in the balance of power, a change that required new symbols.

More important, the Revolution stimulated an ideology sanctioning change and reform. The reformers of the 1920s and 1930s, who believed the Revolution should reject the past, often ignored or even criticized Juárez. They believed that Mexican thought and attitudes should be purged of their racist and capitalist bias, elements of which they found in the Juárez myth. In 1922 one of these men, Felipe Carrillo Puerto, neglected the Juárez commemoration in the Yucatán and thereby provoked *La Raza* to charge his government with cynicism. As governor of the Yucatán in the early 1920s, Carrillo Puerto took the Revolution seriously. Often claiming descent from a Mayan Indian leader who resisted the Spanish, and thereby promoting his own myth, Carrillo Puerto authorized a Mayan translation of the Constitution of 1917 and launched an ambitious program to provide roads and schools for the Yucatán. Supporters of Adolfo de la Huerta assassinated Carrillo Puerto during the revolt in 1923 against Obregón. Narciso Bassols, who in 1931 became secretary of education, also thought the radical and populist aspects of the Revolution should be supported and implemented, and to that end he contributed to the program of socialist education during the Cárdenas years. As a teacher and jurist in the 1920s, he promoted the cause of radical reform and sharply criticized Juárez's failure to perceive the real needs of the "eighty percent of the population converted into a dark and hungry mass." Bassols accused Juárez of disloyalty to his race by overlooking the need to transform the economic condition of the inhabitants of Mexico in his obsession to drive out the French and suppress the privileges of the bishops. Using the anniversary of Juárez's death in 1926 to make these comments, Bassols further accused Juárez of failure to extend independence to the Indians; emancipation of the indigenous races remained to be accomplished. July 18, Bassols thought, should signify the death of a false solution to the causes of Mexico's problems.[9]

Others made similar assessments of Juárez, although for different reasons. An anthropologist who considerably influenced the indianist thrust of the Revolution, Manuel Gamio, questioned Juárez's appropriateness as a national symbol, arguing that his consecration as a hero resulted from the efforts of a minority of Mexicans who always had voice and vote. For the majority of Mexicans, Gamio said, Juárez lacked meaning, for although of the indigenous race, his culture was European and did little for the Indian.[10] Describing Juárez as a symbol of liberalism, a clerical pamphlet entitled *Juárez indio, traicionó a los indios: O el liberalismo en México es una cosa igual a los siete plagas de Egipto* continued the attack on him for failure to understand the nature of Indian culture and problems and thereby lent unintended support to Mexico's more radical revolutionaries. It argued that Juárez's and liberalism's emphasis on private ownership of property had undermined the basis of Indian social and economic life, which was collective.[11]

Rejecting "the cold, dry, glacial individualism of the nineteenth century," as Zapata's former mentor, Antonio Díaz Soto y Gama, put it, the Cárdenas government developed a native socialism that stressed an active land reform program to revive the communal agriculture prevalent in pre-Spanish times, an increased role for peasant and worker groups in national politics, nationalism of such key industries as oil, and a strong presidency. Cárdenas felt little need to use the appeal of Juárez to promote this program, and, as a consequence, he never appeared at any of the Hemiciclo ceremonies. Nevertheless, Cárdenas could regard Juárez as "one of the most outstanding statesmen in the history of Mexico," as he did in a message to the Colombian people on the occasion of the dedication of a Juárez statue in Bogotá.[12]

Despite the regional and ideological biases of Mexican governments in the 1920s and 1930s, some of those closely associated with them attempted occasionally to draw parallels between the work of current revolutionaries and Juárez. In 1925 two members of the Liberal Juárez Committee published a pamphlet for distribution among children, soldiers, workers, and peasants on "the great redeemer Indian" and his importance to the present. Describing Madero as a disciple of Juárez, it said that Juárez lived again in the Constitution of 1917, Carranza, Obregón, and Calles. It linked the agrarian policies of Calles with a statement made by the "Evangelist Juárez" and emphasized the pertinence of Juárez's apothegm "respect for the rights of others is peace" to Luis Morones's defense of Mexican sovereign rights against the claims of foreigners in a speech before the American Chamber of Commerce. According to the authors of the pamphlet, Morones, Calles's secretary of commerce and industry, had stated that privileged concessions contravened the law and had emphasized that foreigners have the same rights as nationals under the law. It hailed the project to create a national Indian boarding school as the best way to honor Juárez, for he provided an example of an Indian's successful integration into the national culture. Juárez, the pamphlet continued, had championed the reorganization and moralization of the army, and by working through his secretary of war Calles shared this ideal. Both Obregón and Calles wanted to create a national guard to deal with military uprisings.[13]

Textbooks continued to project the image of a good Juárez; some of them sustained the tradition begun during the Porfiriato of using history to promote national consolidation, whereas others struck out along the lines suggested by the new philosophy of socialist education to inculcate such values as a classless society, collective ownership of production, fraternity and brotherhood, and class consciousness.[14] An author of one of the socialist-oriented texts, Alfonso Teja Zabre, saw Juárez as the representative figure of the Reform, the Intervention, and the empire, an authentic hero of another era, but, despite confiscation of clerical wealth, not the symbol of social transformation. Longinos Cadena adhered faithfully to official requirements and in his text described Juárez as a man of notable gifts, of great integrity, and of iron will, who despite adversity brought the country great prosperity.[15] Even some of the conservative or traditional texts of the period concurred with the official view. That of Enrique A. Santibáñez acknowledged the importance of Juárez as a valid national hero, for he overcame with honor the threats to the nation from ambitious military leaders, Maximilian, and the French. A hispanist, Abel Gámiz, concluded his assessment of Juárez by calling him a legitimate source of national pride.[16]

As minister of education during the Calles administration, José Manuel Puig Casauranc attempted to relate Juárez to the Revolution, which he interpreted as an attempt to pursue new philosophical and social routes that sought to complete the work of the Reform, by stressing certain personal attributes of Juárez. He described these attributes as love for family, extraordinary scrupulousness in money matters, a rare facility to know men, steadiness of purpose in matters of religion and society, political honor, energy, strength of character, political vision, clear military foresight, a spotless nationalism (despite willingness to sell national territory), and serenity and firmness before enemies.[17]

But it was the new government newspaper, *El Nacional,* that probably did the most to continue the integration of Juárez into a myth of the Mexican Revolution in the 1930s. Establishment of the periodical coincided with creation of an official political party to resolve disputes among politicians and interest groups peacefully and to provide continuity in leadership and policy after the assassination of Obregón in 1928.[18] Much of *El Nacional's* treatment of Juárez in the 1930s exalted him as the hero of the Reform and related him to the Revolution. In July 1931, Arturo García Formentí linked Juárez with Zapata, who, he said, destroyed latifundismo, and Carranza, whom he considered a symbol of the discipline of the law. García Formentí also attributed to Juárez the strength of Obregón. Even though "we find ourselves a little far from the ideology of Juárez's time," García Formentí concluded, the government would do well to maintain the civic fire of a cult of Juárez, for "his example provides a perennial national teaching."[19]

Although earlier revolutionaries had seen differences between Obregón and Juárez, the coincidence of the anniversaries of their deaths and the government's elevation of Obregón to the status of a hero finally prompted a writer for El Nacional, Rafael López, in 1935 to comment on parallels between the two revolutionaries. He wrote that revolutionaries must be taken as social indices and pure indications of collective wishes and then suggested that by separating church and state, Juárez anticipated the revolution of the twentieth century in that he clearly identified with the disinherited of Mexico. With its emphasis on restoration of land to the Indians and peasants, the present revolution was continuing the work of Juárez, López said. Both Obregón and Juárez ought to be considered as links in the great revolutionary chain of Mexican history, he concluded.[20]

In 1937 El Nacional covered extensively one of the speeches given at the Hemiciclo in July by Eloy Montalvo, representing the youth of Mexico. Montalvo had voiced concern about the persistent threats to revolutionary leaders and programs and had suggested that Juárez, despite his shortcomings and contradictions, ought to be taken as a guide and symbol. He described Juárez as a leader in the revolutionary struggle that continued to the present, for even though Juárez and other leaders of the Reform successfully broke the hold on the Mexican economy of colonial institutions such as the church, many of these reformers themselves became large landholders and aristocrats. The Revolution of 1910, according to Montalvo, sought to end their domination of Mexican society, but they continued to occupy positions of power. Referring to the rise of dictators in Europe, Montalvo said the enemies of reform were in league with Francisco Franco, Benito Mussolini, and Adolf Hitler. Mexicans must therefore revive Juárez as an example and an inspiration.[21]

Although Cárdenas did not refer to Juárez in his address to the Mexican people at the time of the petroleum expropriation, writers for *El Nacional* and others noted parallels between it and Juárez's resistance to the French intervention. *El Nacional* quoted extensively from Rubén Gómez Esqueda's speech on the anniversary of Juárez's birth in 1938 in which he emphasized that the force and doctrine of Juárez had risen to new heights in recent days and that his spirit and example should serve as the norm for the reformers and revolutionaries of 1938. Three days before Gómez Esqueda's speech, the Mexican government had announced the petroleum expropriation.[22]

The Cárdenas era closed in 1940, and with it emphasis on radical reform ended. Gradual change and consolidation became objectives of successive governments in Mexico, which thought that Mexico ought to shift from revolution to evolution, emphasizing industrialization rather than reform.[23] Gradually they saw value in reviving and using memories of Juárez as a means to focus the ideology of a restrained revolution. Mexico's entry into World War II followed by increased involvement in international affairs, especially during the administration of Adolfo López Mateos, led to increased invocation of Juárez. In addition, the rise of opposition groups on both left and right, and further consolidation of political power in the official party, which after 1946 was called the Party of Revolutionary Institutions or PRI, and the presidency encouraged further elaboration of the Juárez myth. Like the government of Díaz, Mexican governments after 1940 turned increasingly to the manipulation of historical symbols as a means to promote consolidation, order, and continuity, while at the same time espousing a revolutionary ideology. The process began under the Avila Camacho regime and greatly accelerated with Adolfo Ruíz Cortines and his successors.

Urging Mexicans to turn to Juárez when Mexico entered World War II, a group of patriotic Mexicans organized a program in 1942 to exalt him as a symbol of those values the country should champion by its participation. According to *El Nacional,* these Mexicans recognized that the work of Juárez assumed significance in the context of grave problems that confronted Mexico and the democracies of the world.[24] Newspapers and magazines provided extensive coverage, and Vicente Lombardo Toledano's paper, *El Popular,* queried whether Mexicans were witnessing a resurrection of the cult of Juárez, for the event was indeed glittering.[25] Thirty-four orators from all walks of life spoke in the Palace of Fine Arts. Delegations from the cabinet, congress, and official party participated, along with artists and intellectuals. The minister of the interior and the man destined to succeed Avila Camacho, Miguel Alemán, spoke, as did the philosopher and teacher Alfonso Reyes; the writer friend of Pancho Villa, Martín Luis Guzmán; historian Luis Chávez Orozco; labor leader Vicente Lombardo Toledano; and composer and music director of the National Symphony Orchestra, Carlos Chávez. A 102-year-old veteran of Juárez's army during the French intervention attended and received much attention. Characterizing Juárez as the insignia of the race, insuperable reformer, savior of nationality, and banner of the destinies of the continent, speaker after speaker emphasized the importance of national unity and hostility to those who would subvert national sovereignty. *El Nacional* commented that Mexicans on July 18 viewed Juárez as a typical man of America, self-taught, indigenous, and aware of the destinies of the continent and the world. He appeared in the "sanguinary glare of the bonfires of Europe as a herald who announced on the Cerro de las Campanas the inviolability of the American horizon and that the continent was never to be a field for exploitative expansionism." Maximilian had been a precursor of nazism and fascism, concluded *El Nacional*.[26]

After the war the Mexican government used Juárez to defend and explain its foreign policy, with the full development of Juárez as a symbol of foreign policy objectives coming in the 1960s, when the Castro revolution in Cuba and the conclusion of the Chamizal dispute with the United States encouraged the internationally minded Adolfo López Mateos to affirm a foreign policy independent from that of the United States. In both events the interests of the United States and Mexico conflicted, so that previous examples of resistance to foreign influence took on meaning in the formulation of policy. Fidel Castro's advent and Mexico's response must be seen in the context of the cold war. Characterized by hostility between the United States and the Soviet Union, it required the United States to influence its allies to adhere to a policy of antagonism toward communist governments. The United States encouraged Latin American countries to deal harshly with internal subversive movements and to limit dealings with the Soviet Union and other communist countries.[27]

The United States attempted to use the Organization of American States (OAS) to attain these objectives. Coming shortly before the overthrow of the Arbenz regime in Guatemala, the Caracas meeting of OAS foreign ministers in March 1954 provoked Mexican and other Latin American suspicions of United States motives. The United States participated mainly to secure approval of the Declaration of Caracas, which would pledge the American states to cooperate against intervention by an international communist movement in the hemisphere. The vague language of the declaration aroused concern among many Latins lest it sanction intervention by the United States. The Mexican delegation shared these suspicions and decided to join Argentina in abstaining from a vote on the declaration. That position won approval at home and association with values related to Juárez and the oil nationalization, for it came in March and in the context of both the Juárez and oil anniversaries. Speakers and writers said that Mexico's refusal to endorse the declaration vindicated both Juárez and Cárdenas by affirming once again Mexico's dedication to the cause of national independence and the principle that "respect for the rights of others is peace."[28]

Opposition to meddling by the United States in Mexico's internal affairs provided one justification for refusal to break relations with the Castro government. Headed by López Mateos, the Mexican government maintained that it must be faithful to the twin principles of nonintervention and national self-determination and that Mexico as a free and sovereign state ought not to be a battlefield of international lefts and rights. The newspaper *Excelsior* supported the government's policy, especially to answer criticism of leftist and pro-Cuban groups within Mexico. It described such opposition as anti-juarism. Development and maintenance of the government's policy toward Cuba in face of substantial pressure, both internal and external, encouraged manipulation of Juárez and other symbols associated with the mystique of the Revolution.[29]

The most extensive use of Juárez in the context of Mexico's international relations came during the settlement of the Chamizal dispute with the United States. The conflict involved a small parcel of land that had become detached from Mexico when the Rio Grande River shifted its course between El Paso, Texas, and Ciudad Juárez, Mexico. When López Mateos went before television cameras and radio microphones to announce final settlement on July 18, 1963, he stood before a large portrait of Juárez so that all would understand that both he and Juárez had successfully defended the territorial integrity of Mexico.[30] The United States had returned an insignificant amount of land (only 174 hectares), but the Mexican government exploited fully the fact that for the first time in history Mexico had added rather than lost territory. The commemoration of Juárez's death became an occasion for orators to emphasize this small victory as well as to exalt the devotion of Mexico's incumbent president and government to an important tenet of Juárez's international policy—defense of the territorial integrity of Mexico. López Mateos, editorialized *El Nacional* in anticipation of the president's announcement, manifested the spirit of Juárez in the solution of the Chamizal dispute. The return of El Chamizal had symbolic importance because the United States had shown respect for international law; Mexico's and Juárez's principle that respect for the rights of others is peace had triumphed.[31]

As the Mexican government saw a larger role for Mexico in world affairs, Juárez became an increasingly valuable symbol for the values and policies it espoused. When López Mateos journeyed to Europe in 1963, he saw fit to invoke Juárez before his departure.[32] Other Latin American countries already regarded him as an American symbol, thanks in part to the action of the Colombian congress, which admitted him to the ranks of her heroes. He had become "benemérito de las Américas," and in 1971 a movement began, independent of government initiative, to petition the United Nations to proclaim him well-deserving of the world's adulation.[33] Mexican intellectuals as well as government officials expressed concern about excessive American influence as American money, tourists, and goods poured across the border in increasing quantities after World War II and as the United States sought to share in the Mexican oil bonanza of the late 1970s.[34] In part as a response to the student and worker disturbances that

preceded the 1968 Olympic games held in Mexico City, Luis Echeverría Alvarez, who became president in 1970, assumed the role
of a leader of Third World interests, a position endorsed by his
loyal supporters in the government and the press. In the context
of the July 1975 commemoration of Juárez's death, they proclaimed that the figure of Juárez "obliges us to praise and promote
all that contributes to the strengthening of the thesis of the third
world."[35]

Mexicans found that other countries could pose threats to the
independence and honor of their country. In 1971 the government
proclaimed Juárez's principle that respect for others is peace when
it ordered deportation of five Soviet diplomats shortly after the
arrest of a group of young Mexicans, who, it was charged, had
been trained in North Korea to conduct a guerrilla revolution in
Mexico. Members of the Mexican group had gone to study in the
Patrice Lumumba Friendship University in Moscow and then went
to North Korea, which suggested Soviet collusion in their
endeavors.[36]

Increased sensitivity to Mexico's place in the family of nations
encouraged growth in the power of the Mexican presidency, one
of the most important developments in twentieth-century Mexican
history, and extensive identification with Juárez and other national
heroes accompanied and assisted this growth of power. The behavior of recent Mexican presidents suggests their awareness of
the importance of tradition and faith in the perpetuation of a
system of authority. Extensive travel and participation in national
rituals have been important activities of the president since the
advent of Ruíz Cortines in 1952. Invariably presidents have appeared at the annual commemorations of Juárez's birth and death
in Mexico City or elsewhere. They have found these events useful
for attracting support.[37]

The Mexico City Juárez commemorations often became demonstrations in praise of the current occupant of the presidential
chair. Presidents have sometimes spoken, but more often they
have listened to others heap praise upon them and draw parallels
between their policies and those of Juárez. Beginning in 1953,
the March 21 celebrations included acts of homage to Cárdenas
for his role in the petroleum expropriation, an event that has

assumed even larger dimensions in recent years as Mexico has found itself swimming in a veritable sea of proven or potential oil reserves. Representatives of PRI always took part and usually spoke. During the Miguel Alemán administration, General Rodolfo Sánchez Taboada, president of the PRI, began his speeches by reviewing events of the Reform, continued by stating that the Revolution achieved many Reform goals, and concluded by praising Alemán for carrying on the work of both. Student and labor organizations, usually composed of government employees with the day off, provided the required masses. Sometimes governments found these occasions useful for increasing public exposure of a new official, as happened in July 1971, when the recently appointed mayor of Mexico City gave the principal address.[38]

Improved transportation made travel easier, and presidents often found themselves in Oaxaca on March 21 or July 18 instead of at the Hemiciclo in Mexico City. They have used such visits in Oaxaca or elsewhere to dedicate public works as well as to honor Juárez and assert unity of government and people.[39] In July 1961, López Mateos journeyed to Guelatao, Juárez's birthplace in the mountains of Oaxaca, and on the anniversary of the death of the former president he not only lauded Juárez but also dedicated a new airport, a road, and a new municipal building and met with local politicians. The president appeared at the town hall to have his picture taken next to a bust of Juárez with officials of the state and nearby villages standing on both sides. Then, as the writer for *Novedades* wrote, the president, deputies to the congress, and municipal presidents from Guelatao and surrounding villages mingled with the humble people of the village.[40]

Government publications assisted presidents to exploit and elaborate a Juárez myth by reproducing speeches, newspaper articles, editorials, and documents friendly to both Juárez and revolutionary governments. In the 1960s and early 1970s the finance ministry (Secretaría de Hacienda y Crédito Público) published four books edited by Carlos J. Sierra, which documented the continuing importance of Juárez to Mexicans. One showed the presence of Juárez in governments of Mexico since 1911, and all four contained speeches by important Mexicans and newspaper articles eulogizing Juárez. One anthology included a speech by the son of

Justo Sierra and a high official of the Secretaría de Hacienda in 1959, Manuel J. Sierra, who described Juárez, with Hidalgo, Madero, and Carranza, as the most brilliant constellation in the heaven of the fatherland. The same book contained a speech given in 1960 by the novelist and later minister of education in the cabinet of Gustavo Díaz Ordaz, Agustín Yáñez. He remarked in a ceremony of homage to Juárez that "in the chorus of our immortals the example of Juárez requires of us the civic exaltation of our existence." These and similar views provided the substance of the speeches and articles incorporated in Sierra's anthologies.[41]

The finance ministry also began publishing in the early 1950s the *Boletín Bibliográfico* that devoted itself to recording the major events and heroes of Mexico's past and providing bibliographical assistance for further studies of these subjects. Most of the essays on Juárez treated segments of his career, and a few attempted to relate him to the Revolution. Some essays even provided critical evaluations of Juárez, such as Moisés González Navarro's "Juárez y los indios mayas" in the March 15, 1955, issue. Here González Navarro, a historian at the Colegio de México, said Juárez as governor of Oaxaca had reacted in 1849 to an Indian uprising in a way typical of creoles and liberals of the time. He had recognized the justice of the uprising, but he had also suppressed it ruthlessly.[42] Most articles and editorials have been adulatory, as Maurilio P. Náñez's "El espíritu de Juárez, único en América," which described Juárez as the "father of our constitutionality and our juridical life," or Manuel J. Sierra's essay extolling Juárez as an "immortal abstraction, dogma, banner, and inexhaustible source of energy and faith in the destinies of Mexico to conquer the obstacles that would impede our progress."[43] The entire January 15, 1964, issue treated the Chamizal dispute and its settlement.

During the López Mateos administration and under his personal patronage, a geographer and Oaxacan, Jorge L. Tamayo, began editing a multivolume collection of Juárez documents. A valuable and accessible source of primary material on Juárez, the volumes nevertheless reflect some of the editor's preoccupations with charges that polemicists such as Bulnes have levied against Juárez. One volume. contains only documents relating to the McLane-Ocampo treaties, to support a conclusion that Juárez's patriotism was impeccable during this affair. Tamayo included a section of documents on the assassination of Lincoln in another volume and concluded that the movie *Juárez*, produced by Warner Brothers in 1938, comically distorted history by suggesting a close friendship between Juárez and Lincoln.[44]

Helped in 1959 by a decree establishing the National Commission of Free Textbooks that opened a new stage in the history of Mexican nationalism, school books continued to portray Juárez as a national hero. Under this program official textbooks for the six years of primary education attempted to develop national unity by means of instruction in history and civics. Revolutionary heroes such as Madero, Carranza, and Zapata joined the older ones of the Reform, the independence movement, and the conquest as symbols of important national values to be learned from and emulated by the young.[45]

Beginning in the late 1950s, the Mexican government reminded Mexicans of Juárez and the Reform in more public and dramatic ways by holding centennial celebrations to commemorate the Constitution of 1857, the triumph of the republic, and the death of Juárez. At each centennial publication was encouraged of numerous books on the men, ideas, and events of the Reform and Intervention that argued for a continuity between the Juárez regime and contemporary revolutionary governments.[46] During the centennial of the triumph of the republic, President Gustavo Díaz Ordaz journeyed to Querétaro in June 1967 to dedicate a large monument to Juárez on the site of Maximilian's execution, and on July 15 he led a reenactment of the triumphal entry of Juárez into the Mexican capital. Juárez's small black coach, on exhibit in the Museum of History, served as the principal symbol and object of veneration. It was taken from the museum and moved through the streets of Mexico City to the Constitution Plaza, where a large crowd had gathered to hear Díaz Ordaz read Juárez's 1867 proclamation to the nation from the central balcony of the national palace.[47] In the evening Mexicans heard performances of Hector Quintanar's "Acclamations to the Manifesto to the Nation of Don Benito Juárez" and Salvador Contreras's "Cantata to Juárez" at a gala concert in the Palace of Fine Arts.[48]

The 1957 centennial commemorating promulgation of the Con-

President Gustavo Díaz Ordaz, joined by former Presidents Emilio Portes Gil, Lázaro Cárdenas, Miguel Alemán, and Adolfo Ruíz Cortines, at the dedication of the Juárez monument on the Cerro de las Campanas in Querétaro, May 15, 1967.

The principal symbol and object of veneration during the July 15, 1967, ceremonies in Mexico City commemorating the centennial of Juárez's triumphal
return to the Mexican capital, July 15, 1867; Juárez's small black coach.

President Díaz Ordaz greets the large crowd of people filling the great square, the Zócalo or Constitution Plaza, in front of the National Palace. He stands in the central balcony, where Juárez stood one hundred years earlier to read his proclamation to the nation after returning to the capital following the defeat of the French and Mexican conservatives. The man who was to succeed Díaz Ordaz as president of Mexico, Luis Echeverría Alvarez, stands second to the right of Díaz Ordaz.

stitution of 1857 prompted the government to set aside a portion of the National Palace as a "recinto de homenaje" or place of homage for Juárez. Under the supervision of Manuel J. Sierra and Raúl Noriega, who had been editor of *El Nacional* and was then a high official of the Secretaría de Hacienda, that part of the palace where Juárez had lived while president became a national shrine devoted to perpetuation of his cult. The great-grandson of Juárez, Carlos Obregón Santacilia, provided the architectural design, which included in the recinto a library, a large room with a bust of Juárez at one end for acts of homage, and restoration of part of the living quarters of the Juárez family, including the bedroom where Juárez died.[49]

Government sponsorship of Juárez centennials climaxed by its proclaiming 1972 to be the "Year of Juárez" in Mexico. As in 1906 the government set up a commission to organize activities and sponsor publications to honor Juárez on the centennial anniversary of his death.[50] Describing Juárez as the "nerve and vigor of Mexican nationalism" because of his consolidation of national sovereignty by overcoming "internal and external powers," the Mexican president, Luis Echeverría Alvarez, exhorted the commission to enlist the full support of the governors of the twenty-nine states and two territories to undertake vigorous measures to ensure diffusion of knowledge of the life and works of Juárez.[51]

By the 1970s Mexican governments had emerged as perhaps the most significant agents in the development and perpetuation of a Juárez myth in Mexico. They exploited and shaped images of Juárez as a useful way to further policies of consolidation, order, and peace within the framework of a revolutionary ideology and to reassure Mexicans in time of economic crisis that they are, in the words of Juárez, "arbiters of their fate."[52] Like the 1887 commemoration, the 1953 demonstration signaled the beginning of major government involvement in the myth after a period of relative indifference. The Revolution had already swung to the right; symbolic manifestation of this change came substantially after 1950, when successive regimes endeavored to secure legitimacy through identification with the heroes of Mexico's past.

As in the days of Porfirio Díaz, dissident groups challenged these governments, although in more muted form, for Mexico succeeded where Bulnes observed in 1903 it had failed—it developed an institutional life that made possible opposition without revolution. Many of these groups employed the Juárez myth as a means to criticize and challenge both government and other groups. Despite, or perhaps because of, a continuity of government and policy and hence increasing discontent with what seemed to be a growing ossification or petrification of political life, the argument over Juárez thus continued in Mexico.

9

 Symbol for Dissent

The Juárez myth was used for the purpose of political dissent in twentieth-century Mexico. It has been invoked by many Mexicans of recent decades against the Revolution and against the governments that succeeded the regime of Díaz beginning in 1910 and that tended to turn ever more conservative, all the time announcing their purpose and convictions as revolutionary. Some of the dissenters openly attacked Juárez and thus continued the tradition of conservative unbelievers who would, it often seemed, have had Mexico repeal the nineteenth and twentieth centuries and go back to the golden age of the Spanish viceroys and bishops. Others kept the fires of jacobinism burning by their stress on the need for liberal purity, especially in matters of church and state, and they tended to hold up Juárez as a great historical figure who, they claimed, had represented their jacobin ideal.

The dissenters in the years after 1920, beginning with the era of Alvaro Obregón and reaching to that of Luis Echeverría Alvarez, who presided over the centennial of Juárez's death, and continuing afterward, were opponents of the official party in Mexico, created in 1928 after the death of Obregón, that is, the Party of Revolutionary Institutions, the sole party of the Revolution. Most of the dissenters stood outside the broad coalition of farmers, businessmen, and organized laborers that monopolized power and privilege in Mexico primarily because they had allied themselves with the official party, although some remained within even though they disagreed with government policies. The dissenters all agreed

120

in protesting the government's use of the Juárez myth to prop a new myth, the myth of the Revolution that claimed that what happened in Mexico between 1910 and 1920 and what continued to happen by means of so-called revolutionary institutions was indeed revolutionary.

Two major groupings of dissenters gradually appeared—the rightists, who included those Mexicans who could not accept the Revolution of 1910 with its innovative constitution, and the leftists, who protested the failure of revolutionary governments to carry out the radical provisions of the Constitution of 1917. Both groups agreed in deploring the official manipulation of the historical leader Juárez, describing such behavior as hypocritical, unhistorical, unrighteous, thoughtless, and unpatriotic.

Many of the rightists among the dissenters sustained the traditional conservative-clerical complaint that when Mexican governments adopted and enforced anticlerical or antichurch laws it forsook the country's historical heritage. In the 1920s the government made serious attempts to enforce the anticlerical provisions of the new constitution, and such enforcement became the rightists' principal lament. After the dramatic church-state confrontation of that decade, the government reached an awkward accommodation and relaxed its efforts to require compliance with anticlerical laws, and the rightists then turned to hispanism (maintenance of Mexico's Spanish heritage), nationalism, strict independence from the United States, electoral honesty, and regionalism.[1]

The dissatisfaction of Roman Catholics with the Mexican governments of the 1920s is, of course, well known. Government policies in the 1920s provoked enormous discontent among Catholics, an unrest that led to virtual civil war between 1926 and 1929, when the administration of Plutarco Elías Calles, deciding to enforce the anticlerical provisions of the 1917 constitution, authorized the deportation of foreign priests and registration of remaining priests and the closing of church schools and convents and even accused the Catholic hierarchy of treason. State governments began complying with the constitutional proviso that gave them authority to fix the number of priests who could officiate in local churches, and Tabasco won the prize for diligence in that endeavor by allowing only six priests to administer to congregations numbering altogether some thirty thousand people. Totally out of character with the traditions of Catholicism, priests staged a strike and boycotted their altars. Throughout Mexico fighting broke out between clericals and government officials, especially in strongly conservative Jalisco. Many rural schoolteachers who idealistically had enlisted in the government's ambitious program to bring schools to the countryside were set upon physically, and some were murdered.[2]

In this dismal era for Catholics in Mexico, the Juárez myth played a considerable part. Two groups of laymen helped the Catholic cause. One group, known as *cristeros*, enlisted adherents under the banner of Christ the King. The other took the title of National Defense League of Religious Liberty. On innumerable occasions both groups focused on the Juárez myth as a cause of their woes.

In looking at this Catholic concern for the myth—the manner in which Juárez was used to justify attacks on religion—one should consider the contentions of a remarkable volume published by a cleric, who, along with Montes de Oca, aroused liberals in 1900 to begin organizing against Díaz. In 1927 Regis Planchet presented the case for the *cristeros* and endeavored to provide historical perspective to Catholicism's troubles by careful historical analysis of the transformation of Juárez from man to hero. Planchet argued that Juárez occupied the venerated position of hero only because the liberals won in 1867 and proceeded to use the newspaper press to establish a "soporific juarist literature." With the help of the police, he wrote, Mexican liberalism declared Juárez beyond the criticism of history. Planchet saw Juárez as a vulgar man of ambition, a mistaken governor, a bloody despot. Juárez squandered treasury funds and called foreigners to his aid. Mexicans needed historical studies stressing the truth of Juárez's career to provide "scientific arsenals of war material to destroy the false history written by enemies of the Church and the Fatherland."[3]

The literature of the 1920s pointing up the reprehensible aspects of the Juárez myth—its use by the state to help destroy the church—made a deep impression upon Catholic Mexicans. For many years thereafter one of the founders of the National Defense League of Religious Liberty, Miguel Palomar y Vizcarra, retained battle scars of those years that included an embittered hostility to Juárez and all the values liberals ascribed to him. In an interview in 1964, he admitted that at one time he had been a juarista and had nearly lost his Catholic faith, but he had come to see that Juárez opposed all that the national flag represented. In 1964 he described juarism and Catholicism as antithetical. He saw Cortés as the true founder of Mexican nationality and blamed Juárez for Mexico's agrarian problem, remarking that laws passed during the Reform had destroyed Indian communal villages.[4]

Among the rightists who found the government's use of the Juárez myth troublesome were the outright political movements, among them National Sinarquista Union and the National Action party (PAN). Both of these movements were reactions to the native socialism of Cárdenas. Founded in León, Guanajuato, in 1937, the Unión Nacional Sinarquista, whose members were called sinarquistas, appealed to peasants with a strong Roman Catholic faith and to other lower- or middle-class groups who felt alienated by the Revolution, especially by the social policies of Cárdenas, or, as one of their leaders, Salvador Abascal, put it, "the errors and crimes of Cardenism." For Abascal these crimes consisted of persecution of the church and destruction of the material wealth of the peasants. The sinarquistas held that Mexico should preserve its Spanish and Catholic traditions and develop a Christian social order, a sort of corporate state that would check social fluidity. Like the earlier *cristeros,* the sinarquistas looked upon themselves as soldiers of a militant Roman Catholic faith, and their leaders advocated "open civic action" against cardenism. By 1940 they numbered about five hundred thousand, but after that declined.[5]

Sinarquistas viewed Juárez as a traitor to Mexican nationalism, and what they said about him after 1937 was little more than variations on this theme. Believing that Mexican liberals had abandoned Spanish cultural traditions in favor of those of the United States and other Anglo-Saxon countries, they energetically opposed the United States, even during World War II, when Mexico sided with the Allies. In this context sinarquistas often employed the term "fifth column" to describe Juárez and other liberal heroes. Their newspaper, *El Sinarquista,* cast Valentín Gómez Farías in the role of "chief of the Yankee fifth column, the faithful ally of the invader," and included as accomplices Juárez and Melchor Ocampo. The paper indicted liberal historians for backing the anti-Mexican plan to glorify the villains of Mexican history. An Indian could not be a good Mexican, *El Sinarquista* thought; certainly a man who had ties with the United States could not expect to qualify as a patriot. "Benito Juárez has been called well-deserving of the Americas," *El Sinarquista* complained. Unfortunately, Juárez did nothing but plot against Mexican nationality, cried *El Sinarquista*; in all the cities of the country "we find squatting shamelessly atop pillars this man who, being Indian, attempted to deliver our sovereignty to the United States."[6]

Although sinarquistas sometimes admitted Hidalgo and Morelos to their roster of great Mexicans, they developed alternative heroes to those of the liberals by projecting Cortés as the founder of Mexican nationality and other men of the colonial period as builders. Among the founding fathers they included the first bishop of Mexico, a defender of the interests of the Indians, Juan de Zumárraga; a Spaniard who taught reading, writing, and singing to the Indians, Pedro de la Gante; and the very man who introduced Spanish culture to the New World, Christopher Columbus. From the nineteenth century they chose Lucas Alamán, Félix Zuloaga (who had rejected an offer of money from the United States), and the "liberator and father of the Mexican state," Agustín Iturbide. Indeed, by the end of the 1940s the first emperor of Mexico, who tried to preserve Spanish culture in Mexico after independence, was competing with Cortés as the Jupiter of the sinarquista pantheon.[7]

Because Benito Juárez jeopardized the nation's dignity by the McLane-Ocampo treaties, violated the 1857 constitution, which he had pledged to uphold, and despoiled the church of its rights, he remained a sinarquista villain, and anyone who admired him was automatically a bad Mexican.[8] One of the sinarquista newspapers, *Orden*, used Altamirano's critical assessment to remind Mexicans that Juárez, like the twentieth-century PRI, attempted to establish a system of coalitions with governors of states so as to impose official candidates. The PRI had a glorious tradition, Bártolo Prieto commented sarcastically in *Orden*; Juárez and the PRI shared all that was un-Mexican. The line of bad Mexicans was clear in the mind of Salvador Abascal: Avila Camacho was the son of Calles and Cárdenas and the grandson of Díaz and Juárez.[9]

Sinarquistas expressed their anti-Juárez ideas through actions as well as words, and during the same era as witnessed reverential rallies at the Hemiciclo one could find unbelievers congregating to express their condemnations. Sunday, December 19, 1948, became an especially grim day for juaristas, for about two thousand people marched through the streets of Mexico City and assembled before the Juárez Hemiciclo, and speakers there denounced the role of Juárez in Mexican history. The age of the Reform and the Revolution, said the chief of the sinarquistas in the federal district, Dr. Rubén Mangas Alfaro, was an era of "shame and ignominy, and this great thief Juárez created all the filth of those times by dedicating himself to rob temples such as Corpus Christi in front of us." Nor was this all, for a member of the sinarquista youth organization climbed to the seated figure of Juárez in the middle of the Hemiciclo and, after spitting three times on Juárez's head, covered it with a black cloth, and the master of ceremonies, Carlos González Obregón, then explained: "The sinarquista youth has covered the face of Juárez because we do not want to look at this bandit nor do we want him to look at us."[10]

This noncelebration of 1948, as one might have described it, caused a great outpouring of protest from the followers of Juárez. The sinarquistas said they lacked money to rent a hall for their meeting and hence had to assemble outdoors. Juaristas considered it a planned affront to the dignity of the nation, for not only did the sinarquista orators attack Juárez but they denounced other heroes, describing Hidalgo as a traitorous priest, drunkard, and opportunist, Morelos as a confused agitator in the service of heretics, and Valentín Gómez Farías and Gabino Barreda as vile supernumeraries of bad government and poisoners of education. Juaristas called for dissolution of the sinarquista organization and proscription of its political arm, the Popular Force party, as well as imprisonment of the "parricides." In the Mexican congress Senator Fernando López Arías identified the sinarquistas and the National Action party as opponents to progress and independence. Other senators and deputies overwhelmingly agreed and proceeded to establish March 21, Juárez's birthday, as a national holiday.[11] But the interesting fact is that disbelief had raised its banners.

Sharing many sinarquista views, the National Action party showed more astuteness by avoiding attacks on figures and institutions that most Mexicans regarded as symbols of nationhood and developed a broader appeal so that it eventually established itself as the largest opposition party in Mexico. Founded in 1939 in Mexico City by a group of businessmen, intellectuals, and Roman Catholic university students headed by Manuel Gómez Morín, PAN represented, as one observer has put it, well-to-do Mexicans who feared that the Revolution threatened their status, pocketbooks, or souls, and it drew support from upwardly mobile middle-class people and even from peasants and artisans susceptible to clerical influence.[12] Although PAN and the sinarquistas shared many values (hispanism, Catholicism, limited theocracy, hostility to communism and socialism), the two groups differed in social composition. PAN attacked the founder of the official party, Calles, and his successors as traitors to the Revolution launched by Madero, arguing that these leaders used the Revolution for personal objectives rather than to fulfill the promise of democracy held out by Madero. Political reform had to be achieved before other reforms. PAN portrayed itself as a champion of democracy, which it defined as plurality of opinion and a nonregimented life, and it advocated a fair and impartial election law.[13]

PAN treated Juárez as an official creation, different from the real man, important to those advocates who lauded him only because the false Juárez furthered their interests. It attacked what it considered to be corruption in the Alemán government: "Yes, in accordance with the phrase of his own partisans, Juárez guarded—without applying—the Constitution in order to save it; things were easier that way. And general Taboada, head of the PRI, felt himself disposed to save the Constitution and even democracy, while little gifts from the budget were not missed."[14] PAN's newspaper, *La Nación,* reacted sharply to a celebration in March 1953, in which participants used Juárez to promote their cause. It characterized a 1959 commemoration as a gathering of the family, in which celebrants had ties with the official state machine, and commented that the true meaning of the presence of workers and bureaucrats at the places of homage was synthesized magnificently in a letter sent to the psychological-pedagogical institute, a branch of the ministry of education, that said that all those patriots who attended the anniversary of the Benemérito could take their vacations on Monday.[15] Some years later *La Nación* observed that supporters of the nominee of the PRI, Echeverría, again were tediously celebrating the birth of Juárez to enlist support for their candidate.[16]

In the effort to combat the version of the Juárez myth promoted by the government, some conservative historians joined forces with the ardent Catholics and the two political groups. Rejecting the liberal victory of 1867 and all of its consequences, conservative historians condemned Juárez in much the way sinarquistas and their brethren did at the Hemiciclo or in the press. José Fuentes Mares, an avid hispanist in the 1940s, sustained this tradition in 1949, the year of the dramatic battle of the bones when hispanists and indigenists argued over the authenticity of bones an indigenist claimed were those of Cuauhtémoc. Fuentes Mares condemned men of the nineteenth century as negative factors in Mexican history, agreeing with José Vasconcelos that the titles "Serene Highness," "Benemérito of the Americas," and "Maximum Chief of the Revolution" had been attached to men who supported reductions in the boundaries of Mexico. Decrying the attempts of more than a century to change the history of Mexico into a "species of vulgar anti-Spanish quarrel," Fuentes Mares could not accept the liberal interpretation of the Mexican past.[17]

Naturally there were strong reactions to history read in such a manner. In contrast to Fuentes Mares's view that nothing creative came from the "ungrateful ones" who made the Reform, Roberto Blanco Moheno's *Juárez ante Dios y ante los hombres* characterized such individuals as gods and singled out Juárez as the most godlike. Blanco Moheno found shortcomings even in the most adulatory books on the Reform, including Ralph Roeder's *Juárez and His Mexico*, which he said wrongly characterized Juárez as a weak man. He argued that Spain was not the mother of Mexico, for Spain had behaved as an "adventurer father"; because Juárez and his generation lacked the slightest blemish of dishonor they qualified as gods in Mexican history.[18]

Fuentes Mares persisted in his criticism, even though his books on Juárez and his era sought to refrain from polemic. In the early 1960s Editorial Jus began publishing an extensive collection of these and other monographs called "México heróico." Writing in the first volume of his contribution that his book was the work of an author free from the original sin of contact with political parties, Fuentes Mares felt compelled to point out that government officials had imposed the cult of Juárez. The nineteenth-century leader, he said, was not the author of the Reform.[19] Unfortunately, an argumentative style characterized his volume on Juárez during the empire of Maximilian. In the form of a dialogue, the book concluded that after the execution of Maximilian at Querétaro "three more men joined the ranks of undesired Mexicans," following the fate of Iturbide, who met death after capture by "brave dogs," and Cortés, the hero without martyrdom and the great father who was repudiated by "Indian concubines that bellowed for revenge in the soul of Mexico."[20] Fuentes Mares's last volume in this collection, *Juárez y la república,* pointed out that despite Juárez's role as defender of the constitution, he could not govern with it, and until the very last he alienated himself from the church—"there were no religious ceremonies at Juárez's funeral."[21]

Another dissenting conservative historian was the leading intellectual and revolutionary José Vasconcelos, who after suffering defeat in the election of 1928 rejected his revolutionary position and embraced hispanism and traditional conservatism. His *Breve historia de México,* written in the 1930s, expressed a conservative view of the past and described the myth of Cuauhtémoc as an invention by William H. Prescott and other North American historians. In addition to Cuauhtémoc, "the symbol of independence at all costs," Vasconcelos included the first American minister to Mexico, Joel Poinsett, the hated "initiator of policies that contributed to the destruction of our nationality," and he included that arch adventurer of the nineteenth century, Antonio López de Santa Anna, a man who "represents all the vices of the military caste." He grouped Juárez with these twin nineteenth-century malevolents to make a trinity of villains in Mexican history. Juárez did not come off as badly as the others because he did represent the "aspirations of the century for the suppression of castes and privileges." But he depended too much on the United States, regarded Washington, D.C., as his "mother country," and as a result shared in the nefarious liberal tendency to equate progress with Yankee influence. By seeking reelection he made a joke of the democratic system.[22]

The conservative historian José Bravo Ugarte rejected Juárez by describing the period 1867 to 1910 as the epoch of dictatorship and characterizing the years immediately following 1867 as a time of misery, anarchy, and brigandage. In *México independiente* Bravo Ugarte argued that Juárez used the fact of anarchy to espouse centralism as a guarantee of his continued rule. Maintaining that Juárez was willing to cede Lower California and compromise the sovereignty of Mexico, this noted historian followed the conservative-hispanist view of the relation between Juárez and the United States. The Liberal party, he wrote, made Juárez "an immaculate hero and an untouchable myth," savior of the Constitution of 1857, the republic, of independence itself, and even sought to turn him into a pan-American hero. Alas, Juárez participated in nothing more than a civil war.[23]

Among the dissenting conservative historians was the principal student of the development of the church in Mexico, Mariano Cuevas, whose writings in denunciation of the liberal version of Mexican history conceded little to Juárez. Cuevas described the Laws of the Reform as opprobrious and juarism as immoral and devoted a substantial portion of his *Historia de la nación mexicana* to the McLane-Ocampo treaties and the Anton Lizardo affair of 1860—all to show Juarez's lack of concern for Mexico's sacred sovereignty. Unlike the liberal treatments of Mexican history, his analysis included the 1867–72 period, which he described as a vale of tears, of fifteen revolutions, almost all of them against Juárez. Cuevas even attacked Juárez's masonry, describing it as membership in a foreign alliance, an action obviously against the national interest.[24]

The enemies-of-the-government view of the Juárez myth were indeed extraordinarily numerous. Beginning with an article in *El Universal,* the prominent conservative intellectual Alfonso Junco in 1934 set out to diminish Juárez by considering his similarities to Carranza. He had in mind Antonio Rivera de la Torre's *Juárez y*

Carranza, a book that promoted Carranza by describing parallels between his career and that of Juárez. Junco showed good and bad qualities in the two men. Although both were honest in personal matters and defended the rights of the clergy as Mexican citizens, their democratic talk masked dictatorial actions. They spoke in favor of popular voting and the power of public opinion but disregarded those principles by entrenching themselves in office until death took them out. As civilians, Junco wrote, they headed intensely warlike movements that produced only military leaders like Díaz and Obregón. Both sought the sympathy of the United States, an effort that culminated in the Anton Lizardo affair and the occupation of Veracruz in 1914.[25]

Junco contributed to a series of conservative history textbooks for private schools with interpretations that often conflicted with those of the officially approved texts, and one of his books, published in 1937, criticized Juárez for interventionism caused by the "Yankee-liberal fraternity."[26] Other authors in this series criticized Juárez in favor of such residents of the conservative pantheon as Cortés, Iturbide, and Alamán. The texts of Joaquín Márquez Montiel and Carlos Alvear Acevedo accused Juárez of excessively close relations with the United States and disregard of the constitution after 1867, and Jesús García Gutiérrez remarked outright that Juárez bribed governors to secure his own election.[27]

So much, then, for the use of the Juárez myth by the rightists—the criticism of the Catholics, the rightist political parties, the conservative historians. The myth was put to quite different use by other dissenters from the course of the Revolution after 1920—the leftist dissenters. The old polemic of liberals against conservatives had its uses for Juárez, for after 1929 challengers to the official government party also came from leftist ranks, especially from the group sometimes described as jacobins, and they used commemorations of Juárez as forums against the church and clerical elements in Mexican society as their ancestors had done in the years of the Porfiriato. Events such as the sinarquista meeting at the Hemiciclo in 1948 especially stirred these malcontents.[28]

Leading the jacobins was a former friend of Pancho Villa and author of a famous book of reminiscences of those years, Martín Luis Guzmán, who in 1942 began editing a weekly magazine,

Tiempo, a journal that did much to keep alive the coals of the Juárez myth. Finding Juárez his favorite historical figure, Guzmán advocated the establishment of March 21 as a national holiday. For him Juárez was the symbol of anticlericalism. In 1963 he published an anthology of his views under the title *Necesidad de cumplir las leyes de Reforma*, describing establishment in 1945 of the Mexican Liberal party and his commitment to Juárez as the personification of the triumph of legality; Guzmán had helped found the party, he said, to admonish the government to observe and apply the laws pertaining to clerical activity. Although he remained very much within the broad coalition that supported the successive revolutionary governments, he and his colleagues, including the historian Daniel Cosío Villegas, expressed great dissatisfaction with the laxness of the "revolutionaries" toward the tenets of the liberal faith.[29]

Juárez thus helped the leftist critics of the Revolution. Vicente Lombardo Toledano sounded another dissenting note within the revolutionary coalition, embracing Marxist socialism as an ideological model for the Mexican Revolution. He championed Cárdenas's reforms but toward the end of the Cárdenas presidency became a problem for the government because of his support for the Third International. Enemies accused him of being a tool of Moscow, an Iscariot of the Mexican Revolution.[30] He proclaimed himself a nationalist and took Juárez as his symbol. In 1938 he founded the newspaper *El Popular* to assert his loyalty to Mexico as well as to attack the sinarquistas, whom he regarded as the chief internal threat to Mexico. Considering Juárez one of the creators of Mexico, he expressed his own hostility toward the nation's enemies. "Those who oppose the Revolution oppose Benito Juárez," a writer for *El Popular* cried out in March 1940, "and they are national traitors and interventionists." Miguel Miramón was the first fifth columnist of Mexico, the writer avowed, and "the sinarquistas and panistas are his descendants." Sinarquistas and panistas opposed the Juárez legacy, the paper proclaimed.[31]

Other leftists gave support to the Communist party, and for them, too, the Juárez myth had its usefulness. Founded in the 1920s, the party proved ineffective because of Cárdenas's monopoly of revolutionary sentiment and because of the later alliance of the Soviet Union with the capitalist Western powers during World War II. Mexican communists did all they could to advertise themselves as nationalists. "The history of the fatherland shows us the road," the communist newspaper *La Voz de México* commented in June 1942; the example of heroes was the guarantee of victory. The communists thus pledged their fealty to Juárez, who stood for national unity, the Reform, and defense of independence. "We ought not to forget the example of Juárez in the struggle for national independence," *La Voz* continued in 1943; "he created our nationality."[32] Even in the postwar years the communists supported the heroes of revolutionary Mexico as proof to oppose the accusation that they were receiving their salaries from Russia.[33]

After the war the leftists increasingly complained of conservatism in Mexico, and Juárez became once more their symbol of discontent. Lombardo founded the Popular Socialist party in 1948, and in 1961 it joined the Communist party and the Mexican Farmers and Workers party. The union lasted only until 1962, but it brought together the leftist opposition. A new magazine appeared in the early 1960s, *Política,* accompanying the effort at a leftist coalition, and it attacked the government's use of Juárez, describing the 1967 centennial of the triumph of the republic as a pseudo-juarista carnival "with aspects of tragi-comedy and theatrical teaching that moved no one." It saw the government's use of Juárez as hypocritical; the propaganda exalted the incumbent president, Gustavo Díaz Ordaz, more than Juárez. It described the concert in the Palace of Fine Arts on the evening of the celebration as a mere function, lacking in seriousness or ideological content, for the diversion of the oligarchy.[34]

Other journals of the left displayed similar feelings of disillusion over the revolutionary commitment of the successive governments of the 1950s and 1960s. In an editorial of March 1967, a magazine normally friendly to Mexican governments, *Siempre,* said that the lesson of Juárez lived on in Mexico, despite tendencies of politicians to devote themselves to personal enrichment. It criticized the exhibitionism of Díaz Ordaz and the efforts of government functionaries "to cavort with bankers and businessmen, as documented in the social sections of our daily newspapers." It noted the existence of a false laicism, recalling that Juárez had not denied his Catholicism but had warned of the state's compelling need of laicism.[35]

Such disillusion took a nasty and violent turn—indeed, came to a head—in 1968, when other dissenters took to the streets of Mexico City as preparations concluded for the Olympic games. Beginning significantly with a march in July to commemorate the Cuban revolution, these student and worker demonstrations culminated with a bloody confrontation between students and government troops in the Plaza of the Three Cultures in October. There were antecedents for these demonstrations—the railroad workers' struggles of 1958–59 in Mexico and the student movement in France—but by 1968 the government seemed to have lost its ability to control dissent through institutional manipulation. The government said that about forty people died during the October confrontation in Tlatelolco, but others estimated that upward of two to three hundred were killed.[36]

Mexican intellectuals were alienated by the viciousness of the government's handling of these demonstrations, and in 1972 some of them established *Plural,* a magazine dedicated to art and literary criticism but which also sustained *Politica's* and *Siempre's* cynical analysis regarding official manipulation of Juárez; in the context of the 1972 centennial celebration of Juárez's death one of its writers argued that patriotism often concealed skulduggery. All that official propaganda touched turned to stone, he announced, and as a result of years of canonization and petrification Juárez had become the statue most resistant to the hammers of criticism. By 1972 Juárez had been transformed into a gigantic concrete pyramid covered with official rhetoric. Alluding to a huge portrait of the nineteenth-century leader formed by little tricolor light bulbs displayed on the National Lottery Building, he concluded that the cult of Juárez had the same attraction for Mexicans as lotteries and the Virgin of Guadalupe. From the petrified lips of Juárez on the lottery building issued the red-and-white words, "against the fatherland no one will prevail"—causing, he noted, the passing pedestrian, if a decadent cosmopolite or *malinchista,* to recall the words of Samuel Johnson that politics is the last refuge of the scoundrel.[37]

Dissent from the revolution's myth of Juárez took many forms after 1920, for there were many sources of unrest. Successive governments carefully projected Juárez as a symbol of national and revolutionary unity. But for the many Mexicans outside the benevolences of the nation's official party, outside the embraces of the petrifying revolutionary doctrines, for the dissatisfied, the angry young men who had never known revolution and could not know it, apparently, because so-called revolutionaries had become glutted with the perquisites of power—for these political outcasts Juárez proved ever more useful.

10

Of Mexicans and Myth

Juárez exists primarily as myth in Mexico. Even while he lived, Mexicans regarded him as a symbol of often contradictory values, for he played so many different roles; he was a doer and yet not a doer—he uttered some truths and some seeming untruths, so that the people of his own day hardly were sure what, if anything, he represented. After his death, he became all things to all people, and thus there arose the historical myth, the Juárez that was only in part history and the other part wish fulfillment, the man who represented or did not represent all that was good, or all that was bad, in all of Mexico.

Juárez has been described as enigmatic, probably because he was extremely reticent in matters of state. He seldom told his contemporaries where he was going, or why; he hesitated, seemingly to show his purposes, and one wonders in retrospect whether he had any large purposes. But as the contemporary Juárez, the Juárez of history, was enigmatic, so too was the mythological Juárez as the years passed farther and farther from the minds of men living and as the Revolution of the twentieth century showed the possibilities of using the supposed activities or purposes of the historical Juárez for the purposes of the century that followed his death.

The Juárez myth in Mexico is not the only historical myth in that country; it is one of many and does not stand apart from others. In a country whose culture is extraordinarily well-endowed with myths and is as a consequence defined by them, what people say about Juárez they often say about other historical personalities and about Mexico itself.[1] When people say "Juárez is Mexico" or, as in the *La Prensa* headline the year before the centennial of Juárez's death in 1971, "Juárez lives in the Mexico of today," they mean just that. He is what Mexicans have made him, the embodiment of widely shared values and a vital part of the symbolic or representational aspect of life in Mexico.[2]

Study of this myth, as well as any other, can have value as a means to identify and understand the attitudes, values, and aspirations of Mexicans. Indeed, it and other myths deserve the closest examination, for they both shape and reflect attitudes and can have long-range consequences.[3] For many years anthropologists and other social scientists as well as historians have assumed the importance of myth as a means whereby people have fulfilled psychological, social, and political needs so as to objectify values and assert status. The Juárez myth reveals that several values have appealed to Mexicans during the past century and more and that these values all relate to one event, the liberal triumph of 1867. More important, study of the myth shows that Mexicans have disagreed over historical reality. Again and again they have queried the meaning of this liberal triumph that Juárez headed and the extent to which expectations of that moment were fulfilled. Argument over the values associated with the victory of 1867 has provided the Juárez myth with its vitality.

One important value expressed by the Juárez myth has been the achievement of order within the framework of written law. Although there has been little disagreement over this principle, when discussing Juárez, Mexicans have often debated the expression of constitutionalism in the Constitution of 1857, which contains most of the tenets of the liberal faith: popular sovereignty, sovereignty of the states in their internal affairs, a weak executive and strong legislature, guarantees of civil rights, popular participation in politics by means of public education and universal manhood suffrage, maintenance of private property, and separation of church and state. When portraying Juárez as a defender of the Constitution of 1857 or as a subverter, Mexicans have said they want government by law instead of by men. They have used Juárez as an example of a leader who devoted his career to the constitution, although to do this they have focused on his role during the civil war that followed its enactment and the Intervention and overlooked what happened after 1867. Those Mexicans who have attacked this role during the civil war and Intervention have stressed the post-1867 period, when Juárez and other liberals seemed to modify the constitution to fit a Mexican reality beset by regionalism and its political expression, caudillismo, massive poverty and illiteracy, economic stagnation, and fiscal penury.[4]

Mexicans since 1910 have exalted indigenism as an essential of national life and found Juárez a useful symbol for asserting this value. As defined by writers of both the nineteenth and twentieth centuries, indigenism celebrated the native, the non-European, the pre-Spanish aspects of Mexican culture. Although the writers have used Juárez, they have sometimes disagreed about his authenticity as a symbol of the Indian. Those who have accepted him have pointed to his humble Zapotec background in Oaxaca and said that he represented what the Indian could achieve. Others had difficulty accepting Juárez as an authentic representative of Indian Mexico, concluding that he betrayed his Indian antecedents by embracing European culture and a foreign ideology that supported destruction of such Indian institutions as communal village landholdings.

Not all Mexicans have been indigenists; indeed, many embraced the opposite value, hispanism. They rejected the notion that Indian culture contributed anything of worth to Mexico and argued that Mexico is Spanish. To the extent that Juárez overcame his Indian antecedents and adopted European ways his myth has been tolerable or acceptable, although for some writers, notably Francisco Cosmes in the late nineteenth century, Juárez was a bit awkward to interpret, for he seemed to represent a race that had ability and could achieve. Cosmes solved that dilemma by describing Juárez as an exceptional Indian. Ironically, hispanists and indigenists critical of Juárez sometimes found themselves in agreement concerning the effects of his policy regarding communal landholdings. In general, hispanists have regarded Juárez as the symbol of a hostile ideology—liberalism—and characterized him as an enemy of the church, a Spanish institution, and a friend of Anglo-Saxon culture.

Mexican nationalists have regarded what they called Anglo-Saxon culture, especially that associated with the United States, as anathema, and no Mexican has failed to defend the integrity of the nation through discussions of Juárez. Citing his tenacity in resisting the French during the Intervention and even describing him and some of his associates as "immaculate," they have extolled him as a patriot, a reputation confirmed and reinforced by his refusal to succumb to foreign pressure to pardon Maximilian. Others, also posing as nationalists, have challenged his characterization as a spotless patriot and stressed his dealings with the United States, especially those that resulted in the McLane-Ocampo treaties and the Anton Lizardo affair. They have argued that his liberalism and anticlericalism caused him to deny an important dimension of Mexican culture. All Mexicans agree that Mexico is good and ought to be preserved as an independent entity.

If Juárez has been especially important for the interpreters of Mexican nationalism, they have argued over how the nation ought to be organized and what ideologies should guide. An example is their continuing, although much restrained, disagreement about the place of the church and of Catholicism in Mexico. They have thought that Mexico ought to adopt any ideological model different from those provided by religion and have praised Juárez and other liberals for their part in effecting the separation of church and state. Governments since 1930 have concluded that previous generations completed the task of separation and that they should pursue leniency with respect to anticlerical laws. For them Juárez stood not only for secularism but for conciliation. Other supporters of secularism, often called jacobins for their insistence on a pure liberalism reminiscent of the French Revolution, have been dismayed by the laxity in enforcement of these laws, and for them the Juárez who sponsored the Laws of the Reform has become a symbol of separation of church and state.

Secularism has related to another value, civilianism, one might call it, the exclusion of the military from politics. In the nineteenth century, and after three decades of barracks revolts and opportunistic generals, especially Santa Anna, who simply craved presidential power, Juárez was the model government official. Díaz's appearance in 1876 only confirmed the importance of Juárez.

Mexicans have linked Juárez with such civil heroes of the Revolution as Madero and Carranza and contrasted him with generals like Díaz and Obregón. They regarded the church and the military as banes of Mexican society in both the nineteenth and twentieth centuries and looked to Juárez as the exterminator of both. Mexicans often saw the church and the military as bastions of aristocratic power and therefore associated another value with Juárez—populism. Both the leaders of the republic and those frustrated in their attempts to obtain power have talked about the importance of the people and the need for an open society to permit the humble to rise. They have cited Juárez's lowly origins as an example of what the humble can or ought to do. Government leaders and other Mexicans who control the instruments of power accented the *can;* those who felt excluded have stressed the *ought.* The Díaz regime and its opponents could manipulate Juárez as the representative of their point of view, and so it has been with latter-day regimes and their opponents.

For well over a hundred years all these values have found expression in the Juárez myth. They have both shaped the myth and been influenced by it to produce a multifaceted Juárez, inspiring one historian commenting on opportunities and challenges of nineteenth-century Mexican biography to ask, "Will the real Juárez please stand up?"[5] Myth by its nature is selective and thereby unhistorical. Those who make myths use the material of history to satisfy their own needs. They create myths to reflect attitudes and promote causes, and myths then become parts of history for they can have consequences in such events as elections, debates, wars, revolutions, and diplomatic negotiations, as well as ritualistic commemorations and pilgrimages. The history of the Juárez myth reveals its importance in such events as the twentieth-century Revolution, especially during the process of trying to give that upheaval an ideology or a myth, in Mexico's foreign policy of recent years, the conflict between church and state, the petroleum expropriation of the 1930s, and many other matters. Understanding the Juárez myth is of high importance to any assessment of the liberal model's influence on Mexican reality. Mexicans have been fanatical in their worship of such documents as the 1857 constitution and the Laws of the Reform, often at great cost.

Myth constitutes an essential of the life of man; its argumentative aspect reveals that life on earth is never static. Social relations, values, and needs all change, and so do myths. For Mexicans the Juárez myth proved a way to express values as well as to disagree about them. Political canonizations expressed in statuary, popular and elitist art, school books, and commemorations all worked to advance unity. To the extent that Mexicans agree about Juárez, he is the national symbol. His myth also points to the continuing search by a great people for an elusive identity.

Notes

Chapter 1

1. *Centenario de la proclamación de la independencia: Inauguración del monumento a Juárez en la Alameda de la Ciudad de México; Album gráfico de la República Mexicana;* Moisés González Navarro, "La inauguración del monumento a Juárez."

2. Hubert Howe Bancroft, *History of Mexico,* 5:738–41. During the French intervention Latin American leaders named Juárez "Benemérito de las Américas" as one way to express support. See Robert Ryal Miller, "Matías Romero," p. 234.

3. *Tiempo* 11 (July 25, 1947):3–5.

4. Ibid.; "Rodolfo Sánchez Taboada," in Roderic A. Camp, *Mexican Political Biographies, 1935–1981.*

5. Richard Chase, *Quest for Myth;* Robert Graves, *The Greek Myths,* 1:10; Melville J. Herskovits and Frances S. Herskovits, *Dahomean Narrative,* p. 85; Theodore H. Gaster, "Myth and Story," pp. 197–98; Kenneth E. Boulding, *The Image,* p. 6; Claude Lévi-Strauss, *Structural Anthropology,* p. 208; "Myth and Mythmaking"; Orrin E. Klapp, *Symbolic Leaders;* W. Lloyd Warner, *The Living and the Dead;* John William Ward, *Andrew Jackson;* Henry Nash Smith, *Virgin Land.*

6. Klapp, *Symbolic Leaders,* pp. 211–49; Joseph Campbell, *The Hero with a Thousand Faces;* Dorothy Norman, *The Hero;* Warner, *The Living and the Dead,* p. 14; M. I. Finley, "Myth, Memory, and History," p. 283; Lionel Pearson, "Historical Allusions in the Attic Orators," p. 209.

7. Boulding, *Image,* p. 114. The literature on the relationship between mythologizing and nationalism is substantial. See Frederick C. Turner, *The Dynamic of Mexican Nationalism,* p. 16; Richard W. Van Alstyne, *Genesis of American Nationalism;* Paul C. Nagel, *This Sacred Trust;* Anne M. Cohler, *Rousseau and Nationalism.*

8. Carl Degler, "Reshaping American History," pp. 7–25, esp. 20–21.

9. Lyman Bryson et al., eds., *Symbols and Society;* Hugh D. Duncan, *Communication and Social Order;* Hugh D. Duncan, *Symbols in Society;* Henry A. Murray, ed., *Myth and Mythmaking;* Thomas A. Sebeok, ed., *Myth.* Stephen C. Ausband emphasizes the utility of myth in creating order in *Myth and Meaning,* esp. pp. 1–21.

10. Murray Edelman, *The Symbolic Uses of Politics;* Murray Edelman, *Politics as Symbolic Action;* Charles D. Elder and Roger W. Cobb, *The Political Uses of Symbols.*

11. C. G. Jung, *Psyche and Symbol,* pp. 35–36; see also Edelman, *Politics as Symbolic Action,* p. 80.

12. A. L. Guérard, *Reflections on the Napoleonic Legend;* William F. Sater, *The Heroic Image in Chile.*

13. Samuel Ramos, *Profile of Man and Culture in Mexico,* pp. 170–71; Jorge Carrión, *Mito y magia del mexicano,* pp. 11, 25; Gordon W. Hewes, "Mexicans in Search of the Mexican"; John Leddy Phelan, "México y lo mexicano"; Henry C. Schmidt, *The Roots of Lo Mexicano.* The leader of Mexico's post-1867 literary renaissance, Ignacio Manuel Altamirano, describes in striking detail Mexico's infatuation with the Virgin of Guadalupe in *Paisajes y leyendas,* pp. 55–129. See also M. Gutiérrez Nájera, "El símbolo nacional," *El Universal,* December 12, 1890, p. 1. Juaristas sensed competition from the Virgin of Guadalupe, and in 1887, the year of the first major commemoration of Juárez's death, proposed building a monument to Juárez at the great shrine of Guadalupe so that the thousands of Indians who came to render homage to the Virgin might also reflect upon the contribution of Benito Juárez. See "Benito Juárez," *El Combate,* March 6, 1887, p. 1. A twentieth-century study of the importance of both the Virgin of Guadalupe and Quetzalcoatl, the Indian demigod, is Jacques Lafaye, *Quetzalcoatl and Guadalupe.* See also D. A. Brading, *Prophecy and Myth in Mexican History,* pp. 28–31.

14. Duncan, *Communication and Social Order,* pp. xxiv, 13.

15. Emile Durkheim, *The Elementary Forms of the Religious Life,* p. 2. Clifford Geertz emphasizes the social origins and role of religion in *Islam Observed,* pp. 2, 39.

16. Bronislaw Malinowski, *Sex, Culture, and Myth,* pp. 246, 251, 292.

17. E. R. Leach, *Political Systems of Highland Burma,* pp. 264–78.

18. Edelman, *Politics as Symbolic Action,* pp. 53, 56, 77, 80; David Bidney, *Theoretical Anthropology,* pp. 15, 286.

19. Richard R. Fagen, *Politics and Communication;* Karl W. Deutsch, *Nationalism and Social Communication;* Gabriel A. Almond and Sidney Verba, *The Civic Culture.*

20. Carlos J. Sierra, *Presencia de Juárez en los gobiernos de la Revolución, 1911–1963.*

21. Lévi-Strauss, *Structural Anthropology*, p. 209; see also W. Taylor Stevenson, "Myth and the Crisis of Historical Consciousness," in Lee W. Gibbs and W. Taylor Stevenson, eds., *Myth and the Crisis of Historical Consciousness*, p. 4.

22. Germán Carrera Damas, *El culto a Bolívar*, p. 25.

23. "El finado don Benito," *La Nación*, July 26, 1947, pp. 3–4. *La Nación* has been the principal periodical voice of the National Action party. See Chapter 9 for a discussion of its use of Juárez.

24. Duncan, *Symbols in Society*, p. 64.

25. Rafael Segovia, *La politización del niño mexicano*, p. 91. Children in Roman Catholic schools learn about an alternative set of heroes. See Chapter 9.

Chapter 2

1. "Manifiesto de Benito Juárez al volver a la capital de la República," in Benito Juárez, *Documentos, discursos y correspondencia*, 12:248–50.

2. Albert Hans, *Querétaro*, pp. 191–97; "El Sr. Juárez y la Nación," in Lorenzo Elizaga, *Ensayos políticos*, pp. 165–69; Samuel Basch, *Recuerdos de México*, pp. 301–2; Egon Caesar Count Corti, *Maximilian and Charlotte of Mexico*, 2:821–23.

3. Pantaleón Tovar, "El 15 de julio," *El Siglo Diez y Nueve*, July 16, 1867, p. 1; Gabino F. Bustamante, "El triunfo de la República: La entrada del gobierno constitucional a la ciudad de México," *El Monitor Republicano*, July 11, 16, 17, 1867, in Francisco López Serrano, *Los periodistas republicanos*, p. 134; Daniel Cosío Villegas, *Historia moderna de México: La República restaurada, La vida política*, p. 71.

4. Richard N. Sinkin, *The Mexican Reform, 1855–1876*, pp. 3–5, 98–99, 123–26, 170–73. For discussions of the Lerdo law and its implementation in various parts of Mexico, see Jan Bazant, *Alienation of Church Wealth in Mexico*, esp. pp. 1–58; Thomas G. Powell, *El liberalismo y el campesinado en el centro de México (1850 a 1876)*; Charles R. Berry, *The Reform in Oaxaca, 1856–76*, pp. 31–32, 172–91; Ian Jacobs, *Ranchero Revolt*, pp. 43–45; Robert Wasserstrom, *Class and Society in Central Chiapas*, pp. 151–55; John M. Hart, *Anarchism and the Mexican Working Class, 1860–1931*, p. 15. Jack Autrey Dabbs discusses reasons for the French failure in Mexico in his *The French Army in Mexico, 1861–1867*, esp. pp. 279–86.

5. Sinkin, *Mexican Reform*, pp. 13–29. Donathon C. Olliff argues that the major concern of the liberals, at least those known as *puros*, was

economic change as a basis for liberal reform. See his *Reforma Mexico and the United States*, pp. 1–9.

6. The Warner Brothers film *Juárez* of the late 1930s is an example.

7. Biographical data come from Sinkin, *Mexican Reform*, pp. 40, 43–44, 47, 52–54, 79–80; Walter V. Scholes, *Mexican Politics during the Juárez Regime, 1855–1872*, pp. 25–27; *Diccionario Porrua de historia, biografía y geografía de México*, pp. 1132–33; Bancroft, *History of Mexico*, 5:738–42. There are many biographies in Spanish; perhaps the best known is that of Justo Sierra, *Juárez*. Another biographical study is the four volumes of José Fuentes Mares: *Juárez y los Estados Unidos; Juárez y la Intervención; Juárez y el Imperio;* and *Juárez y la República*. There are three important biographies in English: Charles Allen Smart, *Viva Juárez;* Ralph Roeder, *Juárez and His Mexico;* and Ivie E. Cadenhead, Jr., *Benito Juárez*. For a list of the stops of the Juárez government on its great peregrination, see Pablo C. Moreno, "La ruta de Juárez."

8. Scholes and Sinkin discuss the reform decrees that emanated from Veracruz in their surveys of the period: Scholes, *Mexican Politics*, pp. 43–55; Sinkin, *Mexican Reform*, p. 142. Veracruzanos have been fond of describing Veracruz as the Sinai of Mexico and Juárez the Moses. See Manuel del Río González, *Juárez su vida y su obra*.

9. *El País*, July 18, 1906, p. 1. This conservative Catholic newspaper reproduced the text of the agreement on its front page during the year of the centennial of Juárez's birth.

10. For a full discussion of the McLane-Ocampo treaties, see Olliff, *Reforma Mexico and the United States*, pp. 129–52.

11. Scholes, *Mexican Politics*, pp. 56–72.

12. For a complete discussion of this controversy, see Ivie E. Cadenhead, Jr., "González Ortega and the Presidency of Mexico," and Cadenhead, *Jesús González Ortega and Mexican National Politics*.

13. Scholes, *Mexican Politics*, p. 115.

14. Carlos Pereyra, "Juárez dictador," pp. 681, 700–701; Laurens Ballard Perry, *Juárez and Díaz*, pp. 38–42.

15. Perry discusses the *convocatoria* as it relates to the development of opposition to Juárez in *Juárez and Díaz*, pp. 38–56. See also Cosío Villegas, *La República restaurada: La vida política*, pp. 118–72, and Frank Averill Knapp, Jr., *The Life of Sebastián Lerdo de Tejada, 1823–1889*, pp. 118–23; Antonio G. Pérez, "La convocatoria," *El Siglo Diez y Nueve*, August 21, 1867, p. 1; José Fuentes Mares, "La convocatoria de 1867," p. 442.

16. Pérez, "La convocatoria," p. 1.

17. Knapp, *Life of Sebastián Lerdo de Tejada*, p. 122; Alfredo Chavero, "El convite de Palacio," *El Siglo Diez y Nueve*, October 24, 1867, p. 1.

18. Francisco Zarco, "La reelección de Juárez," *El Siglo Diez y Nueve*, November 22, 1867, p. 1.

19. Cosío Villegas, *La República restaurada: La vida política*, p. 91; Knapp, *Life of Sebastián Lerdo de Tejada*, p. 120.

20. Knapp, *Life of Sebastián Lerdo de Tejada*, p. 120.

21. Perry notes the frequency of insurrections during the restored republic by listing them in *Juárez and Díaz*, pp. 353–54. Francisco G. Cosmes describes them in *Historia general de México*. Gustavo Baz reviews the alignment of the press in his *Vida de Benito Juárez*, pp. 498–505. See also Scholes, *Mexican Politics*, p. 152.

22. Cosío Villegas, *La República restaurada*, pp. 270–82.

23. Ignacio Ramírez, "¡No habrá reelección!" *El Siglo Diez y Nueve*, July 14, 1871, p. 2. Melinda Rankin comments on dissatisfaction with Juárez and describes the revolution of General Trevino in Nuevo León in *Twenty Years among the Mexicans*, pp. 175–80.

24. Cosío Villegas, *La República restaurada*, p. 282; Scholes, *Mexican Politics*, pp. 162–68.

25. Julio Zárate, "La dictadura del Presidente Juárez," *El Siglo Diez y Nueve*, May 22, 1872, p. 1; "La unión del Partido Liberal," ibid., June 21, 1872, p. 1.

26. *El Siglo Diez y Nueve*, July 24 and 25, 1872, reprinted the funeral orations of José M. Vigil, Ignacio Silva, Alfredo Chavero, Francisco T. Gordillo, Victoriano Mereles, Roque J. Morón, and others. See also "Muerte del Sr. Juárez," *La Voz de México*, July 20, 1872, p. 1; "Los presidentes," ibid., July 23, 1872, p. 1. Many Mexicans looked forward to the new administration of Sebastián Lerdo de Tejada and hoped for peace and stability. See Vicente Ortigosa to Mariano Riva Palacio, July 26, 1872, Mariano Riva Palacio Papers, Benson Latin American Collection, University of Texas at Austin.

27. Sinkin, *Mexican Reform*, pp. 176–77. Mexicans have used the name Juárez more than any other to name public libraries; see *Directorio de bibliotecas de la República Mexicana*. After reviewing a questionnaire returned by more than thirty-five hundred schoolchildren in 1969, Rafael Segovia found that even though Juárez was not the only hero by which these children identified their nationality, he was the dominant one (*La politización del niño mexicano*, pp. 89–94).

Chapter 3

1. "La manifestación del lunes," *El Partido Liberal*, July 22, 1887, p. 1; "Después del duelo," *El Siglo Diez y Nueve*, July 19, 1887, p. 1; *El Monitor Republicano*, July 19, 1887, p. 1.

2. México, Congreso, Cámara de Diputados, *Diario de los debates*, 3 (September 17, 1872):10; 5 (April 18, 1873):138–39; "Honors to the Memory of Benito Juárez," *Two Republics*, April 26, 1873, p. 3.

3. *La República*, July 18, 1880, p. 1; Salvador Novo, *Los paseos de la ciudad de México*, p. 38. Textbooks began to incorporate flattering assessments of Juárez. See Luis Pérez Verdía, *Compendio de la historia de México desde sus primeros tiempos hasta la caída del Segundo Imperio*, pp. 312–13; Guillermo Prieto, *Lecciones de historia patria, escritas para los alumnos del Colegio Militar*, p. 618.

4. Baz, *Vida de Benito Juárez*, pp. 5, 10–11, 8, 292–93, 317–18.

5. Marcial Aznar, *Observaciones histórico-políticas sobre Juárez y su época*, pp. vi–vii, xxiii–xxix; see also "El Sr. Marcial Aznar," *La Convención Radical*, July 18, 1887, p. 3.

6. Manuel Ayala, "Nombre inmortal," *El Monitor Republicano*, July 19, 1874, pp. 1–2.

7. José C. Valadés, *El Porfirismo: Historia de un régimen, El nacimiento (1876–1884)*, p. 22; Knapp, *Life of Sebastián Lerdo de Tejada*, pp. 233–54, 184–86; Perry, *Juárez and Díaz*, esp. pt. 2, pp. 203–352; Daniel Cosío Villegas, *Historia moderna de México. El Porfiriato: La vida política interior, parte primera*.

8. Don M. Coerver, *The Porfirian Interregnum*, pp. 23–28.

9. Karl M. Schmitt, "The Díaz Conciliation Policy on State and Local Levels," p. 522; Knapp, *Life of Sebastián Lerdo de Tejada*, pp. 188, 214–22; John Lloyd Mecham, *Church and State in Latin America*, p. 376.

10. Miguel Velasco Valdés, *Historia del periodismo mexicano (apuntes)*, pp. 129–30, 147–52; Henry Lepidus, *The History of Mexican Journalism*, p. 57.

11. "Conversación entre el Sr. Gral. Porfirio Díaz y Mr. H. Bancroft," Mexico City, 1883, in Hubert Howe Bancroft, *Miscellaneous Papers*, p. 46; Jan Bazant, *A Concise History of Mexico from Hidalgo to Cárdenas, 1805–1940*, pp. 98–103.

12. Gabino Barreda, "Oración cívica," in Abelardo Villegas, *Positivismo y porfirismo*, pp. 41–75. William D. Raat discusses the varieties of thought and ideology in his "Ideas and Society in Don Porfirio's Mexico," pp. 32–53, and *El positivismo durante el Porfiriato (1876–1910)*, esp. pp. 39–55, 72–106.

13. Raat, *El positivismo durante el Porfiriato*, pp. 16–19; Josefina Vázquez de Knauth, *Nacionalismo y educación en México*, pp. 48–50.

14. Justo Sierra, "Reorganización de la República," in Justo Sierra, *Obras completas*, 4:175–78; Raat, *El positivismo durante el Porfiriato*, pp. 20–30.

15. Charles A. Hale, "'Scientific Politics' and the Continuity of Liber-

alism in Mexico, 1867–1910," in *Dos revoluciones*, pp. 140–50; Raat, *El positivismo durante el Porfiriato*, pp. 39–55; Cosío Villegas, *Historia moderna de México. El Porfiriato: La vida política interior, parte primera*, pp. 201–2, 428–29.

16. C. de Olaguíbel y Arista, "La reorganización del Partido Liberal," *La República*, June 2, 1880, p. 1; Hilario S. Gabilondo, "Lo que debe hacer el Partido Liberal," *La República*, June 4, 1880, p. 1; Telesforo García, "La unión del partido liberal," *La Libertad*, June 3, 1880, p. 2; Raat, *El positivismo durante el Porfiriato*, pp. 72–106.

17. Justo Sierra, "Liberales-conservadores," *La Libertad*, May 10, 1878, p. 1.

18. "La dictadura," *La Libertad*, September 18, 1878, p. 1; Justo Sierra, "La Libertad y el Señor Vigil," ibid., August 30, 1878, in Sierra, *Obras completas*, 4:147.

19. Justo Sierra, "Sobre las elecciones," *La Libertad*, May 24, 1878, p. 1.

20. "¿Qué debe ser el partido constitucional?" *La Libertad*, May 10, 1878, p. 1; "La no-reelección," ibid., January 11, 1878, p. 1.

21. Juan de Dios Arías, "La constitución y sus adversarios," *La República*, July 7, 1882, p. 1; "El fanatismo filosófico," ibid., June 5, 1882, p. 1; "Los derechos del hombre," ibid., July 15, 1882, p. 1.

22. "Boletín del 'Monitor,' " *El Monitor Republicano*, July 21, 1875, p. 1; *Juárez y los obreros*, pp. 3–5. For a discussion of conflict between radical and moderate factions within the Círculo, see Hart, *Anarchism and the Mexican Working Class*, pp. 48–50.

23. Moisés González Navarro, *Historia moderna de México. El Porfiriato: La vida social*, p. 351; Rodney D. Anderson, *Outcasts in Their Own Land: Mexican Industrial Workers, 1906–1911*, pp. 80–81; "Benito Juárez," *El Combate*, March 6, 1887, p. 1.

24. *La Voz de Juárez*, January 6, 1884, p. 1.

25. "Boletín del 'Monitor,' " *El Monitor Republicano*, July 21, 1875, p. 1; ibid., July 23, 1875, p. 1.

26. Ricardo Ramírez, "Una empresa vana," ibid., March 26, 1886, p. 1.

27. Ignacio M. Altamirano, *Historia y política de México (1821–1882)*, pp. 175–84.

28. Vicente Riva Palacio et al., *México a través de los siglos*, 5:862.

29. "Discurso pronunciado por el C. Diputado Joaquín D. Casasús en la sesión del 20 de abril de 1887 en pro del dictamen de las comisiones unidas 1ª de puntos constitucionales y 1ª de gobernación sobre reelección del Presidente de la República," in *En honor a Juárez*, pp. 121–39.

30. *El Partido Liberal*, July 7, 1887, p. 1; "Los enemigos de Juárez,"

ibid., July 17, 1887, p. 1; *En honor a Juarez*, p. 3; "En honor del Gran Juárez," *El Combate*, July 10, 1887, p. 3; *Biografía del señor Gral. José Vicente Villada, gobernador constitucional del Estado de Michoacán*, p. 98.

31. The newspapers included *Diario Oficial, El Monitor Republicano, El Diario del Hogar, El Partido Liberal, El Pabellón Nacional, El Siglo Diez y Nueve, La Voz de España, El Pabellon Español, Two Republics, La Paz Pública, El Combate, El Lunes, La Federación, El Avisador Comercial, El Correo de las Doce, Cronista Musical, Boletín Postal, Las Noticias, La Convención Radical*, and *El Ferrocarril de Veracruz*. "La manifestación del 18," *El Monitor Republicano*, July 16, 1887, p. 3; "Después del duelo," *El Siglo Diez y Nueve*, July 19, 1887, p. 1; "La manifestación en honor del Benemérito Benito Juárez," *El Diario del Hogar*, July 19, 1887, pp. 2–3.

32. "La manifestación Juárez," *El Nacional*, July 10, 1887, p. 3; "Triste aniversario," *La Voz de México*, July 19, 1887, p. 1; see also "Iturbide," *El Universal*, September 28, 1888, p. 3.

33. "La manifestación del lunes," *El Partido Liberal*, July 22, 1887, p. 1.

34. "Discurso del Sr. Lic. Ignacio Mariscal," *El Monitor Republicano*, July 20, 1887, pp. 2–3; "Discurso del C. Guillermo Prieto," ibid., July 21, 1887, pp. 2–3. Anthologies of essays, speeches, and poetry published for the occasion were *En honor a Juárez* and Daniel Cabrera, *Manifestación a Benito Juárez el día 18 de julio de 1887 promovida y ordenada por la "Prensa Unida" liberal de la Ciudad de México*.

35. *El Hijo del Ahuizote*, July 24, 1887, pp. 5–8; ibid., July 31, 1887, pp. 4–5.

36. José Vasconcelos, *A Mexican Ulysses*, p. 35.

37. *Biografía del señor Gral. José Vicente Villada;* Carlos J. Sierra, *La prensa valora la figura de Juárez, 1872–1910*.

38. Juan Gómez Quiñones discusses the press and its evaluation of Mexico's problems as well as the use by liberals of holidays and commemorations to criticize the regime in his *Porfirio Díaz, los intelectuales y la Revolución*, pp. 129–59.

Chapter 4

1. John F. Berens, "The Sanctification of American Nationalism, 1789–1812"; W. Lance Bennett, "Imitation, Ambiguity, and Drama in Political Life."

2. Jean Jacques Rousseau, *The Social Contract*, pp. 123–25; George L. Mosse, "Caesarism, Circuses, and Monuments," pp. 170–73; James A. Leith, *The Idea of Art as Propaganda in France, 1750–1799*; and Leith, *Media and Revolution*.

3. Mosse, "Caesarism, Circuses, and Monuments," pp. 170–76.

4. Ralph Henry Gabriel, *The Course of American Democratic Thought*, pp. 91–104; Constance McLaughlin Green, *Washington*.

5. Vázquez de Knauth, *Nacionalismo y educación en México*, pp. 81–125; González Navarro, *Historia moderna de México. El Porfiriato: La vida social*, pp. 700–702; "La estatua de Juárez," *El Siglo Diez y Nueve*, February 25, 1891, in Ida Rodríguez Prampolini, *La crítica de arte en México en el siglo XIX*, 3:277; "Juárez, bronce de cañones," *Boletín Bibliográfico*, March 15, 1963, p. 3.

6. Justo Sierra, "Las fiestas de la República," in Sierra, *Obras completas*, 8:37–41; Justo Sierra, "El culto a los muertos," in ibid., 5:29–30; Justo Sierra, "El día de la Patria," *La Libertad*, January 23, 1883, p. 2. The last two articles sustain the idea that Mexico ought to stress conciliation between those who supported the contributions of Spain to Mexican culture and those who rejected the idea that Spain had contributed anything worthwhile. See, too, Francisco Cosmes, *El verdadero Bulnes y su falso Juárez*, p. 65.

7. "Primer centenario de Juárez," *El Diario del Hogar*, March 24, 1903, p. 1; "El centenario de Juárez," *El Imparcial*, March 22, 1903, p. 1; "21 de marzo de 1806 y 21 de marzo de 1906," *Diario Oficial*, March 21, 1906, p. 1; *El Imparcial*, July 19, 1903, p. 1; *En honor de Juárez*, pp. 3–5.

8. *El Diario del Hogar*, July 22, 1904, p. 1.

9. México, Congreso, Cámara de Diputados, *Diario de los debates*, 1904–6. The congress reviewed and approved individual petitions. See also "El centenario de Juárez: El gobierno prepara su celebración," *El Imparcial*, March 21, 1905, p. 1; "El centenario de Juárez," ibid., March 11, 1906, p. 1; "El centenario de Juárez," ibid., March 4, 1906, p. 1.

10. *Centenario de Juárez en el Estado de Tamaulipas*, pp. 51–56.

11. *El Estado de Chihuahua en el centenario de Juárez, 21 de marzo de 1906*, pp. 123, 131, 286; see also Guillermo M. Amezcua, ed., *Juárez en Tabasco*; Comisión Nacional del Centenario de Juárez, *Programa*; Comité Liberal Guanajuatense, *Centenario de Juárez, 21 de marzo de 1906*; *Recuerdo de las fiestas que organizó en esta ciudad la Delegación de la Comisión Nacional del Centenario de Juárez, en honor del insigne patricio*; *A Juárez*; *Al benemérito ciudadano Benito Juárez en recuerdo del primer centenario de su nacimiento*; *Alocución del C. Gobernador del Estado*,

Gral. Bernardo Reyes, dicha con objeto de clausurar las fiestas del Centenario del nacimiento del Benemérito de la Patria, Benito Juárez. Liberals in Guatemala celebrated the anniversary also; see *Centenario de Benito Juárez;* and Manuel Mejía Barcenas, *Homenaje del Partido Liberal de Guatemala al Benemérito de las Américas, Benito Juárez, en el primer centenario de su nacimiento.*

12. Jorge Fernando Iturribarría, *Porfirio Díaz ante la historia*, pp. 284, 313; Victoriano Salado Alvarez, *Informe que en nombre de la Comisión Nacional del Centenario de Juárez leyó en la velada del Teatro Arbeu la noche del 21 de marzo de 1906, el C. Lic. Victoriano Salado Alvarez, Secretario de la misma Comisión; Juárez; Diario Oficial*, March 22, 1906, p. 1.

13. *El Imparcial*, March 15, 1906, p. 1; "La comida popular," *El Mundo Ilustrado*, March 25, 1906; *Diario Oficial*, March 23, 1906, p. 1.

14. Francisco Figueroa, *Biografía del Benemérito Benito Juárez premiada en el concurso que se organizó por la Secretaría de Instrucción Pública y Bellas Artes y destinada a servir de modelo en las conferencias que se efectuarán en las Escuelas primarias el día 21 de marzo de 1906*, pp. 3–5, 10, 15.

15. Ricardo García Granados, *La Constitución y las Leyes de la Reforma en México: Estudio histórico-sociológico*, pp. 38–39, 122–29, 132.

16. Andrés Molina Enríquez, *Juárez y la Reforma*, pp. 6, 3–14; Brading, *Prophecy and Myth in Mexican History*, pp. 64–71.

17. Rafael de Zayas Enríquez, *Benito Juárez*, p. 8; Leonardo S. Viramontes, *Biografía popular del Benemérito de América*, p. 277; Porfirio Parra, *Estudio histórico-sociológico sobre la reforma en México*, pp. 162–63.

18. Sierra, *Juárez*, pp. 438–39; José Bravo Ugarte, *Temas históricos diversos*, p. 169. According to Arturo Arnaiz y Freg, Pereyra wrote three of the chapters of Sierra's biography; see Sierra, *Obras completas*, 13:539, n. 17.

19. *El País*, July 18, 1906, p. 1.

20. "¿Quién fue Juárez?" *La Voz de México*, March 21, 1906, p. 1.

21. Fernando Iglesias Calderón, *Las supuestas traiciones de Juárez*, pp. 126, 509.

22. "La apoteosis de Juárez," *El Dictamen*, March 23, 1906, p. 1; "El centenario de Juárez: Su significancia," *El Nigromante*, April 9, 1906, p. 1; "Boletín del 'Diario del Hogar,'" *El Diario del Hogar*, March 21, 1905, p. 1; "18 de julio de 1906," ibid., July 18, 1906, p. 1; "Ciento un años," ibid., March 21, 1907, p. 1; "El centenario del natalicio de Juárez," *El Paladín*, March 4, 1906, p. 1; ibid., March 25, 1906, p. 1.

23. John Kenneth Turner, *Barbarous Mexico*, pp. 101, 274.

Chapter 5

1. A prelude to this particular debate was what Charles A. Hale calls "Mexico's Great Debate of 1893," when proposals to change the constitution were discussed in the Mexican congress and press. See Hale, "The Científicos as Constitutionalists."

2. *Biografía del señor Gral. José Vicente Villada*, p. 266; "¡Ojo aquí!" *El Combate*, November 2, 1887, pp. 1–2; George Lemus, *Francisco Bulnes*, pp. 6–7; Daniel Cosío Villegas, "A View from Mexico City," in Richard E. Greenleaf and Michael C. Meyer, eds., *Research in Mexican History*, p. 5.

3. "Primera Convención Nacional Liberal: Manifiesto a la Nación," *El Siglo Diez y Nueve*, April 26, 1892, pp. 1–2; "Manifiesto de la Convención Nacional Liberal," *El Partido Liberal*, April 26, 1892, p. 1. Many of those who signed this document, including Bulnes, had collaborated in the publication of *La Libertad* and had advocated a comprehensive reform of Mexican government. See Justo Sierra, "El programa de *La Libertad*," *La Libertad*, January 30, 1879, p. 2. In the late 1880s these same people had associated themselves closely with Manuel Romero Rubio, the father-in-law of Díaz, and his political ambitions. See Cosío Villegas, *Historia moderna de México. El Porfiriato: La vida política interior, parte segunda*, pp. 840–62; Hale, " 'Scientific Politics' and the Continuity of Liberalism in Mexico, 1867–1910," in *Dos revoluciones*, pp. 139–52; Centro de Estudios Históricos, El Colegio de México, *Historia general de México*, 3:222–26; José López Portillo y Rojas, *Elevación y caída de Porfirio Díaz*, pp. 259–77; Walter N. Breymann, "The Científicos"; Hale, "Científicos as Constitutionalists."

4. "Los científicos," *El Paladín*, July 5, 1903, p. 1.

5. Limantour tried to argue that his ties with the *científicos* were not important. After the fall of Díaz, Bulnes wrote a strong criticism of Limantour. See José Yves Limantour, *Apuntes sobre mi vida política (1892–1911)*, pp. 16–17, 21–22; and Francisco Bulnes, *El verdadero Díaz y la Revolución*, pp. 233–50. See also Manuel Calero y Sierra, *Un decenio de política mexicana*; Anthony Bryan, "Mexican Politics in Transition, 1900–1913," p. 51; Francisco Bulnes, *The Whole Truth about Mexico*, p. 366.

6. Bryan, "Mexican Politics," p. 48. A 1979 study of the Liberal Union concludes that it is impossible to identify the *científicos* with precision—that the term was a "slogan and rallying point for the non-participating political factions" and that it lacks objective content except as a term of opprobrium. See Jacqueline Ann Rice, "The Porfirian Elite," p. 2.

7. Emilio Rabasa and Justo Sierra are the two major critics of the

1857 constitution discussed by Daniel Cosío Villegas in his important *La constitución de 1857 y sus críticos.*

8. Ricardo García Granados discusses the uses of *científico* and *jacobin* in his *Historia de México desde la restauración de la República en 1867 hasta la caída de Huerta,* 1:341–48. See Francisco Bulnes, "Los partidos políticos en México: El jacobinismo de imprenta y el partido de la paz mecánica absoluta," *El Universal,* November 18, 1893, p. 1; "Carta del Sr. Bulnes al Sr. Sánchez Santos," ibid., December 23, 1893, p. 1. *El Universal* began publishing in 1888 under the direction of Rafael Reyes Spíndola, another signer of the 1892 manifesto, and with the assistance and blessing of Manuel Romero Rubio. See "'*El Universal*': La nueva dirección y su programa," *El Universal,* November 22, 1893, p. 1.

9. Francisco Cosmes argued that Cortés should be seen as the founder of Mexican nationality in *La dominación española y la patria mexicana,* pp. 8, 26, "¿Fue Cortés el fundador de la nacionalidad?" *El Universal,* October 3, 1894, p. 1. *El Monitor Republicano* and *El Diario del Hogar* were important newspapers for the expression of jacobin points of view, which were often stimulated by Juárez commemorations.

10. Bulnes's two books were *La guerra de Cuba en relación con el criterio americano y los intereses de México* and *El porvenir de las naciones latinoamericanas ante las recientes conquistas de Europea y Norteamérica.* Discussions of Bulnes's ideas about the Indians can be found in Martin S. Stabb, "Indigenism and Racism in Mexican Thought, 1856–1911"; and Thomas G. Powell, "Mexican Intellectuals and the Indian Question, 1876–1911." Many solutions to the "Indian problem" were offered. One, of course, was a better diet. See "Lo que deben comer los indios," *El Universal,* October 11, 1893, p. 1. Another was education and economic development: "La raza indígena," ibid., August 17, 1888, p. 1. Yet another was immigration of Europeans: Luis Alva, "La colonización extranjera y la raza indígena," *La Libertad,* July 2, 1882, p. 2; July 8, 1882, p. 2; July 13, 1882, p. 2.

11. Lemus, *Francisco Bulnes,* pp. 67–76. Further discussion of Bulnes's ideas can be found in William Rex Crawford, *A Century of Latin-American Thought,* pp. 252–60.

12. Cosmes, *La dominación española,* pp. 7, 43–44.

13. "La Convención Nacional Liberal," *El Mundo Ilustrado,* June 28, 1903; "La Convención Nacional Liberal," *El Imparcial,* June 22, 1903, p. 1; Cosío Villegas, *Historia moderna de México. El Porfiriato: La vida política interior, parte segunda,* pp. 753–60.

14. Francisco Bulnes, "Discurso pronunciado en la sesión celebrada por la Segunda Convención Nacional Liberal, el 21 de junio de 1903," in

Andrés Serra Rojas, *Antología de la elocuencia mexicana, 1900–50*, pp. 35–50.

15. Ibid.

16. "Las imprudencias de Bulnes: Algo de historia," *El Diario del Hogar*, June 27, 1903, p. 2; "Boletín 'Diario del Hogar,'" ibid., June 30, 1903, p. 1; "La manifestación a Juárez," ibid., July 9, 1903, p. 1.

17. *Carta de Hilarión Frías y Soto al señor diputado Francisco Bulnes.*

18. "El programa de la Convención Liberal expuesta en un discurso del Sr. D. Francisco Bulnes," *El País*, June 25, 1903, p. 1; "La palinodía del jacobinismo: El problema de la organización política de México," ibid., July 11, 1903, p. 1; "El criterio conservador triunfante en el campo jacobino: Réplica del Sr. Bulnes al Sr. Frías y Soto," ibid., July 20, 1903, p. 1.

19. Francisco Bulnes, *Defensa y amplificación de mi discurso pronunciado el 21 de junio de 1903 ante la Convención Nacional Liberal*, pp. 17–18, 28, 34, 38–40.

20. Francisco Bulnes, *Las grandes mentiras de nuestra historia*, pp. 2–4, 46, 71, 90, 101, 133, 342, 365, 651, 653, 961.

21. Vázquez de Knauth, *Nacionalismo y educación en México*, pp. 81–84, 97–105.

22. Francisco Bulnes, *El verdadero Juárez y la verdad sobre la Intervención y el Imperio*, pp. 82, 114, 141–43, 269, 303, 335–81, 388–423, 475–548, 844, 856.

23. "El verdadero Juárez," *El Imparcial*, August 12, 1904, p. 3; ibid., August 20, 1904, p. 1; "Boletín," *El Diario del Hogar*, August 26, 1904, p. 1.

24. "El verdadero Juárez," *El País*, August 21, 1904, p. 1; "Un libro del señor Bulnes," *La Voz de México*, August 25, 1904, p. 2.

25. *El Imparcial*, August 31, 1904, p. 1; "D. Francisco Bulnes," *El Contemporáneo*, September 5, 1904, p. 2; "La junta de honor," *El Imparcial*, September 4, 1904, p. 1; "Una carta del señor diputado D. Benito Juárez o La junta de honor," *El Diario del Hogar*, September 4, 1904, p. 1; "La reunión de ayer en el Circo Orrín," ibid., September 5, 1904, p. 1; "A los Oaxaqueños," ibid., September 1, 1904, p. 2; "Algunas opiniones sobre el libro de Bulnes," *El Diario del Hogar*, August 31, 1904, p. 1.

26. "Protesta de los juaristas de Cholula," *El País*, October 31, 1904, p. 2; "Gacetilla," *El Diario del Hogar*, September 13, 1904, p. 2.

27. "Una carta del Licenciado Don Juan Dublán," *El Diario del Hogar*, August 31, 1904, p. 1.

28. "El verdadero Juárez," *El País*, August 21, 1904, p. 1.

29. "Próxima refutación," *El Imparcial*, September 7, 1904, p. 2;

"Nuestro verdadero Juárez: Las inculpaciones del Sr. Bulnes," ibid., August 20, 1904, p. 1; "Nuestro verdadero Juárez," ibid., September 8, 1904, p. 1; "Por qué el Sr. Bulnes no puede ser historiador," ibid., September 12, 1904, p. 1; Genaro García, *Juárez,* pp. v–viii, 191, 193. As his response to the book, D. Alfonso Cravioto even wrote a *zarzuela* entitled "El verdadero Juárez," *El Contemporáneo,* September 27, 1904, p. 3.

30. Hilarión Frías y Soto, *Juárez glorificado y la Intervención y el Imperio ante la verdad histórica,* pp. 7–8, 384, 411, 478; Sierra, *Juárez,* p. 449; Carlos Pereyra, *Juárez discutido como dictador y estadísta a propósito de los errores, paradojas y fantasías del Sr. Don Francisco Bulnes;* Carlos Pereyra, "Juárez dictador," pp. 681, 700–701.

31. Ignacio Mariscal, *Juárez y el libro de Bulnes,* pp. 4–5, 7, 10; Cosmes, *El verdadero Bulnes y su falso Juárez,* p. 65. Cosmes sets forth many of his philosophical and historical views in *Historia general de México,* 19:xv–xix, xxx–xxxiii.

32. Juan Pedro Didapp, *Explotadores políticos de México,* pp. 10, 14, 113, 447–49. For additional anti-*científico* reaction see various articles and cartoons in *El Colmillo Público:* "Juárez y Bulnes," November 26, 1905, p. 749; "Juárez y Bulnes: Los científicos y los liberales," September 4, 1904, pp. 542–43; "El libelo de Bulnes," September 11, 1904, pp. 254–55.

33. "Don Benito Juárez y Don Francisco Bulnes," *El País,* September 1, 1904, p. 1; "Otra carta de D. Francisco Bulnes," ibid., September 9, 1904, p. 1. Two other books of significance that attempt to refute Bulnes are Leonardo R. Pardo, *El verdadero Bulnes y la verdad sobre su libro detractor;* and Ramón Prida, *Juárez.*

34. Francisco Bulnes, *Juárez y las revoluciones de Ayutla y de Reforma,* pp. 80–82.

35. Ibid., pp. 3, 18, 26, 31, 80–82, 87, 94, 100, 158, 167, 198, 323–64, 494, 568, 588, 615, 621, 631; Lemus, *Francisco Bulnes,* p. 119.

36. *Refutación del libro de D. Francisco Bulnes, intitulado "Juárez y las revoluciones de Ayutla y de Reforma,"* p. 226.

Chapter 6

1. Michael C. Meyer and William L. Sherman, *The Course of Mexican History,* p. 496; Charles C. Cumberland, *Mexican Revolution,* pp. 150–51.

2. "¡18 de julio!" *El Diario del Hogar,* July 18, 1911, p. 1.

3. Karl M. Schmitt, "The Mexican Positivists and the Church-State Question, 1876–1911"; Schmitt, "The Díaz Conciliation Policy on State and Local Levels"; Robert E. Quirk, *The Mexican Revolution and the Catholic Church, 1910–1929*, pp. 3–20.

4. Cosío Villegas discusses the development of opposition to Díaz in *Historia moderna de México. El Porfiriato: La vida política interior, parte segunda*, pp. 629–908; and James D. Cockcroft focuses on the activities of the Potosí liberals in his *Intellectual Precursors of the Mexican Revolution, 1900–1913*.

5. "Preparativos del Congreso Liberal de San Luis Potosí," *El Hijo del Ahuizote*, February 10, 1901, p. 53.

6. Armando Bartra, ed., *Regeneración, 1900–1918*, pp. 13–83; Howard F. Cline, *The United States and Mexico*, p. 117; William D. Raat, *Revoltosos*.

7. "Programa del Partido Liberal," in *Fuentes para la historia de la Revolución: Planes políticos y otros documentos*, p. 26.

8. *Fuentes para la historia de la Revolución Mexicana: La huelga de Cananea*; Ramón Eduardo Ruíz, *The Great Rebellion*, pp. 68–71; Friederich Katz, *The Secret War in Mexico*, p. 30.

9. James Creelman, "President Díaz, Hero of the Americas"; Ruíz, *Great Rebellion*, p. 29; Stanley R. Ross, *Francisco I. Madero*, pp. 47–50; Cosío Villegas, *Historia moderna de México. El Porfiriato: La vida política interior, parte segunda*, pp. 787–803. Members of the Democratic party named Juárez's son the head of the party; see *Cuestiones políticas de actualidad*, p. 22. See also *Crónica de la recepción que el Club Anti-Reeleccionista "Benito Juárez" hizo a los distinguidos delegados del Centro Anti-Reeleccionista de México en su visita a esta capital el día 16 de enero de 1910*.

10. Francisco I. Madero, *La sucesión presidencial en 1910*, pp. 1, 10–11, 69, 72; José C. Valadés, *Imaginación y realidad de Francisco I. Madero*, 1:95, 200; Cumberland, *Mexican Revolution*, pp. 55–59; Ruíz, *Great Rebellion*, pp. 139–52; William H. Beezley, "Madero: The 'Unknown' President and His Failure to Organize Rural Mexico," in George W. Wolfskill and Douglas W. Richmond, eds., *Essays on the Mexican Revolution*, pp. 2–24.

11. Rogelio Fernández Güell, *El moderno Juárez*; "El moderno Juárez: Estudio sobre la personalidad de D. Francisco I. Madero," *El Amigo del Pueblo*, July 10, 1911.

12. Eduardo Guerrero and Samuel M. Lozano, "Canto a Madero," in C. Herrera Frimont, ed., *Corridos de la Revolución*, p. 24.

13. "Manifiesto a la nación," *El Anti-reeleccionista*, June 13, 1909, pp. 4–5; "¡El pueblo mexicano ve en Juárez un símbolo!" *El Constitucional*,

March 20, 1910, p. 1; "Las cosas de Juárez," ibid., March 23, 1910, p. 1.

14. "El señor Madero es un verdadero liberal," *La Nueva Era*, July 31, 1911, p. 3; *El Diario*, July 19, 1911, p. 6; Jesús Ceballos Dosamantes, *La gran mixtificación maderista*, p. 93. For more anticlerical and anti-Madero views see "Ante el monumento a Juárez," *La Guacamaya*, July 20, 1913, and *El Multicolor*, July 18, 1912.

15. Ross, *Francisco I. Madero*, pp. 215–17.

16. Beezley, "Madero," in Wolfskill and Richmond, eds., *Essays on the Mexican Revolution*, pp. 19–20; John Womack, Jr., *Zapata and the Mexican Revolution*; Michael C. Meyer, *Huerta*, esp. p. 60; Robert E. Quirk, *The Mexican Revolution, 1914–1915*; Charles C. Cumberland, *The Mexican Revolution: The Constitutionalist Years*; Arnaldo Córdova, *La ideología de la Revolución Mexicana: La formación del poder político en Mexico*, pp. 33–34; Peter V. N. Henderson, *Feliz Díaz, the Porfirians, and the Mexican Revolution*, esp. pp. 68–145; Douglas W. Richmond, *Venustiano Carranza's Nationalist Struggle, 1893–1920*; Linda B. Hall, *Alvaro Obregón*.

17. Leonardo M. Ballesteros, *Apuntes biográficos de los señores Lic. Emilio Vázquez y doctor Francisco Vázquez Gómez, el primer ministro de gobernación y el segundo ministro de instrucción pública en la nueva administración*. John Rutherford notes appropriately that a society in revolution presents good conditions for the developments of myths and legends at all levels. See his *Mexican Society during the Revolution*, p. 178.

18. Michael C. Meyer, *Mexican Rebel*, p. 60; "Pacto de la Empacadora (Plan Orozquista)," in *Fuentes para la historia de la Revolución Mexicana: Planes políticos*, pp. 95–106.

19. *La Voz de Juárez*, August 13, 1911, p. 1; "Los renovadores," ibid., November 29, 1914, p. 1; Rosendo Salazar, "Bronce indio," ibid., August 20, 1914, p. 3.

20. Ricardo Flores Magón, "La obra de Juárez," *Regeneración*, June 24, 1911, p. 3.

21. "Venustiano Carranza al abrir el Congreso Constituyente sus sesiones, el 1 de diciembre de 1916, en la ciudad de Querétaro," in México, Presidente, *Los presidentes de México ante la Nación*, 3:119.

22. E. V. Niemeyer, Jr., *Revolution at Querétaro*, pp. 28–29, 58–59, 77–79, 101–33, 134–65; Richmond, *Venustiano Carranza's Nationalist Struggle*, pp. 107–10.

23. Felix F. Palavicini, *Historia de la Constitución de 1917*, 1:234–35.

24. Niemeyer, *Revolution at Querétaro*, p. 28; Palavicini, *Historia*, 2:305.

25. Palavicini, *Historia*, 2:156.

26. Niemeyer, *Revolution at Querétaro*, p. 44; México, Congreso Constituyente, 1916–17, *Diario de los debates*, 1:9–11.

27. "A los honorables miembros del Congreso Americano," *El Demócrata*, August 10, 1913, in Isidro Fabela, ed., *Documentos históricos de la Revolución Mexicana*, 1:106–8; Dr. Atl, "La Revolución Mexicana," *Acción Mundial*, February 5, 1916, p. 1.

28. Richmond discusses manipulation of the press under Carranza in *Venustiano Carranza's Nationalist Struggle*, p. 179. See also *El Pueblo*, March 22, 1916, p. 1; July 20, 1916, p. 1; "El gobierno y el pueblo glorificaron la memoria de Juárez," ibid., July 19, 1918, p. 1.

29. "Juárez fue la encarnación del ideal civilista y demócrata," *El Universal*, July 18, 1917, p. 1.

30. Antonio Rivera de la Torre, *Paralelismo de hombres y carácteres*, pp. 6–7, 14–16, 133–60, 200, 224, 255–56.

31. Linda B. Hall discusses the break between Obregón and Carranza as well as the presidential campaign of 1919–20 in *Alvaro Obregón*, pp. 184–248. See also Richmond, *Venustiano Carranza's Nationalist Struggle*, pp. 219–37; *El Demócrata*, March 16, 1920, p. 12; "Juárez," ibid., March 19, 1920, p. 6; "Los héroes cíviles," *El Liberal*, March 21, 1920, p. 2.

Chapter 7

1. Guadalupe Sanvicente and Antonio Arriaga Ochoa, *Juárez en el arte;* "El rostro de Benito Juárez interpretado por José C. Orozco, Jorge González Camarena, Rivera, Espronceda y González Orozco," *Excelsior*, March 21, 1972; Raúl Flores Guerrero, "Juárez en la pintura," *México en la Cultura de Novedades* (supplement to *Novedades*), March 18, 1956, p. 5; Hector R. Olea, "Imágen de Juárez en el arte," *Boletín Bibliográfico*, July 1, 1973.

2. Jean Charlot, *Mexican Art and the Academy of San Carlos, 1785–1915*, p. 134; Robert H. Patterson, "An Art in Revolution"; David Alfaro Siqueiros, "Historia de la pintura moderna," *El Nacional*, November 4, 1945, sec. 1, p. 2; Raquel Tibol, *Siqueiros*, p. 133; Richmond, *Venustiano Carranza's Nationalist Struggle*, p. 181.

3. Jean Charlot, *The Mexican Mural Renaissance, 1920–1925*, p. 82; José Vasconcelos, "Escultura y pintura," in José Vasconcelos, *Discursos, 1920–50*, p. 85; Tibol, *Siqueiros*, p. 147; Richmond, *Venustiano Carranza's Nationalist Struggle*, pp. 181–82.

4. The text of these artists' manifesto is reproduced in Tibol, *Siqueiros*,

p. 230. See also Laurence E. Schmeckebier, *Modern Mexican Art*, p. 31; Justino Fernández, *Antologías de artistas mexicanas del siglo XX*.

5. José Clemente Orozco, *An Autobiography*, p. 40; Ron Tyler, *Posada's Mexico*, pp. 5, 47–51; Rafael Carrillo A., *Posada y el grabado mexicano*.

6. *Mural Painting of the Mexican Revolution, 1921–1960*, p. 127.

7. Luis Cardoza y Aragón, *Orozco*, p. 107.

8. Diego Rivera with Gladys March, *My Art, My Life*; Bertram D. Wolfe, *The Fabulous Life of Diego Rivera*.

9. Diego Rivera, *Portrait of Mexico*; Bernard S. Myers, *Mexican Painting in Our Time*, pp. 77–79; Schmeckebier, *Modern Mexican Art*, p. 141.

10. Carlos Pellicer, "Sueño dominical en la Alameda Central de la ciudad de México," *México en el Arte*, 1 (July 1948).

11. Justino Fernández, "Obras recientes de Orozco," *México en el Arte*, 6 (December 1948).

12. Cardoza y Aragón, *Orozco*, p. 208.

13. Frances Toor, ed., *Orozco's Frescoes in Guadalajara*.

14. Myers, *Mexican Painting in Our Time*, p. 51.

15. Jose Mancisidor, "Los murales de Siqueiros," *El Nacional*, June 18, 1945, p. 3; "The Siqueiros Affair," *New Politics* 2 (1963):128–31; David Alfaro Siqueiros, *Mi respuesta*. Nevertheless, on the occasion of his death in January 1974, the government decreed a day of national mourning and ordered that his remains be buried in the Rotunda of Illustrious Men. See *Excelsior*, January 7, 1974, p. 1.

16. Myers, *Mexican Painting in Our Time*, pp. 133, 135, 189, 211–15; Tibol, *Siqueiros*, pp. 105–7.

17. *Mural Painting of the Mexican Revolution*, p. 264; Raquel Tibol, *Historia general del arte mexicano*, p. 9.

18. Tibol, *Siqueiros*, p. 164; "El rostro de Benito Juárez," *Excelsior*, March 21, 1972.

19. "El rostro de Benito Juárez," *Excelsior*, March 21, 1972, sec. B, p. 1; Manuel Maples Arce, *Leopoldo Méndez*.

20. Rufino Tamayo, "El nacionalismo y el movimiento pictórico," *Crisol* 9 (May 1933):275–81; Robert Goldwater, *Rufino Tamayo*, p. 7; Octavio Paz, *Tamayo en la pintura mexicana*; *Tamayo*; Rufino Tamayo, *Rufino Tamayo*.

Chapter 8

1. Extensive coverage of the event was provided by major Mexico City newspapers including *El Universal*, *Excelsior*, *El Nacional*, and *La Prensa*.

2. *El Universal,* March 19, 1953, p. 13. General background is provided by Frank Brandenburg, *The Making of Modern Mexico,* pp. 100–108; Howard Cline, *Mexico,* pp. 157–60; Olga Pellicer de Brody and José Luis Reyna, *Historia de la Revolución Mexicana,* pp. 7–30.

3. "Conmemoración petrolera," *El Universal,* March 23, 1953, p. 3.

4. *Novedades,* March 22, 1953, p. 1. The following July 18 commemoration of Juárez's death sustained such links. See "Con Juárez y Ruíz Cortines," *Impacto,* July 28, 1953, p. 33.

5. Many studies emphasize the concept of a restrained revolution after 1940. James W. Wilkie describes the revolution as "economic" or "balanced" to help explain government policies after Cárdenas in *The Mexican Revolution,* pp. 276–85; Cline, *Mexico.*

6. *El Heraldo de México,* March 22, 1921, p. 1; *El Porvenir,* July 19, 1927, p. 1; "El culto a los héroes," *El Siglo de Torreón,* July 21, 1927, p. 3; "¡¡ Se va perdiendo el culto a los héroes!!" *El Dictamen,* July 19, 1934, p. 1; *La Raza,* July 19, 1922, p. 1; Sierra, *Presencia de Juárez en los gobiernos de la Revolución.*

7. Nemesio García Naranjo, "Oaxaquenismo y sonorismo," *Omega,* March 27, 1923, p. 2. The shift may have begun under Díaz, when he selected Ramón Corral of Sonora as his vice-presidential candidate in 1904. See Peter H. Smith, *Labyrinths of Power,* p. 70.

8. General coverage of this period is provided by John W. F. Dulles, *Yesterday in Mexico;* Enrique Krauze with Jean Meyer and Cayetano Reyes, *Historia de la Revolución Mexicana;* Jean Meyer with Enrique Krauze and Cayetano Reyes, *Historia de la Revolución Mexicana;* Lorenzo Meyer, *Historia de la Revolución Mexicana.*

9. Dulles, *Yesterday in Mexico,* pp. 228–35; *El Dictamen,* July 20, 1922, p. 1; Gilbert M. Joseph, "Revolution from Without: The Mexican Revolution in Yucatán, 1910–1940," in Edward H. Moseley and Edward D. Terry, eds., *Yucatán,* pp. 142–71; G. M. Joseph, *Revolution from Without;* Narciso Bassols, "Lo que no vió Juárez," in Bassols, *Obras,* p. 42; John A. Britton, *Educación y radicalismo en México,* pp. 23–30.

10. Manuel Gamio, *Forjando patria,* pp. 317–18.

11. *Juárez indio, traicionó a los indios.*

12. Antonio Díaz Soto y Gama, "Lo mejor de todo: Nuestra constitución," *El Universal,* November 2, 1938, p. 3; "Mensaje del presidente de la República al pueblo de Colombia, en ocasión del descubrimiento de la estatua de Benito Juárez, hecho por el presidente de Colombia en Bogotá, 16 de septiembre de 1938," in *Palabras y documentos públicos de Lázaro Cárdenas 1928–1940,* p. 328. *El Eco Revolucionario,* published by pro-Cárdenas groups during the 1930s, is a good source of the ideology of the Cárdenas regime.

13. Rafael Martínez and Heriberto Frías, *Juárez inmortal*, pp. 19, 22–25, 27–32.

14. Luis G. Monzón, *Detalles de la educación socialista implantables en México*, pp. 9–13; José María Bonilla, *Individualismo y socialismo*; Vázquez de Knauth, *Nacionalismo y educación*, pp. 169–90.

15. Alfonso Teja Zabre, *Breve historia de México*, p. 217; Longinos Cadena, *Elementos de historia general y de historia patria para el primer año de instrucción primaria superior*, pp. 148–49.

16. Enrique A. Santibáñez, *Historia nacional de México desde los tiempos más remotos hasta nuestros días*, p. 323; Abel Gámiz, *Historia nacional de México*, p. 177.

17. José Manuel Puig Casauranc, *Juárez, una interpretación humana*, pp. 5–7.

18. Brandenburg, *Making of Modern Mexico*, pp. 60–66; James Chilton Brown, "Consolidation of the Mexican Revolution under Calles, 1924–1928."

19. *El Nacional*, July 19, 1931, p. 9.

20. Rafael López, "Juárez y Obregón," ibid., July 19, 1935, sec. 2, p. 1.

21. *El Nacional*, July 19, 1937, sec. 2, p. 3.

22. Ibid., March 22, 1938, sec. 2, p. 2.

23. The phrase is Cline's, in his title, *Mexico: Revolution to Evolution*. For a summary and analysis of post-1940 ideology, see Arnaldo Córdova, *La ideología de la Revolución Mexicana: La era del desarrollismo (Proyecto de investigación)*, pp. 59–63.

24. "Juárez, símbolo y ejemplo permanente," *El Nacional*, July 18, 1942, p. 1; ibid., July 19, 1942, p. 1.

25. "¿Resurrección del culto a Juárez?" *El Popular*, July 18, 1942, p. 5. If Mexico was witness to a resurrection of the Juárez cult, *El Popular* from its establishment in 1938 did much to promote it. The paper used Juárez as a symbol of the petroleum expropriation and as a way to attack sinarquistas and panistas. See chapter 9.

26. "Juárez, símbolo y ejemplo permanente," *El Nacional*, July 18, 1942, p. 1. See also *Tiempo*, July 24, 1942, pp. 7–8; *Así*, July 25, 1942; "El aniversario de la muerte de Don Benito Juárez," *Hoy*, July 1942, pp. 16–17; *El Universal*, July 19, 1942, p. 13. The war encouraged the celebration of other national heroes. See Alfonso Camín, "Héroes nacionales," *Todo*, September 3, 1942, p. 19.

27. There are many important studies of United States foreign policy after World War II. A good survey is John W. Spanier, *American Foreign Policy since World War II*.

28. On Guatemala and the Caracas meeting, see Nathan L. Whetten,

Guatemala, esp. pp. 334–37; Stephen C. Schlesinger and Stephen Kinzer, *Bitter Fruit,* esp. pp. 144, 191–204; Richard H. Immerman, *The CIA in Guatemala,* pp. 3–19, 144–51; John Lloyd Mecham, *A Survey of United States–Latin American Relations,* pp. 216–18. For the Mexican reaction, see "Apoyo de los trabajadores a la política nacional e internacional de Ruíz Cortines," *El Nacional,* March 22, 1954, p. 1; "Juárez fue loado en su aniversario: Es y será siempre el símbolo máximo de la nacionalidad," *Novedades,* March 22, 1954, p. 1.

29. Adolfo López Mateos, *Presencia internacional de Adolfo López Mateos;* James C. Carey, "Mexico's 'Hands Off' Policy," p. 232; "El respeto al derecho ajeno," *Excelsior,* March 23, 1961, p. 6; "El respeto al derecho ajeno y la prensa de Cuba," *Todo,* March 31, 1960, pp. 28–29; *Excelsior,* March 22, 1962, p. 1; "La doctrina de Benito Juárez actualizada por López Mateos," *El Nacional,* July 19, 1961, p. 1; Jorge Castañeda, "Revolution and Foreign Policy"; Arthur K. Smith, "Mexico and the Cuban Revolution," p. 294.

30. The dispute had its origin in 1864, when Juárez put the problem before the United States government. In 1911 the United States rejected the decision of an arbitral commission, but in 1931 it began to modify its position. See Sheldon B. Liss, *A Century of Disagreement,* pp. 9, 60, 64–65; *Novedades,* July 19, 1963, p. 1. See also Edelman, *Symbolic Uses of Politics,* pp. 95–113.

31. *El Nacional,* March 22, 1963, p. 1; ibid., July 19, 1963, p. 1. The government published *El Chamizal.*

32. *Excelsior,* March 22, 1963, p. 1.

33. "Benito Juárez en Colombia," *El Nacional,* September 19, 1938; *Benito Juárez y su proyección continental; El decreto de Colombia en honor de Don Benito Juárez;* interview with Eduardo C. Marrufo, president, Comité Ejecutivo Nacional, Movimiento Nacional Cívico Juarista, July 19, 1971.

34. Antonio Carrillo Flores, "La política exterior de México." Appearance of the Warner Brothers film *Juárez* prompted one writer to protest excessive influence by American films in Mexico. See Eduardo Pallares, "Juárez," *El Universal,* July 4, 1939, sec. 1, p. 3; *El Nacional,* March 22, 1978, p. 1.

35. Smith, *Labyrinths of Power,* p. 280; *El Nacional,* July 19, 1975, p. 10.

36. *Novedades,* March 21, 1971, p. 1; *New York Times,* March 29, 1971, p. 58.

37. See Jack Benton Galbert, "The Evolution of the Mexican Presidency." For differing interpretations of the role of the president of Mexico within the political system of Mexico, see Smith, *Labyrinths of Power;*

Robert E. Quirk, *Mexico;* Robert E. Scott, *Mexican Government in Transition,* pp. 244–93; Leon Vincent Padgett, *The Mexican Political System.* Max Weber comments on charisma created by means of manipulation of the past: *Basic Concepts in Sociology,* pp. 81–83. See also T. K. Oomen, "Charisma, Social Structure and Social Change"; and Brading, *Prophecy and Myth in Mexican History,* pp. 81–83.

38. *Novedades,* July 19, 1947, p. 1; "Al rendirse tributo a Juárez, se proclamó su respeto a la ley como su herencia preclara," ibid., July 19, 1950, p. 1; *La Prensa,* July 19, 1971, p. 1.

39. The theme of unity of government and people received much attention in the commentary of *El Nacional* and *Novedades,* especially after 1953. See *Novedades,* March 22, 1954, p. 1; March 22, 1958, p. 1.

40. *Novedades,* July 19, 1961, p. 1. Such trips have been useful for dealing with political crises and dissent with the Mexican political system. See "Echeverría en Oaxaca," *El Nacional,* March 20, 1970, p. 5; *Tiempo,* March 29, 1976, pp. 5–9; March 23, 1981, p. 5; Smith, *Labyrinths of Power,* p. 313.

41. The books edited by Carlos J. Sierra and published by the Secretaría de Hacienda are *La prensa valora la figura de Juárez, 1872–1910; Juárez en la inmortalidad de 21 de marzo; Presencia de Juárez en los gobiernos de la Revolución, 1911–1963;* and *Juárez en su recinto de homenaje.* See Manuel J. Sierra, "Es una obligación cívica el culto a Juárez," in Sierra, ed., *Juárez en su recinto de homenaje,* p. 13; Agustín Yáñez, "La lección de Juárez," in ibid., p. 35.

42. González Navarro, "Juárez y los indios mayas."

43. Maurilio P. Náñez, "El espiritú de Juárez, único en América,"*Boletín Bibliográfico,* March 15, 1957, p. 1; Manuel J. Sierra, "El triunfo de la República," *Boletín Bibliográfico,* July 15, 1967, p. 3.

44. Juárez, *Documentos, discursos y correspondencia,* 3:112, 10:9–10; Mauricio de la Selva, "Precisiones sobre Juárez," *Diorama de la Cultura* of *Excelsior,* March 20, 1971, pp. 8–10.

45. Vázquez de Knauth, *Nacionalismo y educación en México,* pp. 247–49.

46. El Colegio de México published Francisco Zarco's *Historia del Congreso Extraordinario Constituyente, 1856–1857.* Jesús Reyes Heroles found a continuity in Mexican liberalism. See his *El liberalismo mexicano,* 1:xiii. José C. Valadés saw the Juárez regime as a precursor of the "presidential regime" of modern Mexico in *El pensamiento político de Benito Juárez;* see also Brading, *Prophecy and Myth in Mexican History,* p. 82.

47. *Centenario del triunfo de la República.*

48. The weekly *Tiempo* provided extensive coverage of this commem-

oration, including the concert in the Palace of Fine Arts and the men and events of the Reform era during the decades of the 1950s, 1960s, and 1970s.

49. Jaime Alcina, "El recinto de homenaje al benemérito de las Américas," *Magazine de Novedades*, March 24, 1963, pp. 10–11; Carlos J. Sierra, "Natalicio de Benito Juárez,"*Boletín Bibliográfico*, March 15, 1970, p. 3.

50. See the monthly publication of the Comisión Nacional para la Conmemoración del Centenario del Fallecimiento de don Benito Juárez, *Cuadernos Juaristas.* As a sample of the many books published in connection with the centennial, see Jesús Romero Flores, *Lic. Benito Juárez;* Nicolás Pizarro Suárez, *Siete crisis políticas de Benito Juárez;* and Raúl Mejía Zúñiga, *Benito Juárez y su generación.*

51. Pepe Bulnes, *1972.*

52. *Tiempo,* July 25, 1983, p. 5.

Chapter 9

1. A general survey of the radical right in Mexico is Hugh G. Campbell, *La derecha radical en México, 1929–1949.* See also Kenneth F. Johnson, "Ideological Correlates of Right Wing Political Alienation in Mexico"; Lyle C. Brown, "Mexican Church-State Relations, 1933–1940"; Stanley E. Hilton, "The Church-State Dispute over Education in Mexico from Carranza to Cárdenas"; Albert L. Michaels, "The Modification of the Anticlerical Nationalism of the Mexican Revolution by General Lázaro Cárdenas and Its Relationship to the Church-State Detente in Mexico."

2. Quirk, *Mexican Revolution and the Catholic Church,* pp. 145–214; Jean A. Meyer, *The Cristero Rebellion,* esp. pp. 184–91, 212–17; David C. Bailey, *Viva Cristo Rey!;* James W. Wilkie, "The Meaning of the Cristero Religious War against the Mexican Revolution."

3. Regis Planchet, *La cuestión religiosa en México,* pp. 7, 9; see also David L. Graham, "The Rise of the Mexican Right."

4. James W. Wilkie and Edna Monzón de Wilkie, *México visto en el siglo XX,* pp. 419, 483–84.

5. Albert L. Michaels, "Fascism and Sinarquism"; Carlos M. Velasco Gil, *El Sinarquismo,* p. 41; Franz A. von Sauer, *The Alienated "Loyal" Opposition,* p. 38; Frans J. Schryer, *The Rancheros of Pisaflores,* p. 95; Salvador Abascal, *Mis recuerdos,* pp. 141, 144–45, 197.

6. José Victoria, "Traición," *El Sinarquista,* September 12, 1940, p. 3; Abascal, *Mis recuerdos,* pp. 425, 621.

7. Justino Aguicer, "Tres aniversarios," *Orden,* July 16, 1950, p. 3; Abascal, *Mis recuerdos,* pp. 190–91.

8. Julio Abril, "Juárez, el indiscutible y venenoso reaccionario," *Orden,* March 20, 1950, p. 3.

9. Bártolo Prieto, "Juarismo decadente," *Orden,* July 24, 1949, p. 2; Abascal, *Mis recuerdos,* p. 216.

10. *Tiempo,* December 31, 1948, p. 3. Abascal describes an earlier Hemiciclo meeting in *Mis recuerdos,* p. 592.

11. *La Nación,* December 27, 1948, p. 4; *Tiempo,* December 31, 1948, p. 3; *Hispanic World Report,* January 1949, pp. 2–3; February 1949, p. 6; March 1949, p. 5; April 1949, p. 7; México, Congreso, Senado, *Diario de los debates,* 40th Congress, vol. 3 (December 23, 1948), pp. 8–16; Lesley Byrd Simpson, *Many Mexicos,* pp. 337–38.

12. Johnson, "Ideological Correlates of Right Wing Political Alienation in Mexico," pp. 658–59; Albert Louis Michaels, "Mexican Politics and Nationalism from Calles to Cárdenas," pp. 312–15.

13. Donald J. Mabry, *Mexico's Acción Nacional,* pp. 16, 99–112; Sauer, *Alienated "Loyal" Opposition,* pp. 41–60; Martin C. Needler, *Mexican Politics,* pp. 66–67; William Robert Lux, "Acción Nacional," pp. 32–33; James F. Creagan, "Minority Parties in Mexico," p. 58.

14. "18 de julio: Cómo fue el anti-constitucional juramento de la Constitución," *La Nación,* July 24, 1950, p. 24.

15. "21 de marzo," *La Nación,* March 29, 1953, p. 4. Similar criticism came from the left. See *Jueves de Excelsior,* July 23, 1953, p. 3; "La familia en el Monumento," *La Nación,* March 29, 1959, pp. 3–4.

16. *La Nación,* April 1, 1970, p. 8.

17. Simpson provides a description of this episode of the battle of the bones in *Many Mexicos,* pp. 22–24. See also José Fuentes Mares, *México en la hispanidad,* pp. 7, 9, 13.

18. Roberto Blanco Moheno, *Juárez ante Dios y ante los hombres,* pp. 14, 16, 208.

19. José Fuentes Mares, *Juárez y los Estados Unidos,* pp. 4–6. The reviewer for *Historia Mexicana* characterized it as a good book despite its polemical aspect: Carlos Bosch García, "El Tratado McLane-Ocampo," *Historia Mexicana* 10 (1961):660–63. Editorial Jus included the fourth edition in its "México heróico" series.

20. Fuentes Mares, *Juárez y el Imperio,* p. 236.

21. Fuentes Mares, *Juárez y la República,* pp. 22, 160. The other book in the series is *Juárez y la Intervención.*

22. José Vasconcelos, *Breve historia de México,* pp. 14, 105, 315, 325, 364, 386, 400. See Brading, *Prophecy and Myth in Mexican History,* pp. 71–80, for a discussion of the ideas of Vasconcelos.

23. José Bravo Ugarte, *México Independiente*, pp. 149–52.

24. Mariano Cuevas, *Historia de la nación mexicana*, pp. 773–92, 944–46.

25. Alfonso Junco, "Juárez y Carranza," *El Universal*, May 26, 1934, p. 3. The article provoked a minor polemic. See Bernardino Mena Brita, "Juárez y Carranza," *El Universal*, May 30, 1934, p. 3.

26. Alfonso Junco, *Un siglo de México*, pp. 189, 217.

27. Joaquín Márquez Montiel, *Cuestiones históricas*, pp. 135–36; Carlos Alvear Acevedo, *Elementos de historia de México (época independiente)*, pp. 354–57; Jesús García Gutiérrez, *Historia de México*; Vázquez de Knauth, *Nacionalismo y educación en México*, pp. 161–252.

28. A writer for *Novedades* showed some impatience with the persistence of what he called jacobinism. See Gustavo Moa, "Símbolo de unión entre los mexicanos debe ser la figura de Juárez," *Novedades*, July 26, 1965, p. 1.

29. Ermilio Abreu Gómez, *Martín Luis Guzmán*, p. 100; Martín Luis Guzmán, *Necesidad de cumplir las leyes de Reforma*, pp. 120, 131; Charles A. Hale, "The Liberal Impulse," esp. pp. 482–83.

30. Robert Paul Millon, *Mexican Marxist*, p. 13; Brandenburg, *Making of Modern Mexico*, p. 82; *Omega*, July 25, 1942, p. 1; Needler, *Mexican Politics*, pp. 63–66.

31. "Juárez y la reacción actual," *El Popular*, March 22, 1940, p. 3; "Juárez, símbolo de unión revolucionaria," ibid., July 20, 1942, p. 5; "¿Por qué chillan?" ibid., July 23, 1942, p. 5; Vicente Lombardo Toledano, *La izquierda en la historia de México*, p. 73.

32. Karl M. Schmitt, *Communism in Mexico*; "La historia patria nos muestra el camino: El ejemplo de nuestros héroes es la garantía de nuestra victoria," *La Voz de México*, June 12, 1942, p. 9; ibid., March 21, 1943, p. 1; "Juárez, creador de nuestra nacionalidad," ibid., July 18, 1943, p. 1; "En el 75 aniversario de la muerte de Benito Juárez," ibid., July 6, 1947, p. 1.

33. Jorge Tomasini so charged in an article in "Homenaje en memoria de don Benito Juárez," *Todo*, March 22, 1948, p. 8.

34. *Política*, July 15, 1967, p. 14; David T. Garza, "Factionalism in the Mexican Left."

35. "Juárez: lección y camino," *Siempre*, March 29, 1967, pp. 16–17. *Siempre* has been characterized as a semiofficial magazine. See Kenneth F. Johnson, *Mexican Democracy*, p. 74.

36. Córdova, *La ideología de la Revolución Mexicana: La era del desarrollismo*, p. 47; Donald J. Mabry, *The Mexican University and the State*,

pp. 246–70; Judith Adler Hellman, *Mexico in Crisis*, pp.131–80; *1968*, esp. pp. 9–14, 303–6; Arnaldo Martínez Verdugo, *Crisis política y alternativa comunista*, pp. 9–11.

37. "Juárez y el doctor Johnson," *Plural* 1 (August 1972):39–40.

Chapter 10

1. In the collection of reviews and essays in *Prophecy and Myth in Mexican History*, Brading supports this point persuasively.

2. *La Prensa*, July 19, 1971, p. 1.

3. Van Alstyne, *Genesis of American Nationalism*, p. 40.

4. Perry, *Juárez and Díaz*, pp. 3–32.

5. Hugh M. Hamill, Jr., "The Status of Biography in Mexican Historiography," in *Investigaciones contemporáneas sobre historia de México*, pp. 285–304.

Bibliography

The principal sources for this study of the political and ideological uses of Juárez were newspapers, magazines, books, and pamphlets published in Mexico from 1867 to 1983. The dates that follow each newspaper and magazine indicate the period examined. For most newspapers and magazines, I consulted editions published around the dates of the birth and death of Juárez.

Manuscripts

Archivo Bulnes. Archivo General de la Nación. Mexico City.
Archivo Porfirio Díaz. University of the Americas, Cholula, Puebla.
Archivo Vicente Riva Palacio. Colección Genaro García. Benson Latin American Collection. University of Texas, Austin.
Colección Lafragua. Biblioteca Nacional. Mexico City.
"Conversación entre el Sr. Gral. Porfirio Díaz y Mr. H. Bancroft." Mexico City, 1883. In Hubert Howe Bancroft, Miscellaneous Papers. Bancroft Library, University of California at Berkeley.
Hale, Charles A., "The *Científicos* as Constitutionalists: Mexico's Great Debate of 1893." Paper presented at the Meeting of the Latin American Studies Association, October 18, 1980.
Mariano Riva Palacio Papers. Colección Genaro García. Benson Latin American Collection, University of Texas, Austin.

Newspapers and Other Periodical Publications

Acción Mundial (1916)
El Ahuizote (1913)
El Amigo del Pueblo (1911)

El Anti-Reeleccionista (1909)
Así (1942)
La Bandera de Juárez (1872–73)
Boletín Bibliográfico (1954–73)
Boletín de la Sociedad Mexicana de Geografía y Estadística (1867–1984)
El Colmillo Público (1903–5)
El Combate (1887)
El Constitucional (1910)
El Contemporáneo (1904)
La Convención (1914–15)
La Convención Radical (1886–1900)
Cuadernos Americanos (1942–70)
Cuadernos Juaristas (1972)
El Debate (1909–11)
El Demócrata (1918–20)
El Demócrata Mexicano (1911)
El Día (1963–70)
El Diablito Rojo (1912)
El Diario (1911)
El Diario del Hogar (1882–1911)
Diario Oficial (1872–1906)
El Dictamen (1905–38)
El Domingo (1872)
El Eco Revolucionario (1933–35)
El Estandarte (1906–10)
Excelsior (1917–84)
La Guacamaya (1911–15)
Hemisphere (1940–41)
El Heraldo de México (1919–22)
El Hijo del Ahuizote (1887–1913)
El Hijo Jacobino (1904–5)
Hispanic World Report (1948–62)
Hoy (1938–71)
Impacto (1953)
El Imparcial (1896–1914)
El Independiente (1913–14)
El Informador (1921–29)
Jueves de Excelsior (1925–53)
La Juventud Literaria (1887)
El Liberal (1920)
La Libertad (1878–84)
El Machete (1924–29)

Mañana (1967)
Mexican Herald (1908–13)
México en el Arte (1948)
El Monitor Republicano (1867–95)
El Multicolor (1911–14)
El Mundo Ilustrado (1896–1906)
La Nación (1940–83)
El Nacional (1887)
El Nacional (1929–83)
New York Times (1971–83)
El Nigromante (1903–6)
El Norte (1951)
Novedades (1939–76)
La Nueva Era (1911)
Omega (1920–42)
Orden (1946–65)
La Orquesta (1867–72)
El Padre Cobos (1870–71)
El País (1904–14)
La Palabra (1931–34)
El Partido Democrático (1909)
El Partido Liberal (1885–96)
La Patria (1877–1912)
Plural (1972)
Política (1960–67)
El Popular (1938–56)
El Porvenir (1925–28)
La Prensa (1929–72)
El Pueblo (1915–18)
El Radical (1914–15)
La Raza (1922)
Regeneración (1910–17)
La República (1878–82)
Revista Positiva (1901–14)
Siempre (1953–83)
El Siglo de Torreón (1926–35)
El Siglo Diez y Nueve (1867–95)
El Sinarquista (1940–50)
El Socialista (1887–88)
Tiempo (1942–84)
El Tiempo (1887–1912)
Todo (1942–62)

Two Republics (1872–73)
El Universal (1888–1903)
El Universal (1916–72)
La Voz de Juárez (1884–85)
La Voz de Juárez (1909–14)
La Voz de México (1872–1906)
La Voz de México (1938–59)

Government Documents

El Chamizal: Monumento a la justicia internacional. Mexico City: Secretaría de Hacienda y Crédito Público, 1964.
México, Congreso, Cámara de Diputados. *Derechos del pueblo mexicano: Mexico a través de sus constituciones.* 8 vols. Mexico City: 1967.
———. *Diario de los debates.* Mexico City: 1872–1910, 1947–48.
México, Congreso Constituyente, 1916–17. *Diario de los debates.* 2 vols. Mexico City: Imprenta de Gobernación, 1917.
México, Congreso, Senado, *Diario de los debates.* Mexico City: 1872–1910, 1947–48.
México, Congreso, 1912–13, Cámara de Diputados. *Historia de la Cámara de diputados de la XXVI Legislatura Federal.* Edited by Diego Arenas Guzmán. 5 vols. Mexico City: 1961.
México, Presidente. *Los presidentes de México ante la nación: Informes, manifiestos y documentos de 1821 a 1966.* 5 vols. Mexico City: Imprenta de la Cámara de Diputados, 1966.
México, Secretaría de Relaciones Exteriores. *50 años de Revolución: Algunos aspectos de la política internacional de la Revolución Mexicana.* Mexico City: 1960.
———. *Labor internacional de la Revolución Consticionalista de México.* Mexico City: 1918.

Books, Pamphlets, and Articles

Abascal, Salvador. *Mis recuerdos: Sinarquismo y Colonia Auxiliadora (1935–1944).* Mexico City: Tradición, 1980.
Abell, Walter. "Myth, Mind, and History." *Journal of Aesthetics and Art Criticism* 4 (1945):77–86.

Abreu Gómez, Ermilio. *Juárez, su vida contada a los niños*. Mexico City: N.p., 1969.

———. *Martín Luis Guzmán*. Mexico City: Empresas Editoriales, 1968.

Acevedo Escobedo, Antonio. *Asedios a Juárez y su época*. Mexico City: N.p., 1967.

Agencia Benito Juárez. *Laudo arbitral*. Mexico City: N.p., 1908.

A Juárez: Al redentor de una patria y de una raza, en remembranza de su centenario. Toluca: N.p., 1906.

A Juárez benemérito de América en el trigésimo aniversario de su muerte 18 de julio. Chihuahua: Imprenta de C. Alarcón, 1902.

Ake, Claude. "Charismatic Legitimation and Political Integration." *Comparative Studies in Society and History* 9 (October 1966): 1–13.

A la memoria del ilustre Ciudadano Presidente Benito Juárez. Alice, Texas: N.p., 1909.

Al benemérito ciudadano Benito Juárez en recuerdo del primer centenario de su nacimiento. Durango: N.p., 1906.

Album gráfico de la República Mexicana. 2d ed. Mexico City: Müller, 1910.

Alegre, Manuel M. *Muchos pájaros con una piedra*. Mexico City: "La Europea," 1906.

Alfaro Siqueiros, David. *Esculto-pintura*. New York: Tudor, 1968.

———. *Mi respuesta: La historia de una insidia, ¿Quiénes son los traidores de la patria?* Mexico City: "Arte Pública," 1960.

———. *70 obras recientes de David Alfaro Siqueiros*. Mexico City: INBA, 1947.

Algunos episodios de la vida del Benemérito. Pachuca: Impresa Poliglota de Ignacio Madariaga, 1904.

Almond, Gabriel A., and Sidney Verba. *The Civic Culture: Political Attitudes and Democracy in Five Nations*. Boston: Little, Brown, 1965.

Alocución del C. Gobernador del Estado, Gral. Bernardo Reyes, dicha con objeto de clausurar las fiestas del Centenario del nacimiento del Benemérito de la Patria, Benito Juárez. Monterrey: N.p., 1906.

Altamirano, Ignacio M. *Historia y política de México (1821–1882)*. Mexico City: Empresas Editoriales, 1947.

———. *Paisajes y leyendas*. Mexico City: Editorial Porrua, 1974.

Alvarez, Ignacio. *Estudios sobre la historia general de México*. 6 vols. Zacatecas: Impresa de M. Ruiz de Esparza, 1871–77.

Alvarez, Melchor. *Comentarios a la obra del Sr. Lic. Don Justo Sierra, ministro de instrucción pública y bellas artes, titulada: "Juárez: su obra y su tiempo," en la parte relativa a la Guerra de Reforma*. Mexico City: Talleres y Tipografía de "El Tiempo," 1905.

Alvarez Acosta, Miguel. *Juárez, cuatro estancias liberales, discursos.* Mexico City: Ediciones Opic, 1964.

Alvear Acevedo, Carlos. *Elementos de historia de México (época independiente).* 3d ed. Mexico City: N.p., 1958.

Amezcua, Guillermo M., ed. *Juárez en Tabasco: Reseña de los festivales del 21 de marzo de 1906.* San Juan Bautista, Tabasco: N.p., 1907.

Amor y respeto a la Constitución de 1857 y su inmortal sostenedor Benito Juárez. Durango: N.p., 1890.

Anderson, Rodney D. *Outcasts in Their Own Land: Mexican Industrial Workers, 1906–1911.* DeKalb: Northern Illinois University Press, 1976.

Arduz Eguía, Gastón. *El mensaje de Benito Juárez.* La Paz: N.p., 1942.

Arellano Zavaleta, Manuel. *Agonía y muerte de Juárez.* Mexico City: N.p., 1972.

Arenas Guzmán, Diego. *El periodismo en la Revolución Mexicana.* 2 vols. Mexico City: N.p. 1966–67.

Arquín, Florence. *Diego Rivera: The Shaping of an Artist, 1889–1921.* Norman: University of Oklahoma Press, 1971.

Ausband, Stephen C. *Myth and Meaning, Myth and Order.* Macon, Ga.: Mercer University Press, 1983.

Autobiografía del Sr. Lic. D. José M. Iglesias. Mexico City: N.p., 1893.

Aviles, René. *Benito Juarez, el hombre ejemplar.* 2d ed. Mexico City: Sociedad de Amigos del Libro Mexicano, 1957.

Ayala, Miguel de. *Benito Juárez, el indio sublime.* Santiago de Chile: Zigzag, 1939.

Aznar, Marcial. *Observaciones histórico-politicas sobre Juárez y su época.* Mexico City: Tipografía "El Gran Libro," 1887.

Bailey, David C. *Viva Cristo Rey!: The Cristero Rebellion and the Church-State Conflict in Mexico.* Austin: University of Texas Press, 1973.

Baker, Nina Brown. *Juárez, Hero of Mexico.* New York: Vanguard Press, 1942.

Balbas, Manuel. *Los detractores de Juárez, refutación a la obra del señor ingeniero Francisco Bulnes, titulada Juárez y las revoluciones de Ayutla y de Reforma.* Mexico City: Impresa "Victoria," 1916.

Ballesteros, Leonardo M. *Apuntes biográficos de los señores Lic. Emilio Vázquez y doctor Francisco Vázquez Gómez, el primer ministro de gobernación y el segundo ministro de instrucción pública en la nueva administración.* Mexico City: Talleres y Tipografía de "El Tiempo," 1911.

Bancroft, Hubert Howe. *History of Mexico.* 6 vols. San Francisco: A. L. Bancroft and the History Company, 1883–88.

Bartra, Armando, ed. *Regeneración, 1900–1918.* Mexico City: HADISE, 1972.

Basch, Samuel. *Recuerdos de México: Memorias del médico ordinario del Emperador Maximiliano, 1866–67.* Translated by D. Manuel Peredo. Mexico City: N. Chávez, 1870.

Bassols, Narciso. *Obras.* Mexico City: Fondo de Cultura Económica, 1964.

Baz, Gustavo. *Vida de Benito Juárez.* Mexico City: E. Capdevielle, 1874.

Bazant, Jan. *Alienation of Church Wealth in Mexico: Social and Economic Aspects of the Liberal Revolution, 1856–75.* Cambridge, England: Cambridge University Press, 1971.

———. *A Concise History of Mexico from Hidalgo to Cárdenas, 1805–1940.* Cambridge, England: Cambridge University Press, 1977.

Benito Juárez y su proyección continental. Mexico City: N.p., 1962.

Bennett, W. Lance. "Imitation, Ambiguity, and Drama in Political Life: Civil Religion and the Dilemmas of Public Authority." *Journal of Politics* 41 (February 1979):106–33.

Berens, John F. "The Sanctification of American Nationalism, 1789–1812: Prelude to Civil Religion in America." *Canadian Review of Studies in Nationalism* 3 (Spring 1976):172–91.

Berry, Charles R. *The Reforma in Oaxaca, 1856–76: A Microhistory of the Liberal Revolution.* Lincoln: University of Nebraska Press, 1981.

Bidney, David. *Theoretical Anthropology.* New York: Columbia University Press, 1953.

Biografía del señor Gral. José Vicente Villada, gobernador constitucional del Estado de Michoacán. Toluca: Tipografía del Gobierno en la Escuela de Artes, 1895.

Blanco Moheno, Roberto. *Juárez ante Dios y ante los hombres.* Mexico City: Libro Mex, 1959.

Bonilla, José María. *Individualismo y socialismo.* 4th ed. Mexico City: Herrero Hermanos, 1939.

Bosch García, Carlos. "El Tratado McLane Ocampo." *Historia Mexicana* 10 (1961):660–63.

Boulding, Kenneth E. *The Image.* Ann Arbor: University of Michigan Press, 1956.

Brading, D. A. *Prophecy and Myth in Mexican History.* Cambridge, England: Centre of Latin-American Studies, University of Cambridge, 1984.

Brandenburg, Frank. *The Making of Modern Mexico.* Englewood Cliffs, N.J.: Prentice-Hall, 1964.

Bravo Ugarte, José. *México Independiente.* Barcelona: Salvat Editores, 1959.

————. *Temas históricos diversos.* Mexico City: Editorial Jus, 1966.

Breymann, Walter N. "The Científicos: Critics of the Díaz Regime, 1892–1903." *Proceedings of the Arkansas Academy of Sciences* 7 (1954): 91–97.

Britton, John A. *Educación y radicalismo en México: Los años de Bassols (1931–1934).* Mexico City: SepSetentas, 1976.

————. *Educación y radicalismo en México: Los años de Cárdenas (1934–1940).* Mexico City: SepSetentas, 1976.

Brown, Lyle C. "Mexican Church-State Relations, 1933–1940." *Journal of Church and State* 6 (Spring 1964):202–22.

Bryson, Lyman, et al., eds. *Symbols and Society: Fourth Symposium of the Conference on Science, Philosophy, and Religion.* New York: Harper & Brothers, 1955.

Bulnes, Francisco. *Defensa y amplificación de mi discurso pronunciado el 21 de junio de 1903 ante la Convención Nacional Liberal.* Mexico City: N.p., 1903.

————. *Las grandes mentiras de nuestra historia.* Mexico City: La viuda de C. Bouret, 1904.

————. *Los grandes problemas de México.* Mexico City: Ediciones de "El Universal," 1926.

————. *La guerra de Cuba en relación con el criterio americano y los intereses de México.* Mexico City: Imprenta Avenida Juárez, 1897.

————. *La guerra de Independencia: Hidalgo-Iturbide.* Mexico City: Talleres-linotipográficos de "El Diario," 1910.

————. *Juárez y las Revoluciones de Ayutla y de Reforma.* 1905. Reprint. Mexico City: Editorial H. T. Milenario, 1967.

————. *El porvenir de las naciones latinoamericanas ante las recientes conquistas de Europea y Norteamérica.* Mexico City: Imprenta de M. Nava, 1899.

————. *El verdadero Díaz y la Revolución.* Mexico City: Editora Nacional, 1972.

————. *El verdadero Juárez y la verdad sobre la Intervención y el Imperio.* Mexico City: La viuda de C. Bouret, 1904.

————. *The Whole Truth about Mexico.* New York: M. Bulnes, 1916.

Bulnes, Pepe. *1972: Año de Juárez.* Mexico City: B. Costa Amic, Editores, 1972.

Burke, Ulick Ralph. *A Life of Benito Juárez.* London and Sidney: Bennington, 1894.

Caballero, Manuel. *Juárez épico.* Mexico City: A. Carranza, 1906.

Cabrera, Daniel. *Manifestación a Benito Juárez el día 18 de julio de 1887 promovida y ordenada por la "Prensa Unida" liberal de la Ciudad de México.* Mexico City: Impresa de Daniel Cabrera, 1887.

Cadena, Longinos. *Elementos de historia general y de historia patria para el primer año de instrucción primaria superior.* 5th ed. Mexico City: Herrero Hermanos, 1922.

Cadenhead, Ivie E., Jr. *Benito Juárez.* New York: Twayne, 1973.

———. "González Ortega and the Presidency of Mexico." *Hispanic American Historical Review* 32 (August 1952):331–46.

———. *Jesús González Ortega and Mexican National Politics.* Fort Worth: Texas Christian University Press, 1972.

Calero y Sierra, Manuel. *Un decenio de política mexicana.* New York: L. Middleditch, 1920.

Camp, Roderic A. *Mexican Political Biographies, 1935–1981.* 2d ed., rev. and expanded. Tucson: University of Arizona Press, 1982.

Campbell, Hugh G. *La derecha radical en México, 1929–1949.* Translated by Pilar Negrete. Mexico City: SepSetentas, 1976.

Campbell, Joseph. *The Hero with a Thousand Faces.* New York: Pantheon, 1949.

Cardoza y Aragón, Luis. *Orozco.* Mexico City: Instituto de Investigaciones Estéticas, 1959.

Carey, James C. "Mexico's 'Hands Off' Policy." *Midwest Quarterly* 3 (Spring 1962):232–39.

Carrasco Puente, Rafael. *La caricatura en México.* Mexico City: Imprenta Universitaria, 1953.

———. *La prensa en México.* Mexico City: Universidad Nacional Autónoma de México, 1962.

Carrera Damas, Germán. *El culto de Bolívar: Esbozo para un estudio de las ideas en Venezuela.* Caracas: Instituto de Antropología e Historia, Universidad Central de Venezuela, 1969.

Carriedo, Adalberto. *Biografía de Juárez que deberá ser leída en todas las escuelas del Estado de Oaxaca el 21 de marzo de 1906.* Oaxaca: N.p., 1905.

———. *El único Juárez: Refutación a la obra de pretendida crítica histórica que, bajo el título de "El verdadero Juárez," escribió el diputado Francisco Bulnes.* Oaxaca: J. F. Soto, 1904.

Carrillo A., Rafael. *Posada y el grabado mexicano.* 2d ed. Mexico City: N.p., 1981.

Carrillo Flores, Antonio. "La política exterior de México." *Foro Internacional* 6 (October 1965–March 1966):233–46.

Carrión, Jorge. *Mito y magia del mexicano.* Mexico City: Porrua y Obregón, 1952.

Carta de Hilarión Frías y Soto al señor diputado Francisco Bulnes. Mexico City: N.p., 1903.

Castañeda, Jorge. "Revolution and Foreign Policy: Mexico's Experience." *Political Science Quarterly* 78 (September 1963):391–417.

Castillo, José R. del. *Juárez, la Intervención y el Imperio; refutación a la obra "El verdadero Juárez" de Bulnes.* Mexico City: Herrero Hermanos, 1904.

Ceballos Dosamantes, Jesús. *La gran mixtificación maderista: Jesuitas y pseudocientíficos ante la moral y la ciencia.* Mexico City: Imprenta de A. Carranza e hijos, 1911.

Celada, Fernando. *Bronces: Cantos épicos a Juárez.* Mexico City: N.p., 1904.

Centenario de Benito Juárez: Fiestas conmemorativas, 21 de marzo. Guatemala City: Tipografía Nacional, 1906.

Centenario de Juárez en el Estado de Tamaulipas. Victoria: N.p., 1906.

Centenario de la proclamación de la independencia: Inauguración del monumento a Juárez en la Alameda de la Ciudad de México: 18 de septiembre de 1910. Mexico City: Impresa del Gobierno Federal, 1910.

Centenario del triunfo de la República. Mexico City: N.p., 1967.

Centro de Estudios Históricos, El Colegio de México. *Historia general de México.* 4 vols. Mexico City: El Colegio de México, 1977.

Ceremonia conmemorativa del 87 aniversario de la muerte de Benito Juárez. Mexico City: N.p., 1959.

Charlot, Jean. *Mexican Art and the Academy of San Carlos, 1785–1915.* Austin: University of Texas Press, 1962.

———. *The Mexican Mural Renaissance, 1920–1925.* New Haven: Yale University Press, 1963.

Chase, Richard. *Quest for Myth.* Baton Rouge: Louisiana State University Press, 1949.

Chavero, Alfredo. *Discurso pronunciado en los funerales del C. Benito Juárez.* Mexico City: Díaz de León y S. White, 1872.

El ciudadano Benito Juárez, Benemérito de América, juzgado por la prensa extranjera. Mérida: N.p., 1872.

Cline, Howard F. *Mexico: Revolution to Evolution, 1940–1960.* London: Oxford University Press, 1962.

———. *The United States and Mexico.* Cambridge, Mass.: Harvard University Press, 1953.

Cockcroft, James D. *Intellectual Precursors of the Mexican Revolution, 1900–1913.* Austin: University of Texas Press, 1968.

Coerver, Don M. *The Porfirian Interregnum: The Presidency of Manuel González of Mexico, 1880–1884.* Fort Worth: Texas Christian University Press, 1979.

Cohen, Anthony P. *The Management of Myths: The Politics of Legitimation in a Newfoundland Community.* St. John's: Memorial University of Newfoundland, 1975.

Cohler, Anne M. *Rousseau and Nationalism.* New York: Basic Books, 1970.

Colín, Mario. *Juárez.* Toluca: N.p., 1949.

Comisión Nacional del Centenario de Juárez. *Programa.* Monterrey: N.p., 1906.

Comité Liberal Guanajuatense. *Centenario de Juárez, 21 de marzo de 1906.* Guanajuato: Impresa de la Escuela Industrial, 1907.

Contra Bulnes: Recortes y protestas. Mexico City: N.p., 1904.

Córdova, Arnaldo. *La ideología de la Revolución Mexicana: La era del desarrollismo (Proyecto de investigación).* Mexico City: N.p., 1977.

———. *La ideología de la Revolución Mexicana: La formación del poder político en México.* Mexico City: Ediciones Era, 1972.

Corti, Egon Caesar Count. *Maximilian and Charlotte of Mexico.* Translated from the German by Catherine Alison Phillips. 2 vols. New York: Knopf, 1928.

Cosío Villegas, Daniel. *La Constitución de 1857 y sus críticos.* Mexico City: Editorial Hermes, 1957.

———. *Historia moderna de México. El Porfiriato: La vida política interior, parte primera.* Mexico City: Editorial Hermes, 1970.

———. *Historia moderna de México. El Porfiriato: La vida política interior, parte segunda.* Mexico City: Editorial Hermes, 1972.

———. *Historia moderna de México: La República restaurada, La vida política.* Mexico City: Editorial Hermes, 1955.

Cosmes, Francisco G. *La dominación española y la patria mexicana.* Mexico City: Imprenta de "El Partido Liberal," 1896.

———. *Historia general de México: Continuación a la de Don Niceto de Zamacois, Parte contemporánea, los últimos 33 años.* Barcelona: J. F. Parres, 1901.

———. *El verdadero Bulnes y su falso Juárez.* Mexico City: Talleres de Tipografía, 1904.

Crawford, William Rex. *A Century of Latin-American Thought.* Cambridge, Mass.: Harvard University Press, 1964.

Creelman, James. "President Díaz, Hero of the Americas." *Pearson's Magazine* 19 (March 1908):231–77.

Crónica de la recepción que el Club Anti-Reeleccionista "Benito Juárez" hizo a los distinguidos delegados del Centro Anti-Reeleccionista de México en su visita a esta capital el día 16 de enero de 1910. Chihuahua: N.p., 1910?

Crónica oficial de las fiestas del primer Centenario de la Independencia de

México, publicada bajo la dirección de Genaro García, por acuerdo de la Secretaría de Gobernación. Mexico City: Talleres del Museo Nacional, 1911.

Cruz, Francisco Santiago. *Los hospitales de México y la caridad de don Benito.* Mexico City: Editorial Jus, 1959.

Cue Canovas, Agustín. *El Tratado McLane-Ocampo: Juárez, los Estados Unidos y Europa.* Mexico City: Editorial Nueva América, 1956.

Cuestiones políticas de actualidad. Mexico City: Tipografía de "El Tiempo," 1909.

Cuevas, Mariano. *Historia de la nación mexicana.* Mexico City: Talleres Tipográficos Modelo, 1940.

Cumberland, Charles C. *The Mexican Revolution: The Constitutionalist Years.* Austin: University of Texas Press, 1972.

———. *The Mexican Revolution: Genesis under Madero.* Austin: University of Texas Press, 1952.

Dabbs, Jack Autrey. *The French Army in Mexico, 1861–1867: A Study in Military Government.* The Hague: Mouton, 1963.

El decreto de Colombia en honor de Don Benito Juárez. Mexico City: Publicación de la Secretaría de Relaciones Exteriores, 1923.

Degler, Carl. "Reshaping American History." *Journal of American History* 67 (June 1980):7–25.

Deutsch, Karl W. *Nationalism and Social Communication.* 2d ed. Cambridge, Mass.: MIT Press, 1966.

Diccionario Porrua de historia, biografía y geografía de México. Mexico City: Porrua, 1970.

Dickerson, Albert I., ed. *The Orozco Frescoes at Dartmouth.* Hanover, N.H.: Dartmouth College Publications, 1934.

Didapp, Juan Pedro. *Explotadores políticos de México: Bulnes y el Partido Científico ante el derecho ajeno.* Mexico City: Tipografía de los sucesores de F. Díaz de León, 1904.

Diego Rivera. New York: Museum of Modern Art, 1931.

Directorio de bibliotecas de la República Mexicana. Mexico City: N.p., 1970.

Discurso pronunciado por el Lic. Rodolfo Reyes en nombre del Comité Patriótico Liberal en la manifestación organizada para honrar la memoria del C. Benito Juárez. Mexico City: N.p., 1903.

Documentos históricos publicados como un recuerdo de gratitud a la venerable memoria del Gran Reformador C. Lic. Benito Juárez el 18 de julio de 1904. Pachuca: N.p., 1904.

Dos revoluciones: México y los Estados Unidos. Mexico City: Editorial Jus, 1976.

Dromundo, Baltasar. *Juárez, símbolo de eternidad mexicana*. Mexico City: Cámara de Diputados del Congreso de la Unión, 1956.

Dulles, John W. F. *Yesterday in Mexico*. Austin: University of Texas Press, 1961.

Duncan, Hugh D. *Communication and Social Order*. New York: Bedminster Press, 1962.

————. *Symbols in Society*. New York: Oxford University Press, 1968.

Durkheim, Emile. *The Elementary Forms of the Religious Life*. London: George Allen & Unwin, 1915.

Edelman, Murray. *Politics as Symbolic Action: Mass Arousal and Quiescence*. Chicago: Markham, 1971.

————. *The Symbolic Uses of Politics*. Urbana: University of Illinois Press, 1964.

Elder, Charles D., and Roger W. Cobb. *The Political Uses of Symbols*. New York: Longman, 1983.

Elizaga, Lorenzo. *Ensayos políticos*. Mexico City: J. Abadiano, 1867.

En honor a Juárez. Mexico City: J. V. Villada, 1887.

El Estado de Chihuahua en el centenario de Juárez, 21 de marzo de 1906. Chihuahua: Impresa del Gobierno, 1906.

Fabela, Isidro, ed. *Documentos históricos de la Revolución Mexicana*. 14 vols. Mexico City: Fondo de Cultura Económica, 1960–72.

Fagen, Richard R. *Politics and Communication*. Boston: Little, Brown, 1966.

El falso Bulnes: Folleto de actualidades escrito por tres abogados liberales yucatecos. Mérida: Impresa de "El Eco del Comercio," 1904.

Fernández, Justino. *Antologías de artistas mexicanas del siglo XX: Pintores*. Mexico City: Central de B. A., 1958.

————. *El arte del siglo XIX en México*. Mexico City: Impresa Universitaria, 1967.

————. *José Clemente Orozco: Forma e idea*. Mexico City: Porrua, 1942.

————. "Obras recientes de Orozco." *México en el arte* 6 (December 1948).

————. *La pintura moderna mexicana*. Mexico City: Editorial Pormuca, 1964.

Fernández Güell, Rogelio. *El moderno Juárez*. Mexico City: Tipografía "Artista," 1913?

Figueroa, Francisco. *Biografía del Benemérito Benito Juárez premiada en el concurso que se organizó por la secretaría de instrucción pública y bellas artes y destinada a servir de modelo en las conferencias que se efectuarán en las escuelas primarias el día 21 de marzo de 1906*. Mexico City: Tipografía Económica, 1906.

Finley, M. I. "Myth, Memory, and History." *History and Theory* 4 (1965):281–302.

Foix, Pere. *Juárez*. Mexico City: Ediciones Ibero Americanas, 1949.

Frías y Soto, Hilarión. *Juárez glorificado y la Intervención y el Imperio ante la verdad histórica*. Mexico City: Imprenta Central, 1905.

Fuentes Mares, José. "La convocatoria de 1867." *Historia Mexicana* 14 (1965):423–44.

———. *Juárez y el Imperio*. Mexico City: Editorial Jus, 1963.

———. *Juárez y la Intervención*. Mexico City: Editorial Jus, 1962.

———. *Juárez y la República*. Mexico City: Editorial Jus, 1965.

———. *Juárez y los Estados Unidos*. Mexico City: Libro Mex, 1960.

———. *México en la hispanidad: Ensayo polémico sobre mi pueblo*. Madrid: Instituto de Cultura Hispanica, 1949.

Fuentes para la historia de la Revolución Mexicana: La caricatura política. Mexico City: Fondo de Cultura Económica, 1955.

Fuentes para la historia de la Revolución: La huelga de Cananea. Mexico City: Fondo de Cultura Económica, 1956.

Fuentes para la historia de la Revolución: Manifiestos políticos (1892–1912). Mexico City: Fondo de Cultura Económica, 1957.

Fuentes para la historia de la Revolución: Planes políticos y otros documentos. Mexico City: Fondo de Cultura Económica, 1954.

Gabriel, Ralph Henry. *The Course of American Democratic Thought*. 2d ed. New York: Ronald Press, 1956.

Gamio, Manuel. *Forjando patria*. Mexico City: Porrua, 1916.

Gámiz, Abel. *Historia nacional de México*. 4th ed. Mexico City: Aguiles, 1930.

García, Genaro. *Discurso pronunciado en honor de Juárez frente al Panteón de San Fernando el 18 de julio de 1906*. Mexico City: "La Europa," 1906.

———. *Juárez: Refutación a Don Francisco Bulnes*. Mexico City: La viuda de C. Bouret, 1904.

García Granados, Ricardo. *La Constitución y las Leyes de la Reforma en México: Estudio histórico-sociológico*. Mexico City: Tipografía Económica, 1906.

———. *Historia de México desde la restauración de la república en 1867 hasta la caída de Huerta*. 2 vols. Mexico City: Editorial Jus, 1956.

García Gutiérrez, Jesús. *Historia de México*. Mexico City: Buena Prensa, 1946.

Garza, David T. "Factionalism in the Mexican Left: The Frustration of the MLN." *Western Political Quarterly* 17 (September 1964):447–60.

Gaster, Theodore H. "Myth and Story." *Numen* 1 (1954):184–212.

Geertz, Clifford. *Islam Observed: Religious Development in Morocco and Indonesia.* New Haven: Yale University Press, 1968.

Gibbs, Lee W., and W. Taylor Stevenson, eds. *Myth and the Crisis of Historical Consciousness.* Missoula, Mont.: Scholars Press, 1975.

Goldwater, Robert. *Rufino Tamayo.* New York: Quadrangle Press, 1947.

Gómez Quiñones, Juan. *Porfirio Díaz, los intelectuales y la Revolución.* Mexico City: Ediciones El Caballito, 1981.

González Navarro, Moisés. "La inauguración del monumento a Juárez." *Boletín Bibliográfico,* July 15, 1957, p. 2.

———. *Historia moderna de México. El Porfiriato: La vida social.* Mexico City: Editorial Hermes, 1957.

———. "Juárez y los indios mayas." *Boletín Bibliográfico,* March 15, 1955, p. 1.

González y González, Luis; Emma Cosío Villegas; and Guadalupe Monroy. *Historia moderna de México. La República restaurada: La vida social.* Mexico City: Editorial Hermes, 1956.

González Ramírez, Manuel. *Benito Juárez y sus enemigos.* Mexico City: Biblioteca "Los Buenos Libros," 1948.

Graham, David L. "The Rise of the Mexican Right." *Yale Review* 52 (1962):102–11.

Graves, Robert. *The Greek Myths.* 2 vols. Baltimore: Penguin, 1955.

Green, Constance McLaughlin. *Washington: Village and Capital, 1800–1878.* Princeton: Princeton University Press, 1962.

Greenleaf, Richard E., and Michael C. Meyer, eds. *Research in Mexican History.* Lincoln: University of Nebraska Press, 1973.

Guérard, A. L. *Reflections on the Napoleonic Legend.* New York: Charles Scribner's Sons, 1924.

Guzmán, Martín Luis. *Necesidad de cumplir las leyes de Reforma.* Mexico City: Empresas Editoriales, 1963.

Hale, Charles A. "The Liberal Impulse: Daniel Cosío Villegas and the *Historia moderna de México.*" *Hispanic American Historical Review* 54 (August 1974):479–98.

———. "The Reconstruction of Nineteenth Century Politics in Spanish America: A Case for the History of Ideas." *Latin American Research Review* 8 (Summer 1973):53–73.

Hall, Linda B. *Alvaro Obregón: Power and Revolution in Mexico, 1911–1912.* College Station: Texas A & M University Press, 1981.

Hans, Albert. *Querétaro: Memorias de un oficial del Emperador Maximiliano.* Translated by Lorenzo Elizaga. Mexico City: Editorial Jus, 1962.

Hart, John M. *Anarchism and the Mexican Working Class, 1860–1931.* Austin: University of Texas Press, 1978.

Hellman, Judith Adler. *Mexico in Crisis*. New York: Holmes & Meier, 1978.

Henderson, Peter V. N. *Felix Díaz, the Porfirians, and the Mexican Revolution*. Lincoln: University of Nebraska Press, 1981.

Hermida Ruíz, Angel J. *Juárez y la Reforma: El Tratado McLane-Ocampo*. Jalapa: N.p., 1965.

Hernández Cruz, Elsa. *El sentido de la historia en Francisco Bulnes*. Mexico City: Universidad Nacional Autónoma de México, 1964.

Hernández Luna, Juan. *Imágenes históricas de Hidalgo*. Mexico City: Universidad Nacional Autónoma de México, Consejo de Humanidades, 1954.

Herrera Frimont, C., ed. *Corridos de la Revolución*. Pachuca: Instituto Científico y Literaría, 1934.

Herskovits, Melville J., and Frances S. Herskovits. *Dahomean Narrative: A Cross-Cultural Analysis*. Evanston: Northwestern University Press, 1958.

Hewes, Gordon W. "Mexicans in Search of the Mexican." *American Journal of Economics and Sociology* 13 (January 1954):209–23.

Hilton, Stanley E. "The Church-State Dispute over Education in Mexico from Carranza to Cárdenas." *Americas* 21 (October 1964):163–83.

Los hombres del centenario. Mexico City: N.p., 1910.

Homcade, Celestino. *Juárez y Garibaldi*. Mexico City: N.p., 1886.

Homenaje a Juárez: 18 de julio de 1925. Oda y biografía. Mexico City: N.p., 1925.

Homenaje que la Corporación patriótica privada de esta ciudad tributa al Gran Reformador C. Benito Juárez en el XXVIII aniversario de su fallecimiento. Pachuca: N.p., 1900.

Honor a Juárez. Oaxaca: N.p., 1905.

Honras fúnebres decretadas por el gobierno del Estado de Oaxaca a la imperecedera memoria del Benemérito C. Lic. Benito Juárez, presidente constitucional de los Estados Unidos Mexicanos. Oaxaca: N.p., 1872.

Ibarra, Guillermo. *Benito Juárez, forjador de la nacionalidad mexicana*. Mexico City: Ediciones Revista Mexicana de Cultura, 1934.

Iglesias Calderón, Fernando. *Las supuestas traiciones de Juárez*. Mexico City: Tipografía Económica, 1907.

Immerman, Richard H. *The CIA in Guatemala: The Foreign Policy of Intervention*. Austin: University of Texas Press, 1982.

Instituto de Ciencias y Artes del Estado de Oaxaca. *Primer concurso científico-literario en honor de Juárez*. Oaxaca: N.p., 1903.

Investigaciones contemporáneas sobre historia de México: Memorias de la tercera reunión de historiadores mexicanos y norteamericanos. Mexico City: Universidad Nacional Autónoma de Mexico, El Colegio de México, University of Texas, 1971.

Iturriaga, José E. *Pensamiento político y administrativo del Presidente Juárez*. Mexico City: Instituto Nacional de la Juventud Mexicana, 1957.

Iturribarría, Jorge Fernando. *Benito Juárez—Porfirio Díaz*. Mexico City: Populibros "La Prensa," 1966.

————. *Porfirio Díaz ante la historia*. Mexico City: Unión Gráfica, 1967.

Jacobs, Ian. *Ranchero Revolt: The Mexican Revolution in Guerrero*. Austin: University of Texas Press, 1982.

Jimenez, Ramón Emilio. *Panegírico de Benito Juárez*. Ciudad Trujillo, R.D.: Impresora Dominicana, 1948.

Johnson, Kenneth F. "Ideological Correlates of Right Wing Political Alienation in Mexico." *American Political Science Review* 59 (September 1958):654–64.

————. *Mexican Democracy: A Critical View*. Boston: Allyn and Bacon, 1971.

Joseph, G. M. *Revolution from Without: Yucatán, Mexico, and the United States, 1880–1924*. Cambridge, England: Cambridge University Press, 1982.

Juárez, Benito. *Documentos, discursos y correspondencia*. Selection and notes by Jorge L. Tamayo. 15 vols. Mexico City: Secretaría del Patrimonio Nacional, 1965–71.

Juárez and César Cantu: A Refutation of the Charges Preferred by the Italian Historian, in His Last Work, against the American Patriot. Mexico City: Impresa del Gobierno, 1885.

Juárez: Discurso del señor ministro de instrucción pública y bellas artes en la velada del Arbeu. Mexico City: Tipografía de la viuda de F. Díaz de León, 1906.

Juárez en la poesía. Preface, selection, and notes by Vicente Magdaleno. Mexico City: Comisión Nacional para la Conmemoración del Fallecimiento de don Benito Juárez, 1972.

Juárez indio, traicionó a los indios: O el liberalismo en México es una cosa igual a las siete plagas de Egipto. Mexico City: Vargas Rea, 1923.

Juárez y el libro de Bulnes: Alocución leída por el Lic. Ignacio Mariscal. Mexico City: Impresa de Arturo García Cubas, 1904.

Juárez y los obreros. Mexico City: N.p., 1876.

Junco, Alfonso. *Juárez, intervencionista*. Mexico City: Editorial Jus, 1961.

————. *Un siglo de México: De Hidalgo a Carranza*. 2d ed. Mexico City: Ediciones Botas, 1937.

Jung, C. G. *Psyche and Symbol: A Selection from the Writings of C. G. Jung*. Edited by Violet S. de Laszlo. Garden City, N.Y.: Doubleday, 1958.

Katz, Friederich. *The Secret War in Mexico: Europe, the United States and the Mexican Revolution*. Chicago: University of Chicago Press, 1981.

Klapp, Orrin E. *Symbolic Leaders: Public Dramas and Public Men*. Chicago: Aldine, 1964.

Knapp, Frank Averill, Jr. *The Life of Sebastián Lerdo de Tejada, 1823–1889: A Study of Influence and Obscurity*. Austin: University of Texas Press, 1951.

Krauze, Enrique, with Jean Meyer and Cayetano Reyes. *Historia de la Revolución Mexicana: Período 1924–1928, La reconstrucción económica*. Mexico City: El Colegio de México, 1977.

Lafaye, Jacques. *Quetzalcoatl and Guadalupe: The Formation of Mexican National Consciousness, 1531–1813*. Translated by Benjamin Keen. Chicago: University of Chicago Press, 1976.

Lavie, Luis Adrian. *A Juárez*. Mexico City: Impresa J. Chávez, 1910.

Leach, E. R. *Political Systems of Highland Burma: A Study of Kachin Social Structure*. Boston: Beacon Press, 1965.

Leith, James A. *The Idea of Art as Propaganda in France, 1750–1799: A Study in the History of Ideas*. Toronto: University of Toronto Press, 1965.

———. *Media and Revolution: Moulding a New Citizenry in France during the Terror*. Toronto: Canadian Broadcasting Corporation, 1968.

Lemus, George. *Francisco Bulnes: Su vida y sus obras*. Mexico City: Ediciones de Andrea, 1965.

León, Luis G. *Conversaciones y narraciones referentes a Hidalgo y Juárez*. Mexico City: 1909.

Lepidus, Henry. *The History of Mexican Journalism*. Columbia: University of Missouri Press, 1928.

Lerín, Manuel. *Proclama a Juárez*. Mexico City: N.p., 1957.

Lévi-Strauss, Claude. *Structural Anthropology*. Translated by Claire Jacobson and Brooke Grundfest Schoepf. New York: Basic Books, 1963.

Liga Central de Resistencia. *Edicto obrero: Creación de las medallas Calles, Obregón y Juárez*. Villahermosa: N.p., 1929.

Limantour, José Yvés. *Apuntes sobre mi vida política (1892–1911)*. Mexico City: Editorial Porrua, 1965.

Liss, Sheldon B. *A Century of Disagreement: The Chamizal Conflict, 1864–1964*. Washington, D.C.: University Press of Washington, 1965.

Lombardo Toledano, Vicente. *La izquierda en la historia de México*. Mexico City: Ediciones del Partido Popular Socialista, 1962.

López Mateos, Adolfo. *Actualización de Juárez*. Toluca: Ediciones del Gobierno del Estado de México, 1949.

———. *Presencia internacional de Adolfo López Mateos*. Mexico City: Talleres Gráficos de la Nación, 1963.

López Portillo y Rojas, José. *Elevación y caída de Porfirio Díaz*. Mexico City: Librería Española, 1920.

López Serrano, Francisco. *Los periodistas republicanos y su participación en la lucha contra la Intervención Francesa y el Imperio de Maximiliano*. Mexico City: 1969.

Mabry, Donald J. *The Mexican University and the State: Student Conflicts, 1910–1971*. College Station: Texas A & M University Press, 1982.

———. *Mexico's Acción Nacional: A Catholic Alternative to Revolution*. Syracuse, N.Y.: Syracuse University Press, 1973.

Macías, José Miguel. *Paligenesía de Benito Juárez*. Jalapa: N.p., 1891.

Madero, Francisco I. *La sucesión presidencial en 1910*. San Pedro, Coahuila: N.p., 1908.

Malinowski, Bronislaw. *Sex, Culture, and Myth*. New York: Harcourt Brace & World, 1962.

Maples Arce, Manuel. *Leopoldo Méndez*. Mexico City: Fondo de Cultura Económica, 1970.

Mariscal, Ignacio. *Juárez y el libro de Bulnes*. Mexico City: Imprenta de Arturo García Cubas, 1904.

Márquez de León, Manuel. *Don Benito Juárez a la luz de la verdad*. Mexico City: S. Lorenzo, 1885.

Márquez Montiel, Joaquín. *Cuestiones históricas: Apuntamientos de historia genética mexicana*. Mexico City: N.p., 1940.

Martínez, Oscar J. *Border Boom Town: Ciudad Juárez since 1848*. Austin: University of Texas Press, 1978.

Martínez, Rafael, and Heriberto Frías. *Juárez inmortal*. Mexico City: Talleres Gráficos "Seria," 1925.

Martínez Domínguez, Alfonso. *Mexico de hoy; Juárez en 1966*. Mexico City: N.p., 1966.

Martínez González, Marina. *Juárez y Lincoln: Paladines de la libertad y la justicia social*. Saltillo: N.p., 1967.

Martínez Verdugo, Arnaldo. *Crisis política y alternativa comunista*. Mexico City: Ediciones de Cultura Popular, 1979.

Martínez y Aguilar, Apolonio. *Juárez merece bien de la historia*. San Luis Potosí: N.p., 1920.

Mecham, John Lloyd. *Church and State in Latin America: A History of Politico-Ecclesiastical Relations*. Rev. ed. Chapel Hill: University of North Carolina Press, 1966.

———. *A Survey of United States–Latin American Relations*. Boston: Houghton, Mifflin, 1965.

Mejía Barcenas, Manuel. *Homenaje del Partido Liberal de Guatemala al Benemérito de las Américas, Benito Juárez, en el primer centenario de su nacimiento*. Guatemala City: Tipografía Nacional, 1906.

Mejía Zúñiga, Raúl. *Benito Juárez y su generación*. Mexico City: Sep-Setentas, 1972.

Mendoza, Vicente T. *El corrido de la Revolución*. Mexico City: Biblioteca del Instituto Nacional de Estudios Históricos de la Revolución Mexicana, 1956.

———. *El corrido mexicano*. Mexico City: Fondo de Cultura Económica, 1954.

Mexico, cincuenta años de revolución. 4 vols. Mexico City: Fondo de Cultura Económica, 1961–62.

Meyer, Jean A. *The Cristero Rebellion: The People between Church and State, 1926–1929*. Translated by Richard Southern. Cambridge, England: Cambridge University Press, 1976.

Meyer, Jean, with Enrique Krauze and Cayetano Reyes. *Historia de la Revolución Mexicana: Período 1924–1928, estado y sociedad con Calles*. Mexico City: El Colegio de México, 1977.

Meyer, Lorenzo. *Historia de la Revolución Mexicana: Período 1928–1934, el conflicto social y los gobiernos del maximato*. Mexico City: El Colegio de México, 1978.

Meyer, Michael C. *Huerta: A Political Portrait*. Lincoln: University of Nebraska Press, 1972.

———. *Mexican Rebel: Pascual Orozco and the Mexican Revolution, 1910–1915*. Lincoln: University of Nebraska Press, 1967.

Meyer, Michael C., and William L. Sherman. *The Course of Mexican History*. New York: Oxford University Press, 1979.

Michaels, Albert L. "Fascism and Sinarquism: Popular Nationalism against the Mexican Revolution." *Journal of Church and State* 8 (Spring 1966):234–50.

———. "The Modification of the Anti-clerical Nationalism of the Mexican Revolution by General Lázaro Cárdenas and Its Relationship to the Church-State Detente in Mexico." *Americas* 26 (July 1969):35–53.

Miller, Robert Ryal. "Matías Romero: Mexican Minister to the United States during the Juárez-Maximilian Era." *Hispanic American Historical Review* 45 (May 1965):228–45.

Millon, Robert Paul. *Mexican Marxist: Vicente Lombardo Toledano*. Chapel Hill: University of North Carolina Press, 1966.

Moheno, Querido. *¿Hacia dónde vamos?* Mexico City: T. Lara, 1908.

Molina Enríquez, Andrés. *Los grandes problemas nacionales*. Mexico City: A. Carranza e hijos, 1909.

———. *Juárez y la Reforma*. Reprint. Mexico City: Libro Mex, 1956.

Monzón, Luis G. *Detalles de la educación socialista implantables en México*. Mexico City: Talleres Gráficos de la Nación, 1936.

Moreno, Pablo C. "La ruta de Juárez." *Boletín de la Sociedad Mexicana de Geografía y Estadística* 106 (August 1968):143–48.

Moseley, Edward H., and Edward D. Terry, eds. *Yucatán: A World Apart.* University, Ala.: University of Alabama Press, 1980.

Mosse, George L. "Caesarism, Circuses, and Monuments." Journal of Contemporary History 6 (1972):167–82.

Motts, Irene Elena. *La vida en la ciudad de México en las primeras décadas del siglo XX.* Mexico City: Editorial Porrua, 1973.

Mural Painting of the Mexican Revolution, 1921–1960. Mexico City: Fondo Editorial de la Plástica Mexicana, 1960.

Murray, Henry A., ed. *Myth and Mythmaking.* New York: George Braziller, 1960.

Myers, Bernard S. *Mexican Painting in Our Time.* New York: Oxford University Press, 1956.

"Myth and Mythmaking." *Daedalus* 88 (Spring 1959):212–22.

Nagel, Paul C. *This Sacred Trust: American Nationality, 1798–1898.* New York: Oxford University Press, 1971.

Needler, Martin C. *Mexican Politics: The Containment of Conflict.* New York: Praeger, 1982.

Niemeyer, E. V., Jr. *Revolution at Querétaro: The Mexican Constitutional Convention of 1916–1917.* Austin: University of Texas Press, 1974.

1968: El principio del poder. Mexico City: Ediciones de Cultura Popular, 1980.

Noriega, Raúl. *Periodismo revolucionario.* Mexico City: N.p., 1942.

Norman, Dorothy. *The Hero: Myth/Image/Symbol.* New York: World, 1969.

———. *Los paseos de la ciudad de México.* Mexico City: Fondo de Cultura Económica, 1974.

———. *La vida en México en el período presidencial de Manuel Avila Camacho.* Mexico City: Empresas Editoriales, 1965.

Novo, Salvador. *Los paseos de la ciudad de México.* Mexico City: Fondo de Cultura Económica, 1974.

Nuñez, Pedro S. *Corona de pensamientos consagrados al Benemérito de las Américas, Benito Juárez, en el primer centenario de su natalicio.* Mexico City: Sobrerete, Nuñez, 1906.

Ocaranza, Fernando. *Juárez y sus amigos.* Mexico City: Editorial Polis, 1939.

O'Gorman, Edmundo. "Hidalgo en la historia." *Memorias de la Academia Mexicana de la Historia* 23 (1964):221–39.

Olaguibel, Francisco M. *El honor de Juárez.* Toluca: N.p., 1901.

———. *El poema de Juárez.* Toluca: N.p., 1906.

Olliff, Donathon C. *Reforma Mexico and the United States: A Search for Alternatives to Annexation, 1854–1861*. University, Ala.: University of Alabama Press, 1981.

Oomen, T. K. "Charisma, Social Structure and Social Change." *Comparative Studies in Society and History* 10 (October 1967):85–99.

Orozco, José Clemente. *An Autobiography*. Translated by Robert C. Stephenson. Austin: University of Texas Press, 1962.

Ortega y Medina, Juan A. *Humboldt desde México*. Mexico City: Universidad Nacional Autónoma de México, 1960.

Padgett, Leon Vincent. *The Mexican Political System*. Boston: Houghton, Mifflin, 1966.

Padilla Nervo, Luis. *Discursos y declaraciones sobre política internacional ante la OAS, 1948–1958*. Mexico City: Secretaría de Relaciones Exteriores, 1958.

Palabras y documentos públicos de Lázaro Cárdenas: Mensajes, discursos, entrevistas y otros documentos, 1928–1940. Mexico City: Siglo Veintiuno Editores, 1978.

Palavicini, Felix F. *Los diputados: Lo que se ve y lo que no se ve de la cámara*. Mexico City: N.p., n.d.

———. *Historia de la Constitución de 1917*. 2 vols. Mexico City: N.p., 1938.

Pardo, Leonardo R. *El verdadero Bulnes y la verdad sobre su libro detractor*. Mexico City: Imprenta y litografía del autor, 1904.

Parra, Porfirio. *Estudio histórico-sociológico sobre la reforma en México*. Guadalajara: Impresa de "La Gaceta de Guadalajara," 1906.

Patterson, Robert H. "An Art in Revolution: Antecedents of Mexican Mural Painting, 1900–1920." *Journal of Inter-American Studies* 6 (July 1964):377–84.

Paz, Ireneo. *¡Juárez!: Undécima leyenda histórica*. Mexico City: Impresa y litografía de I. Paz, 1902.

Paz, Octavio. *Tamayo en la pintura mexicana*. Mexico City: Universidad Nacional Autónoma de México, Dirección General de Publicaciones, 1959.

———, ed. *Album a Juárez*. Mexico City: Imprenta Mundial, 1931.

Pearson, Lionel. "Historical Allusions in the Attic Orators." *Classical Philology* 36 (July 1941):209–29.

Pellicer, Carlos. "Sueño dominical en la Alameda Central de la ciudad de México." *México en el Arte*, July 1948.

Pellicer de Brody, Olga, and José Luis Reyna. *Historia de la Revolución Mexicana: Período 1952–1960, El afianzamiento de la estabilidad política*. Mexico City: El Colegio de México, 1978.

Pereyra, Carlos. "Juárez dictador." *Revista Positiva* 4 (1904):678–701.

———. *Juárez discutido como dictador y estadista a propósito de los errores, paradojas y fantasías de Sr. Don Francisco Bulnes.* Mexico City: Tipografía Económica, 1904.

Pérez, José T. *Bulnes a espaldas de Juárez.* Morelia: Talleres de la Escuela I. M. Porfirio Díaz, 1905.

Pérez Martínez, Hector. *Juárez el impasible.* Madrid: Espasa-Calpe, 1934.

Pérez Sanvicente, Guadalupe, and Antonio Arriaga Ochoa. *Juárez en el arte.* Mexico City: N.p., 1972.

Pérez Verdía, Luis. *Compendio de la historia de México desde sus primeros tiempos hasta la caída del Segundo Imperio.* Guadalajara: Tipografía del autor, 1883.

Perry, Laurens Ballard. *Juárez and Díaz: Machine Politics in Mexico.* DeKalb: Northern Illinois University Press, 1978.

Peterson, Merrill D. *The Jefferson Image in the American Mind.* New York: Oxford University Press, 1960.

Peza, Juan de Dios. *Benito Juárez: La reforma y la intervención francesa, el imperio, el triunfo de la república.* Mexico City: J. Ballesteros, 1904.

Phelan, John Leddy. "México y lo mexicano." *Hispanic American Historical Review* 36 (August 1956):309–18.

Pineda, Celso. *Juárez en Guadalajara.* Mexico City: N.p., 1906.

Pineda, Rosendo. *Discursos en honor de Juárez.* Mexico City: N.p., 1902.

Pirod Posada, María de Lourdes. *Juárez y la Reforma en la historiografía porfirista.* Mexico City: Universidad Iberoamericana, 1966.

Pizarro Suárez, Nicolás. *Siete crisis políticas de Benito Juárez.* Mexico City: Editorial Diana, 1972.

Planchet, Regis. *La cuestión religiosa en México o sea vida de Benito Juárez.* El Paso: Editorial Revista Católica, 1927.

Poesía: ¡A Juárez! Leída en el meeting anticlerical el 18 de julio del corriente año en la ciudad de México. Zitácuaro: Tipografía La República, 1902.

Powell, Thomas G. *El liberalismo y el campesinado en el centro de México (1850 a 1876).* Translated by Roberto Gómez Ciriza. Mexico City: SepSetentas, 1974.

———. "Mexican Intellectuals and the Indian Question, 1876–1911." *Hispanic American Historical Review* 48 (February 1968):19–36.

Prida, Ramón. *Juárez: Como lo pinta el diputado Bulnes y como lo describe la historia.* Mexico City: Eusebio Sánchez, 1904.

Prida Santacilia, Pablo. *Así fue Juárez: Su vida en láminas.* Mexico City: Editorial del Río, 1954.

———. *Siguiendo la vida de Juárez.* Mexico City: Ediciones Palafox, 1945.

Prieto, Guillermo. *Lecciones de historia patria, escritas para los alumnos del Colegio Militar.* Mexico City: Oficina Tipografía de la Secretaría de Fomento, 1886.

Proyección de México en Latinoamérica: Ciclo de conferencias. Mexico City: N.p., 1960.

Pruñeda, Salvador. *La caricatura como arma política.* Mexico City: Instituto de Estudios Históricos de la Revolución, 1958.

Puig Casauranc, José Manuel. *Juárez, una interpretación humana.* Mexico City: N.p., 1928.

¿Quién fue Juárez? Lagos: Impresa Guadalupana Encarnación, 1894.

Quintanilla, Luis. "La política internacional de la Revolución Mexicana." *Foro Internacional* 5 (July–September 1964):1–26.

Quirk, Robert E. *The Mexican Revolution and the Catholic Church, 1910–1929.* Bloomington: Indiana University Press, 1973.

———. *The Mexican Revolution, 1914–1915: The Convention of Aguascalientes.* Bloomington: Indiana University Press, 1960.

———. *Mexico.* Englewood Cliffs, N.J.: Prentice-Hall, 1971.

Raat, William D. "Ideas and Society in Don Porfirio's Mexico." *Americas* 30 (July 1973):32–43.

———. *El positivismo durante el Porfiriato (1876–1910).* Translated into Spanish by Andrés Lira. Mexico City: SepSetentas, 1975.

———. *Revoltosos: Mexico's Rebels in the United States, 1903–1923.* College Station: Texas A & M University Press, 1981.

Rabasa, Emilio. *La evolución histórica de México.* Mexico City: Porrua, 1956.

Ramillete fúnebre compuesto por el patriotismo mexicano, dedicado a la memoria del ilustre Benito Juárez. Mérida: Impresa de Manuel Aldana Rivas, 1872.

Ramírez de Arellano, General Manuel. *Ultimas horas del Imperio.* Mexico City: Tipografía Mexicana, 1869.

Ramos, Mariano L. *Apoteosis del benemérito ciudadano Benito Juárez, pieza en dos cuadros.* Zaragoza: Imprenta de A. González, 1872.

Ramos, Samuel. *Profile of Man and Culture in Mexico.* Translated by Peter G. Earle. Austin: University of Texas Press, 1962.

Rankin, Melinda. *Twenty Years among the Mexicans: A Narrative of Missionary Labor.* Cincinnati: Chase & Hall, 1875.

Recuerdo de las fiestas que organizó en esta ciudad la Delegación de la Comisión Nacional del Centenario de Juárez, en honor del insigne patricio. Xalapa: Tipografía del gobierno, 1906.

Reed, Alma. *Orozco.* Mexico City: Fondo de Cultura Económica, 1955.

Refutación del libro de D. Francisco Bulnes intitulado "Juárez y las revo-

luciones de Ayutla y de Reforma." Mexico City: Tip. de la Compañía Editorial Católica, 1906.

Reyes Heroles, Jesús. *El liberalismo mexicano.* 3 vols. Mexico City: Universidad Nacional Autónoma de México, Facultad de Derecho, 1957–61.

Richmond, Douglas W. *Venustiano Carranza's Nationalist Struggle, 1893–1920.* Lincoln: University of Nebraska Press, 1983.

Río González, Manuel del. *Juárez su vida y su obra.* Jalapa: N.p., 1966.

Riva Palacio, Vicente, et al. *México a través de los siglos.* 5 vols. Barcelona: Espasa y compañía, 1886–89.

Rivera, Diego, with Gladys March. *My Art, My Life.* New York: Citadel Press, 1960.

———. *Portrait of Mexico.* New York: Covici, Friede, 1937.

Rivera de la Torre, Antonio. *Paralelismo de hombres y carácteres: Juárez-Carranza, Asuntos varios del Constitucionalismo.* Mexico City: Oficina Imprenta de Hacienda, Departamento Editorial, 1918.

Robles Castillo, Aurelio. *Benito Juárez y su yo.* Guadalajara: N.p., 1967.

Rodríguez y Cos, José María. *Canto heróico: México libre o sea Epístola a Juárez.* Mexico City: N.p., 1884.

Rodríguez Prampolini, Ida. *La crítica de arte en México en el siglo XIX.* 3 vols. Mexico City: Imprenta Universitaria, 1964.

Roeder, Ralph. *Juárez and His Mexico: A Biographical History.* 2 vols. New York: Viking Press, 1947.

Romero Flores, Jesús. *Lic. Benito Juárez: Benemérito de las Américas.* Mexico City: B. Costa Amic, Editores, 1972.

Ross, Stanley R. *Francisco I. Madero: Apostle of Mexican Democracy.* New York: Columbia University Press, 1955.

Rousseau, Jean Jacques. *The Social Contract.* Translated and edited by Charles Frankel. New York: Hafner, 1947.

Ruíz, Ramón Eduardo. *The Great Rebellion: Mexico, 1905–1924.* New York: 1980.

Rutherford, John. *Mexican Society during the Revolution: A Literary Approach.* London: Oxford University Press, 1971.

Salado Alvarez, Victoriano. *Informe que en nombre de la Comisión Nacional del Centenario de Juárez leyó en la velada del Teatro Arbeu la noche del 21 de marzo de 1906, el C. Lic. Victoriano Salado Alvarez, secretario de la misma comisión.* Mexico City: Tipografía de la viuda de Francisco Díaz de León, 1906.

———. *Refutación de algunos errores del señor don Francisco Bulnes: El papel de Juárez en la defensa de Puebla y en la campaña del 63.* Mexico City: Tipografía Económica, 1904.

Santibáñez, Enrique A. *Historia nacional de México desde los tiempos más remotos hasta nuestros días.* 2d ed. Mexico City: Aguiles, 1928.

———. *Juárez: Estudio publicado por acuerdo del Club Benito Juárez de Tuxtla Gutiérrez.* Tuxtla Gutiérrez: Imprenta del Gobierno, 1904.

Sanvicente, Guadalupe, and Antonio Arriaga Ochoa. *Juárez en el arte.* Mexico City: N.p., 1972.

Sater, William F. *The Heroic Image in Chile: Arturo Prat, Secular Saint.* Berkeley and Los Angeles: University of California Press, 1973.

Sauer, Franz A. von. *The Alienated "Loyal" Opposition: Mexico's Partido Acción Nacional.* Albuquerque: University of New Mexico Press, 1974.

Scefano, F. *La juareida.* Puebla: Impresa Artística, 1906.

Schlesinger, Stephen C., and Stephen Kinzer. *Bitter Fruit: The Untold Story of the American Coup in Guatemala.* Garden City: Doubleday, 1982.

Schmeckebier, Laurence E. *Modern Mexican Art.* Minneapolis: University of Minnesota Press, 1939.

Schmidt, Henry C. *The Roots of Lo Mexicano: Self and Society in Mexican Thought, 1900–1934.* College Station: Texas A & M University Press, 1978.

Schmitt, Karl M. *Communism in Mexico: A Study in Political Frustration.* Austin: University of Texas Press, 1965.

———. "The Díaz Conciliation Policy on State and Local Levels." *Hispanic American Historical Review* 40 (November 1960):513–32.

———. "The Mexican Positivists and the Church-State Question, 1876–1911." *Journal of Church and State* 8 (Spring 1966):200–213.

Scholes, Walter V. *Mexican Politics during the Juárez Regime, 1855–1872.* Columbia: University of Missouri Press, 1957.

Schryer, Frans J. *The Rancheros of Pisaflores: The History of a Peasant Bourgeoisie in Twentieth-Century Mexico.* Toronto: University of Toronto Press, 1980.

Scott, Robert E. *Mexican Government in Transition.* Urbana: University of Illinois Press, 1959.

Sebeok, Thomas A., ed. *Myth: A Symposium.* Bloomington: Indiana University Press, 1958.

Segovia, Rafael. *La politización del niño mexicano.* Mexico City: El Colegio de México, 1975.

Serra Rojas, Andrés. *Antología de la elocuencia mexicana, 1900–50.* Mexico City: Librería de Manuel Porrua, 1950.

Sierra, Carlos J., ed. *Juárez en la inmortalidad del 21 de marzo.* Mexico City: Secretaría de Hacienda y Crédito Público, 1965.

———. *Juárez en la voz y la palabra de Latinoamérica.* Mexico City: Secretaría de Hacienda y Crédito Público, 1972.

————. *Juárez en su recinto de homenaje*. Mexico City: Secretaría de Hacienda y Crédito Público, 1971.

————. *La prensa valora la figura de Juárez, 1872–1910*. Mexico City: Secretaría de Hacienda y Crédito Público, 1963.

————. *Presencia de Juárez en los gobiernos de la Revolución, 1911–1963*. Mexico City: Secretaría de Hacienda y Crédito Público, 1964.

Sierra, Justo. *Juárez: Su obra y su tiempo*. Mexico City: Porrua, 1970.

————. *Obras completas*. Edited by Agustín Yáñez. 14 vols. Mexico City: Universidad Nacional Autónoma de México, 1948–49.

Simmons, Merle E. *The Mexican Corrido as a Source for Interpretive Study of Modern Mexico (1870–1950)*. Bloomington: Indiana University Press, 1957.

Simpson, Lesley Byrd. *Many Mexicos*. 4th ed. rev. Berkeley and Los Angeles: University of California Press, 1966.

Sinkin, Richard N. *The Mexican Reform, 1855–1876: A Study in Liberal Nation-Building*. Austin: University of Texas Press, 1979.

"The Siqueiros Affair." *New Politics* 2 (1963):128–31.

Smart, Charles Allen. *Viva Juárez: A Biography*. Philadelphia: Lippincott, 1963.

Smith, Arthur K. "Mexico and the Cuban Revolution: Foreign Policy-Making in Mexico under President Adolfo López Mateos (1958–1964)." Ithaca, N.Y.: Cornell University Latin American Studies Program, Dissertation Series 14, 1970.

Smith, Henry Nash. *Virgin Land: The American West as Symbol and Myth*. New York: Vintage Books, 1950.

Smith, Peter H. *Labyrinths of Power: Political Recruitment in Twentieth-Century Mexico*. Princeton: Princeton University Press, 1979.

Sobieski, John. *The Life of Benito Juárez*. St. Joseph, Mo.: Press of Bonner Printing Co., 1919.

Solana y Gutiérrez, Mateo. *Psicología de Juárez, el complejo y el mito: El alma mágica*. Mexico City: Costa Amic, 1968.

Solemnidad cívica con que el Estado de México honró en su capital la memoria del ilustre presidente de los Estados Unidos Mexicanos, C. Benito Juárez, la noche del 27 de julio de 1872. Toluca: N.p., 1872.

Sosa, Francisco. *Biografía de Don Benito Juárez*. Mexico City: Imprenta de F. Diaz de León, 1884.

————. *Las estatuas de la Reforma*. Mexico City: Secretaría de Fomento, 1900.

Spanier, John W. *American Foreign Policy since World War II*. 4th ed. New York: Praeger, 1971.

Stabb, Martin S. "Indigenism and Racism in Mexican Thought, 1857–1911." *Journal of Inter-American Studies* 1 (1959):405–23.

Tamayo: 20 años de su labor pictórico. Mexico City: N.p., 1948.

Tamayo, Rufino. "El nacionalismo y el movimiento pictórico." *Crisol* 9 (May 1933):275–81.

———. *Rufino Tamayo.* Texts by Octavio Paz and Jacques Lassaigne. New York: Rizzoli, 1982.

———. *Tamayo.* Phoenix: N.p., 1968.

Teja Zabre, Alfonso. *Breve historia de México: Texto para escuelas rurales y primarias.* 2d ed. Mexico City: La Impresora, 1935.

Tibol, Raquel. *Historia general del arte mexicano: Epoca moderna y contemporánea.* Mexico City: Editorial Hermes, 1964.

———. *Siqueiros: Introductor de realidades.* Mexico City: Universidad Nacional Autónoma de México, 1961.

Toluca, México, Universidad Autónoma del Estado de México, Extensión universitaria. *El culto a Juárez en Toluca.* Toluca: N.p., 1960.

Toor, Frances, ed. *Orozco's Frescoes in Guadalajara.* Mexico City: Frances Toor Studios, 1940.

Torres Natterman, Elías G. *Presencia de Juárez.* Mexico City: Herrero, 1956.

Turner, Frederick C. *The Dynamic of Mexican Nationalism.* Chapel Hill: University of North Carolina Press, 1968.

Turner, John Kenneth. *Barbarous Mexico.* Reprint. Austin: University of Texas Press, 1969.

Tyler, Ron. *Posada's Mexico.* Washington, D.C.: 1979.

Valadés, José C. *Imaginación y realidad de Francisco I. Madero.* 2 vols. Mexico City: Antigua Librería Robledo, 1960.

———. *El pensamiento político de Benito Juárez.* Mexico City: Librería de Manuel Porrua, 1956.

———. *El Porfirismo: Historia de un régimen, el crecimiento.* 2 vols. Mexico City: Universidad Nacional Autónoma de México, 1977.

———. *El Porfirismo: Historia de un régimen, el nacimiento (1876–1884).* Mexico City: Antigua Librería Robredo, de José Porrua e hijos, 1941.

Van Alstyne, Richard W. *Genesis of American Nationalism.* Waltham, Mass.: Blaisdell, 1970.

Vasconcelos, José. *Breve historia de México.* Mexico City: Editorial Continental, 1956.

———. *Discursos, 1920–50.* Mexico City: Ediciones Botas, 1950.

———. *A Mexican Ulysses: An Autobiography.* Translated and edited by W. Rex Crawford. Bloomington: Indiana University Press, 1963.

Vázquez de Knauth, Josefina. *Nacionalismo y educación en México.* Mexico City: El Colegio de México, 1970.

Velasco Gil, Carlos M. *El Sinarquismo: Su origen, su esencia, su misión.* 3d ed. Mexico City: Editorial Olin, 1962.

Velasco Valdés, Miguel. *Historia del periodismo mexicano (apuntes).* Mexico City: Librería de Manuel Porrúa, 1955.

Villegas, Abelardo. *Positivismo y porfirismo.* Mexico City: SepSetentas, 1972.

Viramontes, Leonardo S. *Biografía popular del Benemérito de América.* Mexico City: Tipografía de la viuda de F. Díaz de León, 1906.

Ward, John William, *Andrew Jackson: Symbol for an Age.* New York: Oxford University Press, 1962.

Warner, W. Lloyd. *The Living and the Dead: A Study of Symbolic Life in America.* New Haven: Yale University Press, 1959.

Wasserstrom, Robert. *Class and Society in Central Chiapas.* Berkeley and Los Angeles: University of California Press, 1983.

Weber, Max. *Basic Concepts in Sociology.* Translated by H. P. Secher. New York: Citadel Press, 1968.

Whetten, Nathan L. *Guatemala: The Land and the People.* New Haven: Yale University Press, 1961.

Wilkie, James W. "The Meaning of the Cristero Religious War against the Mexican Revolution." *Journal of Church and State* 8 (Spring 1966):214–33.

———. *The Mexican Revolution: Federal Expenditure and Social Change since 1910.* 2d ed. rev. Berkeley and Los Angeles: University of California Press, 1970.

Wilkie, James W., and Edna Monzón de Wilkie. *México visto en el siglo XX.* Mexico City: Instituto Mexicano de Investigaciones Económicas, 1969.

Wolfe, Bertram D. *The Fabulous Life of Diego Rivera.* New York: Stein and Day, 1963.

Wolfskill, George W., and Douglas W. Richmond, eds. *Essays on the Mexican Revolution: Revisionist Views of the Leaders.* Austin: University of Texas Press, 1979.

Womack, John, Jr. *Zapata and the Mexican Revolution.* New York: Knopf, 1968.

Zarco, Francisco. *Historia del Congreso Extraordinario Constituyente, 1856–1857.* Mexico City: El Colegio de México, 1956.

Zavala, M. *Juárez y la Reforma.* Mérida: Imprenta de la Ermita, 1896.

Zayas Enríquez, Rafael de. *Benito Juárez: Su vida—su obra.* Mexico City: Tipografía de la viuda de F. Díaz de León, 1906.

Zerecero, Anastasio. *Benito Juárez: Exposiciones (Como se gobierna).* Mexico City: F. Vázquez, 1902.

Dissertations and Theses

Brown, James Chilton. "Consolidation of the Mexican Revolution under Calles, 1924–1928: Politics, Modernization and the Roots of the Revolutionary National Party." Ph.D. dissertation, University of New Mexico, 1979.

Bryan, Anthony. "Mexican Politics in Transition, 1900–1913: The Role of General Bernardo Reyes." Ph.D. dissertation, University of Nebraska, 1970.

Creagan, James F. "Minority Parties in Mexico: Their Role in a One-Party Dominant System." Ph.D. dissertation, University of Virginia, 1965.

Galbert, Jack Benton. "The Evolution of the Mexican Presidency." Ph.D. dissertation, University of Texas, 1963.

Lux, William Robert. "Acción Nacional: Mexico's Opposition Party." Ph.D. dissertation, University of Southern California, 1967.

Michaels, Albert Louis. "Mexican Politics and Nationalism from Calles to Cárdenas." Ph.D. dissertation, University of Pennsylvania, 1966.

Rice, Jacqueline Ann. "The Porfirian Elite: Life Patterns of the Delegates to the 1892 Unión Liberal Convention." Ph.D. dissertation, University of California at Los Angeles, 1979.

Index

About the Author

Charles A. Weeks is Chairman of the Upper School Humanities Department, St. Andrew's Episcopal School, Jackson, Mississippi. He received his B.A. from Dartmouth College, his M.A. from the University of Michigan, and his Ph.D. from Indiana University.